DOING

GIRLFRIEND

THEOLOGY

- storytelling
- critical social analysis
- theological reflection

Roz,
I have enjoyed being in classes w/ you—I will always remember. — Deborah W.

story theology

struggle

Stories of empowerment?

celebrations of

traditional religious education begins with scripture + moves toward life experience

Theologies grow out of stories

kids need free telling of stories

Is the Wild Child active? I love your Rebekah/Dobbins chapter

Hey Roomie:
Thanks for sharing
your story with me and
for listening to mine with an
open heart!
I can't wait to hear how
your vocation unfolds in your new
ministry! In Christ's ♡, Linda

lpurves@gt.rr.com
409-896-5009 (h)
409-651-4701 (c)

DOING
GIRLFRIEND
THEOLOGY

GOD-TALK WITH YOUNG WOMEN

DORI GRINENKO BAKER

THE
PILGRIM
PRESS
Cleveland

Handwritten inscriptions:

Roz, you thank you's
I can't thank you
presence, shall always

Dear Roz!
Blessings
on your
way!

S. McKenna

Roz,
I can't wait
to see you
again!

you are such a joy
to be with and I
don't want to lose touch.
My prayers and love go
with you! Ginger ginevans@sync.com

This book is dedicated to my daughters,
Erin Adeline Baker and Olivia Marie Baker

It is written in memory of
Sophia Marie Baker and Jean Kellett Otte

The Pilgrim Press
700 Prospect Avenue
Cleveland, Ohio 44115-1100
pilgrimpress.com

© 2005 by Dori Grinenko Baker

A portion of chapter 3 originally appeared in *Religious Education,* Summer 2000.

Citation from *I Know Why the Caged Bird Sings* by Maya Angelou copyright © 1969 and renewed 1997 by Maya Angelou. Used by permission of Random House, Inc.

Citation from *Pilgrim at Tinker Creek* by Annie Dillard copyright © 1974 by Annie Dillard. Reprinted by permission of HarperCollins Publishers Inc.

Citation reprinted with permission from *Zami: A New Spelling of My Name* by Audre Lorde. Copyright 1990 by Audre Lorde, The Crossing Press, an imprint of Ten Speed Press, Berkeley, CA. www.tenspeed.com.

10   09   08   07   06   05   5   4   3   2   1

Library of Congress Cataloging-in-Publication Data

Baker, Dori Grinenko, 1963–
    Doing girlfriend theology : God-talk with young women / Dori Grinenko Baker.
    p.   cm.
    Includes bibliographical references and index.
    ISBN 0-8298-1616-X (pbk.)
    1. Feminist theology.   2. Young women – Religious life.   I. Title.

BT83.55.B35 2005
268'.433'082 – dc22

2005040548

Contents

Foreword by Rosemary Radford Ruether   vii

Acknowledgments   ix

Introduction   1

1. Vespers Whispered under a Full Moon:
   The Feminist Theological Education of Adolescent Girls   9

2. Future Homemakers and Feminist Awakenings:
   Methods of Theology, Education, and Research   27

3. God-Talk across Religious Borders   42

4. Collecting Sea Glass: Building and Sharing the Usable Past   67

5. God Talk in the Midst of Violence and Death   91

6. Slipping through the Barbed Wire Fence:
   Crossing the Borders of Women's Emancipatory Theologies   118

7. Breast-Feeding Women and Vegan Girls:
   Girlfriend Theology as Embodied Pedagogy   142

8. God-Talk at the Crossroads of Souls   161

Appendix: Guidelines for Facilitating Girlfriend Theology,
and Frequently Asked Questions   177

Notes   189

Bibliography   209

Index   219

Foreword

I first had the pleasure of reading and discussing Dori Baker's manuscript on girlfriend theology as a doctoral dissertation in the joint program in Religious and Theological Studies of Garrett-Evangelical Theological Seminary and Northwestern University, in Evanston, Illinois, in the late 1990s. It has lost nothing of its freshness in being translated into a book. I felt touched and moved to read its insightful stories a second time.

Dori Baker's development of the themes and methodology of girlfriend theology is based on a poignant social reality in U.S. American culture. The feisty "tomboy" girl of ten gets shut down by thirteen and loses her voice. As she moves from childhood to adolescence, the girl learns to conform to the expectations of gender roles. In myriad ways the message comes to her that she must quiet down, lower her voice, learn to make herself pleasing to others, no longer express her own feelings.

This fact reminds me of a vivid scene in my own young mothering. It is a spring day in 1969. The sounds of boys playing ball in the street rise from outside. I am standing in a second-floor bedroom in our house in Washington, D.C., when I overhear an African American eleven-year-old friend say to my daughter of the same age, "We are becoming young ladies now. We can no longer shout and play with boys in the street." My daughter appeared to silently concur. I remember being astonished at how this socialization into gender conformity was being inculcated by one eleven-year-old girl into another.

As Dori Baker makes clear, adolescent girls pay a heavy price to learn these lessons of silence and submission. Eating disorders, cutting, depression, even suicide are some of the more extreme ways that the stresses of this process of conformity express themselves. A high level of violence affects the youth of our society. Murder and suicide are the second- and third-leading causes of death of young people from the ages of fifteen to twenty-four. Yet there is little outlet in our culture, whether in churches, in families, or in schools, for young women to share their experiences of tragedy or explore their groping efforts to make meaning in the midst of confusing messages.

Girlfriend theology is about providing the safe space for adolescent women to tell their stories and to probe the emerging horizons of hope in their lives. Girlfriend theology is about hearing young women into speech. Its methodology is one of storytelling and small-group reflection on stories. Stories that have often been bottled up inside young women find a place where they can be shared in a gathering of friends who can hold one another in grief and in joy and ask about the deeper meaning of the patterns of young lives.

Through such storytelling, young women can ask, "Where is God in this story?" Is God in the abusive father, pastor, or teacher, or rather in the friendship of two hurting young people who reach out their arms to one another? Is God in the judgmental views of adults about the young father struggling to overcome drug addiction? Or is God in that young father giving his life to save his baby girl by shielding her under his body when his gang friends firebomb the house where he and his girlfriend are living? These kinds of stories are the stuff of girlfriend theology. They have to do not with "childish things" but life-and-death matters.

A few theological principles emerge from such explorations of the hidden stories of young women. One of them is that God is mysteriously, but not omnipotently, present with us in our struggles. Another is that God is accessible through our bodily experiences. Church is found in communities of compassion that allow us to search for meaning or sometimes simply to grieve together when meaning cannot be found.

Girlfriend theology is an invaluable contribution to reclaiming the voices of one of the most silenced groups in our society, the teenaged girl. It offers the remarkable conclusion that such girls are not only grappling with deeply serious issues. They also can be reflective theologians with much to teach the adult world that so often finds them opaque and hard to understand. The key lies in learning to listen. Dori Baker shows us how to do that.

ROSEMARY RADFORD RUETHER

Acknowledgments

Many people labored with me to bring this project to birth. I am deeply grateful to those midwives of body, mind, and soul who caressed, prodded, and nudged the process along. I am especially thankful for the constant support and nurture given to me by Laurel Brown Andrews, who helped birth babies and ideas, almost simultaneously. This book could not have been written without the friendship of Eleiza Braun, whose tireless activism helps me raise daughters with voice and vision.

My parents, Dee and Don Grinenko, along with my in-laws, Ron and Barbara Baker, are generous souls who lovingly entertained my children so I was free to write. I have been blessed with great neighbors: Pattie MacKenzie, Debby Braun, Joan Myra Polikoff, and their families provided soul food. They, along with Marsha Hott, Sue Smock-Lawson, and Kathy Smith made up a female cluster in Evanston, Illinois, that continues over e-mail, phone lines, and occasional reunions.

I thank the Clinical Pastoral Education (CPE) staff at the Rush-Presbyterian-St. Luke's Medical Center in Chicago. My colleagues there in 1990–91 were wonderful storytellers and creative theologians. The rich sharing of our life stories changed the way I do theology. I am especially grateful to Beth Burbank for developing and sharing the story theology model and, again, to Laurel Brown Andrews for sharing the wisdom she has gained through the sustained practice of story theology in local congregations. Working closely with dying children and their families during this year of CPE blessed me to my core. These gracious souls taught me to grieve well and to sit attentively with others who grieve. During this year, while ideas for this book were incubating, I lived in the household of Milton and

Vella Bass of Skokie, Illinois. The warmth, humor, and kindness of
their home provided infinite nurture.

I am thankful for the generous support from the American Association of University Women's American Fellowship and the United
Methodist Church Board of Higher Education's Dempster Fellowship. The Association of Professors and Researchers in Religious
Education provided a forum for the presentation of early drafts of
two chapters. The Youth Theology Initiative, a Lilly Endowment
project at Candler School of Theology, welcomed me as a research
partner. The Valparaiso Project, under the excellent guidance of
Dr. Don Richter, provided a grant to explore the practice of testimony
in the lives of girls and women. Minnie Lane of Altavista, Virginia,
provided boundless enthusiasm and ongoing support of girlfriend
theology as I was readying this book for publication.

The First United Methodist Church of Arlington Heights, Illinois,
especially the United Methodist Women, the Rev. Bill Cull, and the
Rev. Linda Hollies, challenged and nurtured my emerging call to
translate emancipatory theologies for laity. Jill Templeton Murphy,
Sarah Lofstedt, Katie Predick, John and Donna Kroupa, Josh Mika,
Jason Janczak, and the other youth of Cheers taught the immense
gift of listening to voices of the young. My good friend Paul Saltz-
man taught me to love two things — the act of writing and the city
of Chicago. Both have figured largely in the path my life has taken.

This book began as a dissertation. To my mentors and colleagues at
Garrett-Evangelical Theological Seminary (G-ETS) and Northwestern University, I am grateful. My advisor, Dr. Jack L. Seymour, held
a belief in me that provided motivation. Dr. Linda J. Vogel pointed
me in fruitful directions. They inspire my teaching practices. My colleagues in the PhD program, especially the Rev. Reginald Blount,
Dr. Debra Washington, Dr. Steve Kang, and Dr. Evelyn Parker, shared
support and encouragement along the way. My students in youth
ministry courses gave me an early forum in which to practice leading
story theology. Several former students became friends who helped in
this project's unfolding. I am especially grateful to the Rev. Jenny Gorman, the Rev. Jenny Edwards-Bertrand, Angie Williams, and Lynn
Peck. I am thankful for Dr. Dwight D. Conquergood's seminar in
critical ethnography and Dr. Fran Paden's seminars on women and

autobiography, both at Northwestern University. Dr. Rosemary Radford Ruether's ideas have shaped my thought. I am grateful for the way her presence influenced the G-ETS community, drawing women from around the world who have become my friends and allies.

Without my new friends in Altavista, Virginia, I never would have found time to write. I wish to thank Jenny Roark and Jane Green for providing more than their share of carpooling and playdates. Kelly Wheeler, Lana Lowe, Laurie Gossler, the Rev. Jeff Allen, and Susan Allen read portions and gave me much-needed encouragement. Elizabeth Hawkins provided careful editing. Two female clusters — the Thursday night book club and the Monday morning contemplative prayer group — helped me remember myself in a sometimes alien culture and provided nourishing moments of Sabbath. If my faith in the brilliance of teenaged girls ever flags, I need look no further than my babysitters, Hannah and Julia Dudley. I thank them for gracefully mentoring the younger girls in their realm with such strength and sweetness.

In the late 1980s, a group of seminarians started gathering to eat dinner together on Thursday nights. We have sustained life-giving community through the birth of a dozen children and despite numerous migrations. They are like extended family to me. The oldest of those children are preparing to enter college. I count myself fortunate to have watched this small segment of the Millennial Generation come of age. I especially thank the Rev. Jeff Williams for responding to two early chapters; Lindsey Williams for giving me an annual summer reality check; and Cassidhe Pavy Hart for resolutely holding on to childhood pleasures. I thank the others in this group — Amanda, Cameron, Colin, Delaney, Evan, Nolan, Ryan, Sarah, and their parents — for their constant support and thoughtful conversations.

The adolescents and women who were part of this project entered my life in powerful ways. I thank them for opening their lives to each other and to me. Many of my companions during my teenage years remain my friends today. I am grateful for the lives of my sisters, Dr. Dawn Grinenko and Dr. Deidre Grinenko; my childhood friend, Tavia Naset Cowell; and the rest of my girlfriends from Plant City, Florida. Because of a group of girls with whom to laugh, explore, and play, I look back on those years with a smile. Indeed, this project has been a journey of smiles, the latest of which are due to the pure pleasure of working with my editor at Pilgrim Press, Ulrike Guthrie.

Finally, I owe special thanks to my husband, Lincoln Baker, who also accompanied me through adolescence. Words cannot convey the appreciation I have for the long history and joyful present we share. Erin Adeline and Olivia Marie, you are all the world to me.

DOING
GIRLFRIEND
THEOLOGY

Introduction

I believe in parables. I navigate life using stories where I find them, and I hold tight to the ones that tell me new kinds of truth.
— Barbara Kingsolver, *Small Wonder*

This project began with a vision of girls and women changing the world through changing the church. At its heart is the belief that communities of faith can bring justice, compassion, and peace to a hurting world. The place to begin, I believed then, was in helping girls unearth the long-hidden treasures of the feminine divine within the Judeo-Christian story. *Girlfriend theology* doesn't go searching for archeological fragments of a dying tradition; it searches out seeds of hope for a new earth.

Women passionately transformed church in the 1970s, 1980s, and 1990s. They claimed pulpits. They created liturgies. They danced and spun and wove and painted new ways of knowing God in quiet pockets of safety that spread to embrace ever-widening spheres of influence. Women envisioned a church rebirthed by the divine feminine and set about creating it.

But often *girls* got left behind. Psychological literature depicted dire circumstances on the adolescent girl's journey to adulthood. Depression, suicide, cutting, eating disorders, sexual promiscuity, and related diseases plagued girls. While academic, athletic, and professional arenas opened wide to support and encourage girls, their spirits seemed to be quietly growing smaller, snuffed out by a culture that demanded that they be "smart, strong, and bold" as well as thin, athletic, and, above all, nice. Sometimes, the onslaught of a hyperconsumptive culture left the most resilient of girls overwhelmed, confused, and vulnerable to soul shrinking.

This book is about soul expansion. Girlfriend theology begins by creating "female clusters" in which a girl tells a story from her life. A circle of peers and mentors listens to the story, paying attention to the feelings it evokes. Powerful feelings of awe, fear, grief, and horror, or mundane feelings of comfort, safety, and contentment arise and are shared. Then the group looks at the story for glimpses of God. What images in the story remind us of the holy as seen through scripture and other sacred stories which give life meaning? Do we hear echoes of the gospel woman at the well? Teresa of Ávila? Catherine of Siena? Hildegard of Bingen? Or — as happened at one recent gathering recounted below — *The Lion King*? Last of all, the group asks how the story and its connection to other stories might change the way we live.

Throughout the research for this project, I found that girls' spirits are alive and well. Girls are connected to a living, breathing, almost-tangible divine presence. They question, they doubt, they sometimes call themselves atheist. But they remain in conversation with a church they seek to hold accountable to their innate desires for community, connection, and meaning in the face of crisis. The girls I met are hungry: hungry for adults who will not be intimidated by their youthful insouciance; hungry for mentors who will not be in a hurry to give pat answers to their questions; hungry for people who will admit to their own surprised moments of standing on holy ground, barefoot, wide-eyed, and mouth agape.

Girlfriend theology is a method of religious education that helps adults be present to these adolescent hungers. At the heart of this book is a four-step method that teaches participants to see life theologically. I used this method to invite girls and women to tell true stories from their lives. Such stories are thick, messy, scary, and awesome. When we lift the lid, we never know what will come out. I've heard girls' stories that come rushing out like a mighty grace-filled wind, but others that slip out sadly to reveal suicide, murder, sexual abuse, and badly distorted visions of potential futures. Girlfriend theology is about girls and women creating spaces in which it is safe to share these stories — the good, the bad, and the ugly — so that we might discern the trace of a living, breathing divine presence who seeks our companionship as much today as on the fresh new dawn of creation. It is a daunting task, but one that is incredibly rewarding.

In the hundreds of girlfriend theology sessions I have led in workshops across the United States, I always walk into the room hopeful and expectant — knowing in my gut that women and girls have stories they are aching to tell. But I am also always aware of the skeptic in the room. She is skeptical that a process as seemingly simple as storytelling can lead us into the complex web where faith, spirituality, and everyday life intersect.

On one particular day, the skeptic was a middle-aged woman. Her eyes became glued to the circle as a girl's story unfolded. On this day, I had been asked to share the method with an interfaith group of girls who began gathering as part of a women's peace initiative following the 9/11 tragedy and its aftermath. Katie told her story to a circle of Jewish, Christian, Muslim, and Hindu teenagers in a church fellowship hall. The story was about an accident that happened during a youth group's downhill snow-skiing trip. The crux of Katie's story was this: "I didn't know what to do. Emma's sister was halfway up the ski slope, being carried down by medics on a stretcher. I didn't know what to do, what to think. So I put my arms around Emma and started singing 'Hakuna Matata,' you know, from *The Lion King*."

The skeptic was swept into the story and the meaning-making that ensued. The song "Hakuna Matata" is well-known to anyone born after 1980. Sung by the comic meercat Timon and his warthog friend Pumba, a duo who befriend the orphaned lion cub Simba in the movie *The Lion King*, it translates from the Swahili to mean "no worries, for the rest of your days." In the mind of the teenagers who began to interpret Katie's instinct to hug her friend and sing this song, "Hakuna Matata" was seen as a generation's mantra, something they know by heart and to which they return when the world is a scary place. For them, singing "Hakuna Matata" is like reciting the Twenty-third Psalm or singing "Amazing Grace" was to their grandparents' generation. Adults in the group teased out connections to passages in the Hebrew Bible and the Koran. "Hakuna Matata" *isn't* scripture. It *isn't* the Lord's Prayer or the Nicene Creed. But it functioned, like the best of scripture and creed, to give comfort and hope in the midst of a tense and scary moment. The skeptic came up to me after experiencing girlfriend theology that day to tell me how amazed she was at the girls' stories and their ability to tease profound meanings out of them.

On another day in a different city, *I* was the skeptic. I had been invited to share girlfriend theology with the women's group of a United Methodist church I had formerly pastored. I had carefully arranged the event, soliciting stories in advance and choosing one that seemed particularly evocative. It was about a grandmother enjoying a beautiful day on a boat with her extended family. When a sudden change of weather brought fear of a tornado, the grandmother was elected to wade to shore with her young grandson, leaving her grown daughters with their father behind to tend the boat. I knew it was a story ripe with meaning. But, as I looked around the room at a sea of faces ranging in age from mid-twenties to late sixties, I felt fear. Perhaps these women will choose to remain silent? Perhaps they are too invested in preexisting notions of each other, God, and the church to play with fresh, interesting, but untried images? I had the distinct feeling that I had thrown a party to which no one was going to come. But as the story unfolded, the skeptic in me took a long vacation. *I* was swept up, left amazed and weak in the knees at the profound conversation about the Trinity that ensued.

Time and again girlfriend theology surprises and refreshes those who take part. In the following pages, you will hear girlfriend theology unfolding, beginning each time with a true story told by a person in the group. It allows for participants to feel what they feel, know what they know, and revisit old memories that the story calls to mind. It moves from the story, feelings, and memories to images, meanings, and theology. Who is God in this story? Where does *this* story intersect with *holy* stories, religious traditions, or spiritual imaginations? Each session ends with the "so what" question. If "Hakuna Matata" can be sung as a mantra during a crisis, so what? If a grandmother taking her grandson to safety can remind us of a creator God sending his son on a life-saving mission with an unknown outcome, so what? How do new images of God, scripture, and our relationships to one other help us reshape our religious traditions? Can those transformed traditions help us lead more faithful and fulfilling lives?

The method described in this book will help pastors and laypeople to lead groups into thoughtful reflection that can spark action in the church, our communities, and our world. The book concludes with a practical guide, giving step-by-step advice for using the method in a group. I have included handouts, answers to frequently asked questions, and ideas for different contexts in which I have found the method to be helpful.

It is important while reading this book to understand two purposes. The first is to share a method of religious education that girls and women can use to create a world that fosters human flourishing. An underlying purpose is to probe this method for application beyond the realm of girls and women. The other half of the human population — boys and men — stand at a historic crossroad at the beginning of the twenty-first century. For the first time in the history of the modern church, they are not the ones always in charge. An unintended result is that many men and boys are not showing up at church. As one student of mine — who attends a large, mainline church led mostly by women — remarked, "Boys look around church on Sunday morning and get the clear message that they don't belong here."

As I neared the end of my research, I became particularly aware of concerns facing boys coming of age in North America. Douglass Rushkoff's PBS *Frontline* documentary "Merchants of Cool" well depicts their plight.[1] Merchandising giants such as MTV have sold an image of maleness that robs boys of respect and dignity. Best-selling books popularized the plight of girls in the 1980s. Those that followed in the 1990s showed the distinct ways in which boys also suffer from a culture with rigid gender expectations, hyper-consumptive lifestyles, and too little interaction across generations.[2] Each time I teach girlfriend theology to seminary students, they update my understanding of the particular ways in which boys suffer from a lack of adequate alternatives to the caricatures of adulthood offered by much of popular culture. Boys, too, need gatherings of peers and mentors willing to create safe spaces where they can learn to become caring, compassionate men with a capacity for emotional intimacy and a rich life of the spirit. The method in this book is especially suited as a tool for boys because of its focus on enlarging emotional vocabularies, a task specifically named as missing from many boys' educations.[3] Boys in a mixed-gender fifth-grade Sunday school class I teach have embraced the method and enter into it expectantly. While preteens require more active guidance through the process, I find them always able to make biblical connections and mull over new meanings they discover. When this theological method is practiced with boys or mixed-gender groups, I call it *story theology* and follow the same steps.

Girlfriend theology emerged first as a theological response to psychological research that called attention to the lives of adolescent girls. It brings to that task insights informed by women's theological voices from around the globe. It borrows from methods of religious education that honor the learner as a holder of sacred knowledge. It always and everywhere errs on the side of a playful God who prefers a reflective curiosity to a staid ingestion of traditionally held belief or dogma.

In the following pages, you will find the windows of ancient Judeo-Christian tradition thrown open to the fresh air of contemporary girls' and women's wisdom, wit, and experience. When the girls and women laugh, remember, pause, reflect, and wonder, girlfriend theology is happening.

As girlfriend theology happens, the Christian practice of testimony is illuminated and enlarged. Testimony is one of twelve Christian practices chosen by Dorothy Bass for the focus of her book *Practicing Our Faith: A Way of Life for a Searching People*. The author defines practices as "those shared activities that address fundamental human needs and that, woven together, form a way of life."[4] Following that book, a companion volume cowritten with teams of teens and adults adapted these practices for younger audiences. In this book, *Way to Live*, the practice of testimony is explained as telling the truth of your life out loud to another and speaking the truth to power.[5]

When I think of testimony, I think of the Southern Baptist church I often visited as a teenager. There on Wednesday evenings, laypeople took center stage to tell the stories of how God was active in their lives. Often these testimonies, while truthful, seemed a bit predictable and staged. They usually followed a pattern, telling of sinful living, followed by salvation, followed by an easier life walking a straighter path. Despite their scriptedness, those events were moments in which the church carved out space for laypeople to tell their stories. Far too little of that kind of space exists in the churches I experience today.[6] In girlfriend theology, learners engage in the practice of testimony. Here testimony expands to include not just the big stories, the conversion experiences, and mountaintop moments, but the significant little stories of God's work in the lives of everyday people, every day. Here testimony arises not as predictable stories of religious conversion, but as a shared process of finding glimpses of God in everyday acts such as a summer swim, a surprising friendship, or the death of a best friend. When it invites people to speak the truths of their lives out loud to one another, girlfriend theology helps the church provide answers to the spiritual hunger, passion, and curiosity that today's adolescent girls bring to the generations of women who came before them.

My hope is that this book will lead the church to new kinds of truth, new stories by which to navigate life. These stories do not "go flying off solo somewhere,"[7] but are rooted and grounded in the stories of our faith — those that have stood the test of time, and return, refreshed, when seen through new eyes.

Chapter One

Vespers Whispered
under a Full Moon

*The Feminist Theological Education
of Adolescent Girls*

*What would it mean for a girl — against the stories read,
chanted, or murmured to her — to choose to tell the truth of
her life aloud to another person at the very point when she is
invited into the larger cultural story of womanhood — that is,
at . . . adolescence?*   —Lyn Mikel Brown, "Telling a Girl's Life"

Our tent stood a mere three feet from the lake's edge. The gentle
lapping of the waves upon the shore bathed us in a comforting rhythm
as we snuggled in our sleeping bags and began our evening whispers.
During the course of a week in the remote Minnesota wilderness, my
tentmates and I had fallen into this ritual. Bedtime became a time
to reflect — in unflinching detail — on what that particular day of
portaging canoes over muddy trails and paddling through winding
rivers might mean for ourselves and our relationships.

This night, as we bumped around searching for the theme that
would emerge, one of us happened to look out the open window
of the tent. What we saw took us by surprise. The moon, rising
gently over the tree-lined horizon, shone full and bright, reflecting
perfectly on the water below. Throughout the next few hours, our
conversation carried us toward morning in contented wakefulness.
We spoke of the joys of being seven women ages fourteen to forty,
confronting the challenges of canoeing and camping in a wilderness

with no phones, no motors, and no men. We spoke of the mystical moose whose eyes had met our own during an early-morning walk to the latrine. We spoke of the wholeness — body, mind, and spirit — which emerged as we communed with God in God's creation, surrounded by sisters who were always there to help when the mud grew too deep or the canoes became too heavy. That night, as our conversation lingered on unusually late, we watched the progress of the steadily journeying moon as it drew its reflection on the calm skin of the water.

That night I was reminded — nestled as I was in the comfort of my woman friends and the wideness of God's creation — of the ever-changing, yet constant nature of the moon. It became for me a symbol of my Creator — always changing face, always revealing a new aspect, but always present. I can, as Mary Chapin Carpenter sings, "rely upon the moon."

For centuries, women have relied upon the moon. Our physical cycles are tied to its changing phases. Our bodily tides move in sync with its rhythms. The moon symbolizes the bond that connects women today with women of centuries past: women who walked to the deep well each morning to draw sustaining water for the day; women who struggled against the overwhelming odds of male power structures to claim their strength and voice; women who found ways to name their personhood and pursue their callings. That night in the moon's full glow, my tentmates and I were telling new stories, but speaking an old, old language. We were joining our particular voices with a chorus of women that began long ago. Joining this chorus is the beginning of a process I call *girlfriend theology*. Girlfriend theology begins with the bold act of adding new voices to the strong chorus of women who have gone before us. It is adult women meeting adolescent girls in the light of a full moon. It requires the creation of safe spaces within faith communities for the stories of female adolescents to be told, heard, honored, and reflected upon. It views those stories in light of the stories of the Judeo-Christian canon, the long tradition of faithful mystics and saints, the legends of women whose stories have been only scantily recorded, and the wider corpus of texts that shape the reality of a postmodern world.

The Problem: Missing Voices of Youth, Silenced Selves, and Girls in the Footnotes

Missing Voices of Youth

The three teenaged girls in the tent that night came from a predominately white United Methodist church in a middle-class suburb of Chicago. This church, the first place I served following seminary and a residency in Clinical Pastoral Education, was not a place that invited adolescent girls to tell their stories. From their point of view, church was something their parents required, and confirmation was the ticket out. Once confirmed, local custom affirmed, they could decide for themselves whether they wanted to continue participating in the outward trappings of the Christian faith. Unfortunately, youth in mainline churches often view confirmation as the way *out* rather than the way *in* to more adult involvement in the church.

I ordered the curriculum and entered the confirmation class with much higher expectations. I imagined relationships forming, questions getting tossed about, minds opening wide, and hearts expanding. All of these things happened over the course of our yearlong confirmation quest and beyond as those confirmands formed the core of an active youth ministry. More often than not, however, the truest teaching and learning happened in moments of frustration when we tossed the curriculum aside and proceeded spontaneously. The life-giving expressions of theology I had experienced in seminary were absent from the confirmation and youth ministry curricula I perused. I found myself working too many hours trying to figure out ways to translate to my pupils the God I had come to know through the writings of feminists, Latin Americans, and people of color. Listening to those voices — particularly those of people struggling for emancipation from various types of oppression — reminded me of what was missing in youth ministry resources. All emancipatory theologies begin with concrete life experience. Then they reflect on that experience in the context of the Bible and society. Finally, they seek callings in which to practice faith and engage in action. But without that crucial first step, they would not have transformed so much of the landscape of contemporary theology. I became convinced that the first step in youth ministry should be hearing the voices of the youth themselves. This is not a new idea, but it became a deeply rooted conviction for me, shaping my research into the faith lives of adolescent girls.[1]

In addition to a lack of resources for youth ministry in general, the specific needs of female adolescents motivated my research. Unique problems also face adolescent boys. A culture of violence, access to guns, and rigid gender expectations combine to form combustible environments for boys struggling to reach adulthood. If ever there was a time for the church to provide boys with role models to help them develop rich emotional lives and the capacity for intimacy, now is such a time. However, my feminist passion requires that I start where I live, in this female body, addressing the particular issues that society, culture, and the church bequeath to women. In the end, forming faithful, liberated Christian women who are able to claim their full voice carries the potential of transforming all of church and society, beyond the bounds of gender.

As I grew close to young women, I found their life stories echoing the research of Carol Gilligan, Lyn Mikel Brown, and their colleagues in the field of women's psychological development. Not only were girls being silenced in early adolescence, they were having difficulty regaining their voices and shaping their identities well into adulthood. If a girl raised within an American church is lucky, she may encounter the writings of feminist theologians, a substratum of the faith community that, among other things, reclaims biblical women's history in an effort to empower women today. But girls are not likely to encounter these voices of hope with any consistency in their local churches, and I could not find much evidence that feminist theologians have taken any interest in their adolescent sisters. Addressing these two themes of silenced selves and girls in the footnotes of feminist theology helps to further describe the problem this book seeks to address.

Silenced Selves

On the way to womanhood, some girls in contemporary American culture experience a dramatic loss. The vivacious, feisty ten-year-old who is unafraid to stand up for herself goes underground; a tempered, silenced thirteen-year-old emerges with a veneer of "nice and kind" that covers turbulent feelings churning within.[2] As adolescence unfolds, some girls shed previous identities-in-the-making — ones that allowed for complex and relatively unfixed expressions of selfhood — absorbing instead dominant cultural norms of what it means to be female.[3]

Recent research into the lives of predominately white, middle-class adolescent girls has unearthed "the loss of voice" as a primary psychological marker of the move into junior high school and beyond. This is shorthand for a series of transitions that seem to occur as girls begin to belie their inner sense of knowing, internalizing voices — often the voices of adult women in their lives — that run counter to their own experience. Internalizing cultural cues, girls begin to "not know" and to behave in ways deemed "nice and kind."[4] Conventional gender stereotypes seem to creep into the mind of the early-adolescent girl, catching her unaware. Subtle forces operate to tie the blindfold and tighten the gag. Descriptors such as "vivacious," "spunky," and "willful" give way to adjectives such as "nonconfrontational" and "pleasing." Wildflowers dry up; wallflowers emerge.[5]

My project seeks to fashion a theological response to the psychological research calling attention to the lives of adolescent girls. If girls internalize voices that limit their potential to be active agents forming and transforming their world, they are living less than fully human lives. This has not only psychological, emotional, and political implications, but spiritual ones as well. As Carol Lee Flinders notes, a secular framework alone is not adequate to "strengthen girls enough so they can look patriarchy in the eye and keep walking." Like Flinders, I believe faith traditions bring vital resources to the task of getting girls across that threshold so that they "stand a good chance of remaining whole and safe."[6]

Because I believe people are inherently theological — often struggling to make sense of ultimate issues in relation to life's sacred dimension — I assumed at the outset of my research that girls are already quietly employing their spiritual selves in whatever acts of resistance to mainstream culture they are able to muster.[7] Whatever voice, whatever authority, whatever self-reliance, and whatever self-esteem they exhibit, I hold, must at root draw from resources of spirit.

My goal, then, is to tease out of the stories of girls the embodied strategies they use to confront oppressive forces that seek to diminish their humanness. Thus, I endeavor to articulate a spirituality of resistance — resistance that moves toward empowerment, subjectivity, and agency shaped in the image of God.[8]

The silence of adolescent selves, however, is not a universal female experience. To some African American and Asian American women, research conclusions about "silencing" and "losing voice" appear askew, bearing little resemblance to the life they knew as girls. As African American educator Beverly Jean Smith writes, psychological research on women reflects her knowledge of white, middle-class women, but leaves out the experiences she had as a young woman, which taught her not to be passive but to resist. "Raised as a resister, I am able to question these paradigms. I see spaces that need filling, so that a more complete picture of women's development emerges."[9]

When researchers make central the experiences of girls from varying class and ethnic backgrounds, different psychological wounds bear testimony to added oppressive forces of dominant culture, including race and class ideology.[10] Thus, while mindful of the phenomenon of silencing, I remain aware of other manifestations of dominant culture in the lives of adolescent girls. I seek to avoid lumping all adolescent girls into one master narrative, which would belie the particularities of class, race, and ethnicity.

Girls in the Footnotes

White feminists have been critiquing dominant Western theological models for more than thirty years. Alongside them, but often unacknowledged by them, women of color have been constructing their own models of theology and ethics based on the truths of their embodied lives and critiques of racism, sexism, and classism. This discipline, known as womanist thought and grounded in the experience of black women, offers critical insight to broader theological and ethical discourse.[11]

Within *white feminist* theology, the lives of adolescent girls have been largely ignored. Within *womanist* literature, however, young girls are pervasive. White feminist theology has traditionally focused on adult issues. Teenage girls, if they appear at all, show up as footnotes. An example of such a footnote appears in Nelle Morton's book, *The Journey Is Home*. In acknowledging the political voice she inherited from her mother, Morton writes, "When she was young, she wrote a prize-winning oration, 'The Woman I Want to Be.' It anticipated the woman movement today. When I was in my teen years, she gave it to me to use in an oration contest. I, too, won a prize with it." Morton does not mention that brief story, which might contain seeds for a tradition of educating girls into feminist consciousness, again. This provides evidence that, although we may be indebted to our mothers for the educations that helped us struggle toward our own voices, white feminists frequently forget to turn an intentional eye toward feminist socialization of younger generations.[12]

The possible reasons for this are many. Perhaps they have been too busy juggling the demands of professional life and the still-imbalanced burden of women's familial responsibilities to turn attention to girls coming into womanhood. Perhaps they have been too busy struggling for ordination, tenure, and publication to attend to the practical application of feminist theology in the lives of adolescents. Perhaps as the language of academia isolates them in towers ever-closer to the pinnacles of white male power, they have forgotten the painful memories of their own adolescence and can no longer speak the language or feel the pain of a teenage girl. Perhaps feminist theologians have gravitated away from practical theology (i.e., Christian education) because it was traditionally relegated to women who were not welcomed in the more powerful roles of priest and pastor.[13] Thus, practical theology, especially when related to youth and children, took on a kind of "ghetto" status within church structures. Whatever the reasons, it is clear that feminist consciousness, as appropriated within the context of the Christian church, has not been translated intentionally into an "explicit curriculum" for the girl sitting in the pew, walking to class through the crowded hallway, hiding away in the safety of her bedroom, preparing an evening meal for her siblings and parents, or learning to care for a new infant of her own.[14]

Despite the lack of direct attention on the part of white feminists, new generations of girls are meeting God in churches where some things have changed: women's voices speak from the pulpit and the lectern; when used, inclusive language chips away at the centuries of patriarchal imagery contained in the Christian tradition; and female imagery and metaphorical language enter God-talk more regularly. But the intentional teaching content of the church has rarely gone beyond surface level, falling short of equipping girls with the tools of feminist consciousness. It is time to turn our attention to adolescent girls in the church, using the best of what the social sciences are telling us about their lives to fashion a response that resonates with the best of our faith tradition, while at the same time serving as a corrective to the worst of it.

Womanist thought provides a corrective to white feminist theology's tendency to render invisible the lives of adolescent girls. From its very inception, womanist thought has made girls not only visible, but prominent. In fact, Alice Walker's classic definition of the term "womanist" points to the existence of precocious girls. It includes these often-quoted words:

> From the black folk expression of mothers to female children, "You acting womanish," i.e. like a woman. Usually referring to outrageous, audacious, courageous, or willful behavior. Wanting to know more and in greater depth than is considered "good" for one. Interested in grown-up doings. Acting grown up. Being grown up. Interchangeable with another black folk expression: "You trying to be grown." Responsible. In charge. Serious.[15]

Although womanists are thus defined as being "not girls," inherent in the definition is a sideways glance of affirmation to girls who act womanish. Although uppityness may bring rebuke from a black mother, it may also, as in this definition, be highlighted as a virtue in the same breath. In two other stories told in her definition of "womanist," Walker refers to conversations between "Mama" and a child. Thus, the very definition of womanist has its roots in the education provided by a mother to her female offspring.

Beyond this definitional acknowledgment of adolescent girls, womanists have a tradition of interpreting domestic life as a place of power, power that emanates from instilling values in new generations.

Womanists retrieve evidence of black women cultivating "homeplace" as a site of resistance out of which emerge women with high self-esteem.[16] Within this view, "The common understanding of women's psychological state as rooted in her powerless existence as homemaker and childrearer, or a pedestal queen, carries little weight."[17] In this homeplace, attention is given to adolescent girls and sometimes results in the ability to "observe the social world critically and to oppose those ideas and ways of being that are disempowering to the self."[18] However, this capacity for high self-esteem — existing as it does within structures of oppression that operate to limit hope for positive futures in African American adolescent females — does not always translate into self-fulfillment, or a sense of agency or empowerment.[19] A model of religious education aimed at the spiritual and psychological health of all girls would encourage feminists to learn from womanist practices of cultivating healthy resistance in adolescent girls. It might also assist some African American girls in positively incorporating the sass, unctuousness, and healthy resistance they have inherited into their identities-in-process. Beyond black and white women's strategies, this education model engages voices from other margins, including the voices of *mujeristas,* Asian feminists, and others writing liberatory theology out of life experiences of oppression.

Girlfriend Theology Defined

Girlfriend theology attempts to address the problems of silenced selves, missing voices, and girls in the footnotes. It does so by constructing a method of religious education that begins with the voices and life stories of adolescent girls. It engages those stories with the stories of adult women who have found voice, and translates the resources of women's theological thought into the context of female adolescence. It is a meeting at the crossroads between adolescence and adulthood. It is a relational model of producing meaning. It moves from making meaning to taking action, as girls and adults emerge changed, able to identify new callings, and take steps toward unfolding vocation. It is a process designed to bring young women's development as feminist theologians into central focus.

Girlfriend theology is shorthand for a method of eliciting girl's autobiographical stories and reflecting theologically upon them. It is a method that grows out of research in the fields of women's emancipatory theologies, critical ethnography, religious education, and critical pedagogy. Literature from these fields will enter this conversation to provide a theoretical basis for the practical theological act I am describing, but first I want to make clear my use of two words: "girl" and "theology."

During my own feminist awakening in my early twenties, I learned to stop referring to myself and other adult women as "girls." My ears grew sensitive to that word's derogatory nuance. When used by someone in a position of authority, "girl" vs. "woman" carries negative connotations. I reclaim that word here, just as many adult women have found power in reacquainting themselves with the "girl within."[20] We may grow up and gain power, voice, and authority, but at some level we remain girls, and that deserves to be celebrated. Girls need girlfriends — those special bonds that form when females of any age develop deep and abiding, playful, and creative relationships of respect and nurture with each other. Within recent years African American girls have influenced the English language with their use of the term "girl," as in "You go, girl!" I am indebted to them, as well as to the African American adult women who taught me to think of ourselves as "girlfriends," for helping me shed the negativism white feminism has brought to the word.[21]

"Theology" is the second word I reclaim, rescuing it from the exclusive domain of the professionally trained and naming it more broadly as the process of making meaning of our lives in relation to God.[22] Theologians in mosques, seminaries, and synagogues *write* theology; people in pews, laborers walking home at sunset, and women nestled in moon-drenched tents *do* theology.[23] In the words of Rebecca Chopp, "Theology no longer uncovers unchangeable foundations, or hands down the cognitive truths of tradition, or discloses the classics, or even figures out the rules of faith. Rather, theological work is a communal process of bringing scraps of materials used elsewhere and joining them in new ways."[24] Sometimes we do theology on purpose, intentionally setting out to create rituals or write songs articulating our encounters with the divine. Sometimes we stumble into it accidentally, as my tentmates and I did on that moonlit night. Naming those conversations as vespers, an ancient term for prayers recited at the end of the day, grants them theological authority, claiming traces of the sacred in the midst of the everyday. When we lead others into the act of making meaning, intentionally creating spaces where new theological awareness emerges, we are about the task of religious education.

Girlfriend theology, then, is not a new set of ideas systematized and categorized. Rather, it is a process of bringing to voice the "God-talk" that emerges when adolescent girls and adult women "meet at the crossroads" to share everyday experiences.[25] Psychologists Carol Gilligan and Lyn Mikel Brown, in their study of female adolescent moral development, advocate that kind of meeting in order to combat the loss of voice that adolescent girls sometimes experience. Adult women, however, often feel ill-equipped to bridge the chasm separating girls from women. Girlfriend theology is what *could* happen if a group of faithful, feminist, adult women — those of us who have painstakingly constructed a "usable past" that reconciles our spirituality and our feminism — decide it is time to pass that tradition on to a new generation of young women.[26] Naming the content and practices of feminist theology as a tradition that transforms Christian community is in keeping with Mary Elizabeth Moore's definition of a "traditioning" model of religious education.[27]

Carol Lakey Hess acknowledges the importance of transforming Christian community so that it might aid in the moral development of women. She writes, "Rather than being a place that colludes with our sexist culture, [the community of faith] can be a place that holds on to women in affirmation, appropriately challenges and lets go of women as they grow, and stays put as these supported women celebrate their distinctiveness and exercise their voice."[28] As adult women retrieve the "hidden texts" of faith traditions, it is the task of the religious educator to develop methods by which those hidden texts become part of the curriculum, enabling Hess's vision of faithful communities as "holding environments" to take shape. My work is an attempt to cultivate such a method for the moral development of adolescent females within faith communities.

The Research

The research for this project involved eliciting autobiographical stories and engaging in conversation around them in three small-group settings in Chicago and Atlanta. We told stories to each other in groups of five to eight people, meeting in a home, a church, and a church-related institution. After hearing the story, we listened to our feelings, our emotions, and our memories — more or less in that order. Then we plumbed the depths of the larger stories available to us — stories from scripture, from our particular cultures, and from history and tradition — seeking to name the connections and discontinuities between our lives and the stories embedded in our psyches.

For each of the sessions, I solicited the participation of an adult woman with a graduate-level theological education and a feminist commitment. In addition to bringing a story from her own life to begin the series, the woman joined me in the role of a participant-observer who engaged in conversational give-and-take.

Themes emerged. Often these themes resonated with themes appearing in the world of contemporary, professional, Christian theology. Echoes of feminist theology, liberation theology, and process theology drifted to the surface, to be teased out and heard by the trained ear of the professional theologians listening and participating. With the participants' permission, I audio-recorded and later transcribed each of the ninety-minute sessions.

This research is a type of ethnography that proceeds in awareness of the interventions taking place. I acknowledge that the adults and adolescents are in ministry with one another, reflecting Margaret Ann Crain and Jack L. Seymour's assertions that ethnographic knowing is connected and that mutuality is crucial.[29] In their terms, the ethnographer is a minister. This kind of "passionate scholarship" is echoed in the feminist stance of intersubjectivity, which seeks to break down hierarchical and potentially exploitative relationships between researchers and collaborators. This kind of scholarship acknowledges desired outcomes.[30] The desired outcome of my research is the ability of girls to lead more fulfilling lives because of a connection to their feminist inheritance.

Adolescence as the "Field,"
Auto/Ethnography as the Method

To speak of adolescence as a stage of life is to engage in dialogue with developmental theory, the discipline in which Gilligan trained and which her body of work critiques for its lack of gender inclusiveness. In 1904, G. Stanley Hall first coined the term "adolescent." In doing so, he shaped underlying assumptions about this time of life as one fraught with "storm and stress" and full of unique emotional upheaval, mood swings, and psychological crises.[31] Setting off decades of conversation and debate about this period of transition from childhood to adulthood, Hall was a precursor to the clinical observations of Jean Piaget, Erik Erikson, and Lawrence Kohlberg, whose work supports the view of adolescence as a time when converging biological, emotional, and cognitive transitions cause unparalleled developmental difficulties.[32]

To speak of essential characteristics of adolescence that transcend cultural boundaries or to understand maturation as an unvarying sequence of developmental stages overlooks differences based on race, class, and culture. In light of this critique, scholars have turned their attention away from stage theory in recent decades and toward narrative as a key to understanding moral development.[33] Throughout this project, I frequently adapt key concepts from developmental theory to analyze my ethnographic research. However, like Gilligan, I see stage theory models growing out of developmental psychology as social constructs that are thoroughly imbued with modernist assumptions. These models present possible windows through which to view reality, but are just as likely to blind our view to alternate realities. Qualitative research, particularly critical ethnography, supports a turn toward narrative as a means of understanding the ways in which adolescents mature and develop.[34]

Critical ethnography, an area of scholarship emerging from the discipline of anthropology, informs my work in two ways: first, as I turn to the "field" of adolescent girlhood, and second, as I interrogate my own connection to that field through memories of my own adolescence.

As I turn to adolescent girls to elicit their autobiographical stories and theological reflection, I resemble an anthropologist entering a foreign land. I enter that land steeped in the political agenda of feminism and aware of a power dynamic at play between my collaborators and me. I am older, more educated, and the designated interpreter of events. Although committed to sharing my interpretations with my participants, I have the final say in the way they are represented. Critical ethnography supports the acknowledgment of these dynamics. As opposed to traditional anthropologists, critical ethnographers do not pretend to be invisible, detached observers collecting neutral data.[35] By situating myself in the research space, I name myself as a player. Along with my tape recorder and notebook, I bring my empathic personhood. The result of such qualitative research does not pretend to be scientific or universal. Rather, it seeks to be about "particular and specific embodiment." The result of this is "situated knowledge."[36]

As a person who once lived in this foreign land of female adolescence, I am both an insider and an outsider. Kamala Visweswaran writes that "fieldwork" becomes "homework" as we, through auto/ethnography, expose our own entanglements of race, gender, and power. This kind of scholarship explicitly addresses the tensions between the self and other and between the personal and the political, allowing those connections to become visible.[37] It sees the researcher's own engagement with another culture as part of the story, rather than an invisible fact read only between the lines, as traditionally has been the case. In adopting auto/ethnography as my method, I introduce myself into the lives of my subjects and introduce my subjects into my theorizing. Auto/ethnography challenges researchers to "interrogate our reasons" for immersion in a particular "field."[38] I do this throughout my project by weaving autobiographical fragments of my own adolescence into my discussion of the theory and practice of girlfriend theology. This is in keeping with feminist objectivity, which is defined by Diane Wolf as being about

> limited location and situated knowledge, which allows for a multiplicity of viewpoints. This perspective not only allows and encourages feminist researchers to bring their own particular location and position into the research, to acknowledge and build on their partial perspective, but makes it imperative for

them to do so before any discussion of another's reality can be introduced.[39]

Throughout this project, my ethical and theological commitment toward helping girls come into ownership of voice and moral agency is visible. I adopt this reflexive practice in line with a long list of scholars who have chosen to break from the anthropological tradition of the unbiased observer. In acknowledging my desire to "create meaningful change" as part of my research and to "do research for and with women," I follow the lead of scholars who adopt participatory and action research. The research model I use is action-oriented because it allows participants to define the agenda, creating a reciprocal event in which there is greater potential for the research subjects to become empowered by the process.[40] Although I bear responsibility for the finished product, subjects of my research become authors of their own meaning, entering into a cooperative venture with me in which they are more collaborators than informants.[41] The result of this collaboration is a practical, constructive theology. In this way, girlfriend theology moves from research to adult/adolescent encounters that become a guide for the creation of such relationships.[42]

Many of the girls and women who assisted in this project remained part of the process of interpretation. As I transcribed sessions, coded them for theological themes, and wrote my analyses, I turned to the girls and women as conversation partners both formally and informally.[43] The girls, most of whom were high school juniors at the time of our meetings, were college freshmen during the months I was writing. They kept me posted on dorm life and campus feminist movements. The women, most of whom were former students of my youth ministry course at Garrett-Evangelical Theological Seminary, were engaged in the frontlines of local parish ministry during the months I was writing. They constantly reminded me of the pressing issues facing their youth, especially in the wake of the killings at Columbine High School in Littleton, Colorado, and the ripple effect of such violence. They also reminded me of the need for the translation of emancipatory theologies into youth ministry curricula. In chapter 2 I will provide a fuller description of my collaborators and the groups we formed.

An Overview

This project is a dialogue between practice and theory. This chapter began with an autobiographical account of a group of girls and women doing theology in a tent at the end of a day and then moved into a review of literature identifying the need for the creation of similar spaces for communal meaning-making. The following chapters will follow a similar course, constantly weaving practice — often in an autobiographical mode — into the discussion of methodology and theory.

Chapter 2 begins with an autobiographical account of my own adolescence, for the researcher is also a research tool out of which grow convictions regarding methods of theology, education, and research. I describe two key theological metaphors guiding my method. I then introduce my collaborators, tell how they came to participate in the project, and share seven theological assertions that arose during the thirteen sessions. Specifically, two themes emerged: the necessity of being able to share interreligious dialogue and the centrality of stories about violence and death. These two themes provide a structure around which I organize the analysis of four of the story sessions.

Chapter 3 begins that analysis, bringing the voices of the girls in the form of two stories. These stories show the value of encouraging theological conversation across religious borders and about our bodies. As these girls engaged their life stories with persons of varying faith traditions, theological imaginations broadened and a reshaping of Christian tradition, especially as it regards female bodies, took place. This chapter begins a thick description of the practice of girlfriend theology.

Chapter 4 begins with an autobiographical account of my experience of deeply ingrained misogyny in U.S. culture. Fashioning a response to such a culture is an act of practical theology informed by key sources within feminism's usable past: women's autobiographical literature and women's emancipatory theologies. Here I share three stories from the autobiographies of two black writers and one white writer. These stories provide examples of women mentoring adolescent girls. They also widen the conversation to include issues of race, ethnicity, and class.

Chapter 5 delves back into the worlds of contemporary girls, engaging again in the practice of girlfriend theology. The two stories here relate to death and violence, issues of overwhelming import in adolescent lives today. When girls are given the opportunity to tell a story from their lives in a safe space, tales of violence and death often spill forth. Making meaning of the Christian tradition in light of tragic loss, the girls who collaborated with me rejected neo-orthodox images of God and instead echoed motifs inherent in theologies emerging from third-world and other subjugated contexts.

Chapter 6 explores these contexts, bringing girlfriend theology into dialogue with three key movements in contemporary theological literature: *mujerista* theology, womanist theology, and Asian-feminist theology. The ways this literature engages feminist theology and becomes a guide for moving toward liberatory praxis forms the basis of this chapter. Here I define my theological biases and identify key theological sources that inform my practice of girlfriend theology.

Chapter 7 turns to bodies. As I concluded my research, I realized that "the female body" was not one theme among many for the girls and women in my groups; rather, body issues surfaced continuously. In this chapter, I argue that girlfriend theology is an embodied pedagogy, a term I use to describe ways of teaching and learning that engage bodies as a primary source of knowing. Using the postmodern critique of education advanced by scholars of cultural studies and critical pedagogy, I describe the girlfriend theology classroom as one in which bodies matter.

Chapter 8 brings this focused conversation between women's emancipatory theologies, critical ethnography, critical pedagogy, and religious education to a conclusion. I construct a model of God in relationship to humanity that grows out of the theory and practice of girlfriend theology. I call this a meeting at the crossroads *of souls*.

The book ends with an appendix giving guidelines for starting girlfriend theology groups and for adapting the method to other contexts.

Living the Method

In writing this book, I followed a method similar to the one used in my research. I avoid the standard format of reviewing the literature, formulating a hypothesis, and building a linear argument. Instead, I reflect autobiographically, situating myself historically and culturally — especially in regards to race, gender, class, and age. This mirrors the story-telling step of the method. I then move to larger discourses, bringing my life experience into conversation with the wider culture's texts, especially those of academic theological discourse. This models the second and third steps of the method. At this intersection of lived experience and intellectual encounter, I construct theory and theology, which affects future actions by providing a framework for the next lived experience. This step reflects the fourth part of the story theology. Thus, I move in my writing from story to theory, theology, and action. I return to story, all the while making and discovering meaning in a process more akin to a spiral than a straight line.

Chapter Two

Future Homemakers
and Feminist Awakenings
Methods of Theology, Education, and Research

*You heard me. You heard me all the way. I have a strange feeling
you heard me before I started. You heard me to my own story.
You heard me to my own speech.*

—Nelle Morton, *The Journey Is Home*

When I entered Turkey Creek Junior High in 1976, women were
participating in consciousness-raising groups all across the country
and were experiencing liberation from the idea that life held no more
than marriage and motherhood. But my cohorts and I knew nothing of that. Cindy, Donna, Kay, Tavia, and I joined an organization
called Future Homemakers of America (FHA). We were drawn by
the promise of an annual weekend trip to Orlando—an exotic ticket
away from our families—even if it was only a two-hour jaunt. Being
a Future Homemaker held zero status, especially compared to being
a Future Farmer, which meant you made thousands of dollars selling
prize-winning steer at the county fair. But subtly, subversive acts were
taking place where that group of women and girls gathered.

In this chapter, I will harvest memories of those subversive acts,
showing how the method I use in girlfriend theology grows quite
naturally out of my own life experience as a girl. Then, I will describe
two key theological supports of the method, explain my research, and
introduce the girls and women who collaborated with me in it.

In FHA, we learned to sew. We learned to cook. We dressed in red
and white. But that is not what I remember most about my years in

FHA. I remember Kay learning Robert's Rules of Order and presiding with grace over large gatherings of girls. I remember Cindy creating subcommittees, Donna organizing phone trees, and Tavia learning to account for the money we raised selling calendars and stationery. Mostly, I remember Mrs. Margaret Ann Doak, our adviser, asking me on one particular occasion to get up in front of a large group of people to speak. She provided the text. I memorized it, and, to the awe of my friends who feared public speaking, I delivered the morning devotion to a room of a thousand people at the state convention. In FHA, I learned something fundamental about my self: I have a voice that carries and no fear of using it.

Whether or not she did it purposely, Mrs. Doak was planting seeds of feminist consciousness. She gave us the basic skills of political involvement, packaged in a club ostensibly devoted to the private realm of homemaking. She helped to awaken our voices, laying groundwork so that we might be "heard to speech."[1]

When we reached Plant City High School, we tried our best to become savvy. We ditched the FHA and branched out into different areas of expertise, still encircled by the community of care we had created in the shadow of Mrs. Doak. In high school, Mrs. Suzette Thompson — whose rolling tongue pronounced Spanish, French, and English most beautifully — provided the next words for my fledgling voice to speak: "Córdoba. Lejana y sola. Jaca negra, luna grande...."[2] I would yell these words loudly into the wind as I performed the dreaded chore of mowing and disking my father's orange grove. I won first prize reciting that poem in a contest sponsored to celebrate Tampa's Cuban heritage. While learning the nuances of Spanish inflection, I caught a glimpse of myself tractoring someday to places far beyond my father's orange grove. Having encountered wanderlust, I began collecting the many words I might need to describe the world I would find, the feelings Córdoba's full moon might evoke in me.

It would be years after graduating from high school that I would come into fullness of voice as a woman and a political being equipped with tools of critical thinking, a social conscience, and a feminist commitment to Christianity. With a Midwestern seminary degree and ordination papers to gird me, I returned to the South, accepting an invitation to preach at my home church. I naively assumed the invitation was a commonplace courtesy. Much later I learned that it was hard-won. It came only after months of persistence by none other than Mrs. Thompson. My high school Spanish teacher persuaded, cajoled, and wielded the power of her United Methodist Women to see that I would be the first ordained woman to preach from the pulpit of that stately red-brick church. Having helped me find voice as a teenager, a decade later she provided a forum and ensured an audience for my more mature voice.[3]

In my journey from adolescence to adulthood, I was fortunate. There were women who threw lifelines that pulled me in and helped me to continually add the pieces of myself I would need to survive and flourish, to find a life of meaning and a calling.[4] To paraphrase Nelle Morton, "They heard me. They heard me all the way." It happened, however, in fits and starts. A teacher here, a powerful peer there. Cumulatively, they mentored me. Looking back as an adult, I am grateful. Looking ahead as a feminist religious educator, I hope for more for the young women I see coming of age today.

Theological Method: Hearing to Speech and Saving Work

Although teachers in public schools happened to be *my* salvation, I look to communities of faith to be agents of change in girls' lives today, bringing them out of the footnotes and into focus. In the intervening decades since my awakening, feminists have changed school culture. Thanks to the work of groups such as Girls Inc. and AAUW, girls are more likely to encounter networks of support and affirmation for their emerging public selves. Teachers with feminist commitments need not look far for research and accompanying curricula to help them advocate for girls' needs. As a pastor ever mindful of the church's role as educator and catalyst for social change, I see faith communities as an important additional sphere in which to nurture girls' emerging public voice. In ancient times, the church operated in such a way. A teenaged girl named Catherine found a way to change the world through the church in Siena, Italy, in the fourteenth century. Another teenaged girl named Teresa found her path to politics through a convent in Ávila, Spain. Motivated by saints like these, I began to envision contemporary Teresas and Catherines finding strength to transform church and communities. I began to envision an educational method that would help churches provide pockets of resistance to dominant cultural norms. I began to imagine churches creating zones of safety in which adolescent girls could reflect upon their identities-in-the-making and be "heard to speech." This method would do consistently and self-consciously what my beloved teachers did spontaneously and sporadically.[5] I knew the key was not in *providing* the texts, as Mrs. Doak and Mrs. Thompson had done for me, but in *evoking* the texts lying within girls' lives.

Story is the opposite of silence. Girlfriend theology is story theology. Two feminist theologians provide guiding metaphors that support this method. Nelle Morton's concept of "hearing to speech" and Rebecca Chopp's concept of "saving work" help articulate a theological method consistent with my educational and research methods.[6]

Hearing to Speech

Nelle Morton describes a moment in her educational career when a student brought her to a new understanding of hearing. Several days into a workshop that spanned the course of a week, a reserved woman hesitantly began to speak, relating a painful story. "No one interrupted her. No one rushed to comfort her. No one cut her experience short. We simply sat. We sat in powerful silence. The women clustered about the weeping one went with her to the deepest part of her life as if something so sacred was taking place they [dared] not withdraw their presence or mar its visibility." Afterward, when the woman described this experience, she said, "You heard me to my own story. You heard me to my own speech." Morton relates the recurrence of such liminal moments on different occasions where women gathered to accompany one another "into the depths...where sound is born." She tells of a "depth hearing that takes place before speaking — a hearing that is more than acute listening. A hearing that is a direct transitive verb that evokes speech — new speech that has never been spoken before. The woman...had indeed been heard to her own speech."[7]

Morton goes on to affirm that "Hearing to speech is political. Hearing to speech is never one-sided. Once a person is heard to speech she becomes a hearing person."[8] A commitment to this kind of depth hearing, whenever it is possible, is foundational to the method I use in girlfriend theology. When we gather as a circle of women and girls to hear each others' stories, we enter a space where we learn to sit in powerful silence and listen in ways that evoke new speech. Naming this as sacred space affirms God's presence in the act of holy listening. Being called forth into speech is not a solitary act of personal devotion, but a political one; it names a new reality and creates a community with the potential to effect change.

This community resembles the "community of resistance" described by Sharon D. Welch. Being grounded in a community of resistance, Welch writes, enables and sustains transcendence of the multiple oppressions that cripple human life. Stories of renewal and transformation written to "save ourselves" emerge from such communities of resistance.[9] In girlfriend theology, we tell stories and hear one another to speech. These stories and this speech offer transformation to both the speaker and the listeners. For, as in Morton's case, it is often the student who does the teaching.

Saving Work

From Rebecca Chopp, I borrow the metaphor of "saving work" to articulate the second foundation of my theological method. Derivations of the word "salvation" usually bring to mind the lexicon of neo-orthodox Protestant evangelicalism. In this lexicon, salvation often denotes an individual objective, an exchange between self and God. Especially within fundamentalist interpretations of Christianity, "being saved" connotes a particular set of understandings. For me, growing up in the Southern Baptist Bible Belt, "being saved" meant making a "personal confession of Jesus Christ as Lord and Savior." This limited understanding of salvation cuts us off from more relational understandings. Chopp reclaims this word. For her, to participate in "saving work" is to join the communal process of continually reshaping the Christian tradition.[10] This understanding of "saving work" allows us to reclaim the theological motif of salvation in a way that makes sense in a postmodern world.

By "saving" our stories, I refer to the intentional recounting of the life experiences that shape and form us. The existential philosopher Martin Heidegger reminds us that to be human is to experience an essential "thrownness." This thrownness is a seemingly arbitrary set of particulars: an abusive parent, an attentive older sibling, a violent neighborhood, or a chubby physique. It diverges into an ever more intricate web of specific events, surroundings, and interactions that combine to make up an individual life. This thrownness is the raw material out of which all of our openings to the world are shaped. Psychologists name it as the stuff out of which we endeavor to construct a self.[11]

To be human is to give meaning to these raw materials. Experiences lead us to "address basic questions about the nature of the world, of God, of relationships, of the presence of evil, and of our life commitments."[12] This task, whether it takes place within a religious community, inside an individual's head, or in dialogue with family, friends, and professionals, can be called theology. Each of us theologizes as we filter our experiences through our "temples of meaning" — unfinished buildings that house our ongoing processes of meaning-making.[13]

By telling our stories and enlisting the help of others in making sense of our stories — especially as they relate to the larger stories of our sociocultural and religious contexts — we save our stories from the oblivion of isolation within our own referential boundaries. When we engage in the sharing of stories, we engage in a communal, saving work of reinterpreting our inherited traditions into forms and shapes that make sense in an emerging landscape. By saving our stories, we participate in saving our selves, connecting our lives to the evolving Christian tradition, and engaging with Christ in the ongoing incarnation of God's word in the world.

This act is especially important in youth culture today. Contemporary girls need spaces in which to make sense of their faith traditions as they intersect the horizons of a postmodern world. Generation X and those who follow, termed the Millennial Generation, harbor a deep distrust of institutions, especially the church.[14] Inviting girls to examine what their stories have to say to the story of their faith tradition holds promise as a way for the church to remain relevant to this generation, especially if these methods allow youth to "produce their own representations, narrate their own stories, and engage in respectful dialogue with others."[15]

The method I am about to describe is an educational method of storied theological reflection. Written between the lines are the theological convictions arising out of the concepts of "hearing to speech" and "saving work." After explaining the method and my history with it, I will introduce my collaborators and describe the research I conducted.

The Story Theology Method

The method begins with a person telling a story from her life to a group of four or five others, one of whom is a designated facilitator. In advance of each session, one participant agrees to prepare, in writing, a story to read aloud. When time allows, we distribute copies of the story to each participant to refer to after the reading. The group then reflects upon the story in two ways: "experience near" and "experience distant."

The first half of the session is "experience near." During this time, the storyteller and the group share feelings and associations that the story evokes. Related stories and memories surface, and group members respond. Participants ask and answer questions as they tease out of the story the range of emotions and associations it suggests. Central symbols, themes, or messages may arise. They are named and held for the second part of the session.

The second half of the session is "experience distant." During this time, conversation turns to themes, theological concepts, and issues embodied in the story. Participants may voice related stories from scripture or myth, or they might respond to the question "How is God present (or absent) in this story?" Although this method was developed within a Christian context, its designer, a Quaker woman, was attempting to create a model that would allow for interfaith theological dialogue.[16]

When used within a Christian context, this model attempts to cast the broadest net possible in order to include the most varied interpretations of that tradition. As a Christian theologian committed to encouraging ecumenical and interfaith dialogue, I intentionally recruited girls from different Christian denominations and from outside the Christian church. I was especially interested in finding girls who identified themselves as religious seekers, those who come to the Judeo-Christian faith critiquing or questioning their affiliations with organized religion, yet self-consciously on a spiritual journey. Such seeking is both a developmentally appropriate step for adolescents and a culturally appropriate response to postmodernity. Because of the interplay between my beliefs and those of my collaborators, I alternate between the terms "church" and "faith community," depending upon the religious mix of the group.

"Going forth" is the final step in the process. Here we ask the question, "How might this story and our conversation around it change any future action?" The aim of this process is not to end with grand conclusions, but to have each participant leave the storytelling space with her own awareness or set of conclusions, some of which may be communally agreed upon and some of which may be individual. The final step of naming a potential change completes an action/reflection educational model and helps reinforce portions of the story/conversation that stood out as particularly meaningful.

This process was designed by Beth Burbank, a supervisor in a Clinical Pastoral Education program (CPE) at Rush-Presbyterian St. Luke's Medical Center in Chicago. It was conceived as a way for seminary-trained persons involved in clinical training as hospital chaplains to engage in theological reflection as a group. The groups using this method are working, learning, and reflecting together in a variety of didactic and clinical settings. The CPE method relies heavily on an action/reflection model of learning, in which experience is the basis for critical thinking. Learning, in this method, is a result of reflection on praxis guided by individual supervision and group interaction. The story theology method reflects this educational philosophy embraced by, but certainly not unique to, CPE.

I encountered this method when I was a CPE student at Rush-Presbyterian St. Luke's Medical Center in 1990 and 1991. At the time, I was a resident in the pediatric unit, helping young oncology patients and their parents deal with issues of grief and loss. As I used the method with my peers, I was able to articulate new theological understandings, growing spiritually while also maturing in my capacity to provide pastoral care in a clinical setting. As I moved from the crisis-driven ministry of chaplaincy to the more varied ministry of a suburban parish, I realized that the practice of story theology had changed fundamentally my views of theology. Theology once meant reading other people's work and integrating it into my own thinking: it became a process that started in my own life experience, moved out to the intersecting worlds of scripture, reason, and tradition, and ended with action in the world. I began to use the method with groups I led — first, with a group of single adults in their late twenties and later with a group of adolescents. When I began teaching youth ministry at the seminary level, I introduced this method to my students as a way of teaching youth to engage in theological reflection. It thus became a method for religious education as theological reflection.

Having lived with this method for more than a decade, I have liberally adapted it, moving it from the realm of trained theologians into the realm of laypersons and youth. I also have discerned connections between story theology — as Burbank conceived it and practices it with her colleagues — and the writings of several religious educators.

As a model of religious education, story theology echoes the movements of Thomas Groome's "shared Christian praxis." Groome's model provides a five-part process for leading communities through an action/reflection educational method. It begins with naming a present action and moves to critical reflection on that action. Then, it draws on scripture and tradition to evaluate the present action and to guide future actions. Next, participants converse with their tradition and decide on a response in the form of future action. Groome's model has as its goal that "participants appropriate the faith Story/Vision to their own lives and contexts, to know for themselves through judgment," and to thereby make that story their own.[17] Story theology has a similar trajectory of theological reflection, as well as a similar goal of reinvesting scriptural traditions with new meaning.

Story theology also finds much in common with Anne Streaty Wimberly's method in its use of life stories as a primary source of group theological conversation.[18] It shares with Wimberly's method a conviction that religious education needs to offer "a process that has as its center our lived stories" and helps connect them to biblical/faith traditions. It also resonates with Wimberly's desire to enable "persons to break the silences into which they have often been relegated." The most important distinction between Wimberly's method and story theology is the role of facilitator. In Wimberly's method, the leader strategically brings stories from African American heritage and from scripture into conversation with everyday stories. In the method I use, the introduction of themes and stories is not planned before the session. The larger canon of stories from women's history, literature, tradition, and scripture flow in and out of the discussion and may be brought in by the facilitator or by one of the participants.

Zora Neale Hurston, a writer who crosses the disciplines of literature, anthropology, and ethnography, writes, "there is no agony like an untold story inside you."[19] As girls and women in my research groups moved through the steps of this method, they often shared stories never told before. In releasing those untold stories, they were heard to speech by the sheer presence of safe space. Girls and women in my research groups often reported leaving the story theology space with a new sense of ownership in their religious tradition. Having saved their own stories from obscurity within their individual frames of reference and having made powerful connections to the larger stories of their faith traditions, they felt emboldened to claim their rightful place as ongoing interpreters, engaged in the saving work of making old, old stories relevant to a new day.

The Girls: My Research Partners in Girlfriend Theology

At the heart of this book are the voices of fifteen females — eleven girls and four women. The research began in May 1997 after a student in one of my youth ministry courses expressed an interest in learning how to use story theology with the youth group she was serving in an upper-middle-class suburb of Chicago. Lisa introduced the idea to three girls, two of whom agreed to take part in a series of two-hour sessions over the course of a month. Leila and Maggie, both sixteen-year-olds at the end of their junior years of high school, participated in three sessions with Lisa, twenty-three, and me, thirty-four, during the following weeks. Although both Leila and Maggie were confirmed members of the Lutheran church where we met, neither of them attended church or youth group regularly. They both expressed doubt about Christianity and described themselves as "spiritually seeking." Both are whites who define themselves as middle- to upper-middle-class.

The second group formed in the home of my neighbor, Elaine. A gregarious and politically active sixteen-year-old, Elaine heard about my research and offered to take part. She was interested in the conversations that might take place with her colleagues in Future Leaders Chicago (FLC), a leadership development program funded by the Community Trust. Through a competitive selection process, thirty high school juniors from the Chicago area are selected annually to take part in monthly immersion learning events related to public life. Elaine told me that often during their animated conversations, questions of spirituality and religious conviction surfaced. We sent invitations to the fifteen female participants, asking them to come to a weekend retreat at Elaine's home. Of the seven girls who responded with interest, four were able to commit to the entire weekend. Emma, Katie, Hannah, and Elaine joined me and Peg, a twenty-four-year-old adult seminary student I recruited to be a part of our conversations, for two days of story theology sessions on June 28–29, 1997. Katie, Hannah, and Elaine, all seventeen, were preparing to enter their senior years of high school. Emma, also seventeen, was preparing to move away to college. I will discuss the pertinent religious, ethnic, and socioeconomic backgrounds of the girls in this group when I relate their stories and sessions. Our meeting took place outside the auspices of FLC. Although I informed the director that I would be using the FLC mailing list, the organization was simply a common thread that brought these girls together.

The third group took place in Atlanta, Georgia, in July 1998. Every summer, sixty rising seniors gather at Emory University for a program called Youth Theology Institute (YTI). Funded by a Lilly Foundation Grant and the Candler School of Theology, this four-week intensive learning event provides theological education for a select group of youth already steeped in religious thought and language. The five girls who participated did so voluntarily, giving up their free time in the afternoon. Cathy, Mary, Holly, Tina, and Kaitlin were all sixteen or seventeen years old. I recruited Sarah, twenty-six, from the staff of YTI to take part in the conversations. I will discuss the pertinent religious, ethnic, and socioeconomic backgrounds of the girls in this group when I relate their stories and sessions. Our meetings were part of YTI's officially approved research component.[20]

Taken together, these three groups are in no way meant to be representative of teenage girls in general. In many ways, the latter two groups are unique in their high level of sophistication and ability to articulate concepts. By being chosen for FLC and YTI, respectively, these girls were preselected as educationally and theologically elite. At the outset, I envisioned groups that would be racially, ethnically, religiously, and economically diverse. In the end, I achieved a desirable ethnic, religious, and economic diversity, but only minimal racial diversity. Although both FLC and YTI are racially diverse, all but one of the girls who participated in my research are white. I attempt to supplement this lack of ethnic diversity by drawing on the writings of African American, Latino, and Asian writers, especially as they recall their own adolescent experiences.

Much of the research documenting loss of voice in girls points to early adolescence as a particularly ripe moment for intervention. Although I intend this method to be a potential intervention tool aimed at helping girls find and maintain voice, I also was interested in documenting the God/human relationship from an adolescent perspective. I chose an older population to ensure a wider breadth of life experience from which to draw. Although a younger population might have allowed me to better test this method as an intervention, the literature documenting the phenomenon of silencing describes it as beginning in early adolescence and often continuing well into adulthood. My choice of an older population also reflects a simple truth of fieldwork:

I sought teens with whom I had some connection, assuring quicker and more authentic access into their worlds.

In alternating the time element of the groups — weekly, weekend, and weeklong — I was attempting to assess which format would best provide an environment for thinking that was "lithe and beautiful and immensely generative."[21] Thus, I engineered three different educational environments, hoping to compare the success of the method among environments.[22] Although I have ideas about which environment was the most fruitful, in the end, the generative capacity of each session depended more on the individual makeup of the group rather than the type of setting. At the same time that I was orchestrating the learning moment, I was creating a space where I would also be a participant. The method was thus simultaneously an ethnographic research method, in which data was recorded for later analysis, and an innovative educational method, which was being tested for its ability to generate theological thought.

All the participants and their parents completed consent forms. I tape-recorded and transcribed the sessions, with particular attention to the subtleties of adolescent conversation, including body language, overall mood, and facial expressions.[23]

Theological Assertions of Girlfriend Theology

In interpreting the text of the thirteen story sessions, I chose four of them for careful analysis here. Within those four story sessions, I identified seven theological assertions I heard my collaborators making. In many situations, the girls articulated these assertions on their own, bringing their implicit and explicit religious learning into conversation with their life stories. At other points, one of the two adults made the assertion and received a resounding "aha" from an adolescent.

Each of these assertions grew out of my analysis of one or more of the story sessions and will appear in later chapters, when the accompanying story session is related. For ease in tracking these assertions, I have included the number of the story session out of which each assertion grew. The seven theological assertions are as follows:

1. God is mysteriously omnipresent, but not magically omnipotent. Although we cannot explain it, God *is* at work within human tragedies to create healing potential. God may not fix things, but neither does God abandon us (story #3 and story #4).

2. God feels our pain and cries with us (story #3 and story #4).

3. We have direct access to God through our bodies (story #1 and story #2).

4. Our lives are like "fifth gospels." Our life stories are sacred texts where God continues to reveal God's self (story #1 and story #2).

5. We go to church to "*share* God, not find God."[24] Religious institutions affirm our hunches about God but do not usually introduce us to God for the first time (story #1 and story #2).

6. God is most fully alive (incarnated) in us when our eyes are open to the pain of others (story #4).

7. Church, at its best, is a community of compassion, a resource in our healing, and a potential agent of change in the world (story #1 and story #4).

I see these seven assertions as the beginning of an inclusive list that will grow and mutate. The list is heuristic and is in no way static. Often a theme or assertion voiced in one group setting was echoed by a different group of girls in another time and place. The ensuing chapters will examine these themes in detail, using the stories and accompanying conversations to illuminate the method by which the girls "heard to speech" their emerging theological understandings and by which adult feminist theologians provided support at the crossroads of female adolescence.

In the next chapter, I will relate two stories and summarize the conversations that followed. Liberally quoting the transcripts when appropriate, I will demonstrate how themes emerged and God-talk ensued. I will then draw connections between the assertions of girlfriend theology and themes in contemporary feminist theology.

In recounting these sessions, I make every attempt to stay as close as possible to the actual words spoken by my adolescent collaborators, so that the girls' inherent theological voices might be claimed and heard. However, their words were constantly co-mingling with words and images offered by the adult women. What emerges is a thick description, a richly nuanced portrait of the meaning-making moment, both its content and its method. My hope is that this detailed snapshot will enable, not precise duplication of the teaching/learning event, but creative adaptation of the method. Ideally, women who care about the development of girls in their communities of faith might endeavor to do saving work, creating safe spaces where more girlfriend theology might take place.

Chapter Three

God-Talk across Religious Borders

God's story is revealed in our story in myriad and mysterious ways. Each of us is the pen with which God writes a fifth gospel.
— Judith Siqueira, *In God's Image*

The two stories I have chosen for analysis in this chapter stand in stark contrast to one another. The first, "Will You Be My Friend?" is a seventeen-year-old's story about the suicide of her childhood friend. The second, "Tomorrow, Then," is a sixteen-year-old's story about one of those shining moments when all is right with the world and God is near at hand. From theodicy to epiphany, these two stories, and the accompanying conversations, show teenage girls doing theology out of tragic pain and ineffable beauty — themes that surface frequently in adolescent lives. In both of these stories, the conversations about God transcend the boundaries of a single religious tradition, landing "someplace between religion and spirituality, at a crossroads where tradition, tolerance, and universality intersect."[1]

Story #1: Will You Be My Friend?

Emma, a seventeen-year-old girl from a suburb of Chicago, told the following story. Present in the session were myself, an adult collaborator, and two other girls, Hannah and Elaine. Hannah is a seventeen-year-old Roman Catholic who joined the church as a third-grader after "succumbing to the pressure" of nuns at a parochial school to which she had been sent by her Baptist mother and Jewish father. Elaine, also seventeen, is an active member of her Conservative

Jewish synagogue and takes part in national Jewish youth organizations. Emma, whose extended family is Roman Catholic, was not raised in the church. She describes her beliefs as foreign to organized religion, but having affinity with Native American belief systems. The adult collaborator, Peg, and I are both ordained United Methodist clergywomen.

We were gathered at the home of Elaine, who was my neighbor at the time. Elaine and I frequently enjoyed theological conversations over the back fence. After hearing about my dissertation project, Elaine volunteered her home for a weekend retreat. We met on Friday and Saturday and were joined by three additional girls for portions of the retreat. We worked around job schedules, figure skating practice, and a Shabbat dinner, meaning the makeup of our group occasionally changed. The core group of girls knew each other through an urban leadership program in which they had all taken part during the previous school year. Emma was a friend of Elaine's who did not know the others, but was interested in our project and decided to take part.

Before gathering, I asked each participant to prepare a story from her life to share with the group. I asked them to choose an event or moment in their life about which they were curious, and not necessarily a pivotal or life-changing moment. I also asked the group to keep within our circle any part of the conversation that one of us named as confidential. Emma told the following story.

WILL YOU BE MY FRIEND?

My story begins back in first grade. I met this girl named Rachel, and she was the first person that I ever met in first grade. The first friend that I ever really had.

She came up to me on the playground and she said, "Hi, who are you? I'm Rachel. Will you be my friend?" I said, "Okay." And we were friends from then on. From forever. For twelve years we were friends. She moved to the city a year ago, and she got her own apartment. We kind of lost touch a little bit this past year, but we were still really good friends. We've been best friends for so many years that to lose touch, like one, maybe two years didn't really matter. Every time we saw each other it was like — click — we were friends again.

So, this was about a month ago. It was about one-thirty in the morning. The phone rang, and I didn't really pay any attention to it. My mom answered it apparently, because it stopped ringing. I went back to sleep. Then, my mom comes in and wakes me up. She tells me I had a phone call. I was disturbed a little bit. I picked up the phone, and it was my other friend Lori, who was the second friend that I met, right after Rachel, in the first grade. The three of us had been friends for twelve years. She was crying. I asked her what was wrong, and she said, "Rachel's dead." I didn't believe her. Rachel had hung herself.

A few hours before, she had been in a play. She was an actress, and she went to a school for acting and visual arts, a school where you have to audition to get in. She was a theater major. She was a senior. She was just about to graduate. It happened right after a performance, the last performance of the play she was in. She was still in her costume. There were people still filing out of the theater. Someone found her right after the play in a costume room. She had hung herself from a pole in the costume room. There were still hundreds of people there when this happened, when they found her.

So, Lori is friends with her roommate. And her roommate called Lori, and Lori called me. And then Lori came over. It was about two in the morning at that point. And we just sat there the whole night. We didn't sleep. We just kind of held each other the whole night. We had that support.

The story doesn't really have an end. It's like day by day we have to deal with the fact that we never got to say good-bye. We never got a chance to say anything to her. That night I went through about four stages. It was interesting, almost all the stages. The first was just hysteria. I cried and cried and cried for hours. And the second stage was denial. Like, I recognized all this afterward. I was just like — "No." I blocked it out of my mind for the next few hours, "just go eat something." Nothing happened. And then the third stage was just anger at her — for doing that. This was like continuing on to the next day. I didn't sleep for two days. I'd throw pillows at the wall and punch the wall and just scream. I have pictures of my friends, a wall of pictures. And I would just talk to the picture of her I have on the wall and just scream at her in anger. And then the next stage, I was just depressed. It was like, you know, I'll never get over it.

So, then I went to her service. Her parents had a service. She wanted to be cremated. She told me that beforehand. Her parents had a service for her at her grandparents' church. I went to that. I guess this is where the story ends.

It was a very frustrating service. She was not a religious person at all. She didn't believe in God at all. Yet, they had this service for her at this church where they passed out a program for her saying that "Rachel is now with God." The whole service was like, "She is now in heaven with God, where she belongs." Blah, blah, blah. The preacher was saying all these wonderful things about her, but he didn't know her at all. I felt bad, because I didn't even really cry at the service. It angered me a lot, thinking that this was how people were going to remember her.

I don't believe she is in heaven. Because for her, there wasn't a heaven. So, I don't believe that she's in a place that she didn't even believe in. It just totally angered me.

Later on we found out different clues that kind of brought everything together. She hadn't told anybody this. Not me or Lori or her roommate or any of her friends, but she had been diagnosed with clinical depression and had been on medication and going to therapy for six months. She kept all of that a secret from everyone but her parents. She kept everything inside.

She was beautiful. She looked like she was straight out of a magazine. She was gorgeous. She was talented. She had a boyfriend. She seemed to be so happy, and then this happened. I don't know. It made me question. It made me thankful that I don't feel how she did, that I can see through my problems. Whatever problems she had, she kept inside her. I know she could have worked through them, but I guess she didn't feel like she had the strength to do that. The whole experience made me thankful that I'm able to work through my personal problems.

Doing Story Theology with "Will You Be My Friend?"

Experience Near: Feelings, Emotions, and Associations

Often the initial moments after the storyteller finishes are filled with an awkward silence. It sometimes takes a few minutes to move from the immediacy of our feelings to the ability to formulate speech around them. It can be a vulnerable moment for the storyteller, who perhaps has just shared intimate details of her life. I told the group ahead of time that this silence is benign — perhaps even a thing to befriend. "We don't have to jump in right away and fill up the silence," I said. "We can just be in it until someone begins to speak." Someone always does.

At the end of Emma's story, everyone was silent, and some were tearful. One participant reached out and touched Emma's hand. After a few moments, people started sharing their feelings, beginning with sadness and moving on to anger. At one point early on, a participant asked how long ago this had happened, and Emma clarified the timeline of the death and the memorial service. Those kinds of questions and clarifications, although not explicitly part of the process, are often necessary during the initial conversation. Also, this is a time when participants may refer back to a written copy of the story, if it is available.

A moment later, a participant introduced the question of theodicy by saying, "Why did this have to happen?" I noted the comment, then interrupted that chain of thought by saying, "I want to remind you to try to stay on feelings for now. We'll come back to that as we move on."

The predominant feelings expressed were those of sadness for Rachel, for Rachel's family, and for Emma in her loss. Several people connected with Emma's anger about the service. Two people shared associations of funerals that had left them feeling angry or empty.

Experience Distant: Images, Symbols, and God

The talk naturally flowed away from the immediacy of our feelings to the level of thoughts, symbols, and larger connections. When that happened, I drew attention to it by saying, "We've moved on to the second step of the process now. I just want to remind you to open your mind up to the wider traditions, scripture, and stories that are part of us. Let's bring them into the conversation now."

A metaphor emerged that was later incorporated into conversation about the nature of the church. The metaphor was that of life as a stage or a play, where a girl diagnosed with clinical depression could temporarily live out an alternative existence. The Rachel whom people saw on the outside — a gorgeous, talented actress — hid a deeply troubled and closely guarded interior life.

Emma: One of the last times I saw her, she was complaining about how she was "a big, fat pig." She weighed ninety-eight pounds. I'm not blaming the media, but something had her convinced she wasn't good enough, that she wasn't pretty enough, that she needed to be better than she was. I mean, she was straight out of a magazine. She wore plastic miniskirts.

Elaine: The play was another world where she could be. It's a place where, when you change your costume, you change yourself. She could totally step out of this life, wanting to step into a whole other setting. When I play the character, I am the character. It's not the story of Rachel.

Emma: People could watch her —

Elaine: And she was the star —

Emma: She could be a completely different person in a completely different world. I think she had a realization that this was the only place people could watch her and praise her and love her.

Elaine: And when it's over, she can't go back to where the problems are....

Peg: And, following the metaphor of the actor, people who are mentally ill are not themselves. It's not the Rachel you met on the playground in the first grade.

God-Talk: A Covenant, a Minyan, an Icon

God-talk emerged straightforwardly at this point, as we discussed the disjunction between the official religious ceremony and the gathering of friends and family immediately after the tragedy. In the process, three images — a covenant, a *minyan,* and an icon — surfaced, bringing motifs from Judeo-Christian, Jewish, Christian traditions into the conversation of girlfriend theology.

To Emma, the church service felt like a betrayal of Rachel's truest self, the self hidden behind the beautiful actress facade. The service angered Rachel's closest friends and alienated them at a time when they longed for closure. The "true church" in this story was the group of friends who sought each other out, instinctively knowing their need to be together. They made a promise to each other regarding their own future acts, becoming a covenant community in the wake of this tragedy. Emma recounted: "My friends and I all got together. We didn't go to school, obviously, the next day. So, they all came over to my house and I made everyone promise. It was a dumb promise, well, not a dumb promise. I made them promise never to do anything like this. To always find a way of working through our problems."

Emma received overwhelming support from the other girls present that this was no "dumb promise," even though it reminded them of the seemingly hokey teachings from junior-high health class. Elaine said, "It's the kind of thing you think will never happen, until it hits home."

Building on the image of promise-making, I pointed to the covenant as a predominant theme in Hebrew literature. Often, at pivotal moments or in the wake of tragedy, people make covenants with each other and with God. I also focused on Emma's description of friends and parents who gathered at Rachel's home two days after her death. "That's an incredible image," I said.

Elaine gave a theological name to this image, bringing her Jewish heritage into conversation with the Christian context of Emma's story. "This is like a *minyan,* the community gathered," she said. She explained that a *minyan* is the quorum of ten men necessary for a ritual of celebration or mourning to take place in Judaism. In Reform Judaism, women worshipers are included in the number to form a *minyan.* In Conservative Judaism, individual congregations decide for themselves whether to include women in the quorum.[2] Elaine took the word out of those contexts, freeing it to conform to a non-Jewish, nonmale adaptation: people need a community of support in a time of loss. Emma and her friends created a *minyan* that moved in and out of the grief-filled days following Rachel's death. Perhaps, Elaine conjectured, it would continue to function in the months and years to follow because "in Judaism, it's important for us to remember that there's no set grieving period. You can never say someone's time of mourning is up."

Here the image of the play and the God-talk about a *minyan* converged, leading to a conversation about religious icons.

Dori: So in your story, there's the "play" community — the church and all the people gathered there — and there's the "real" community. And if I were to say where the church is, in my best image of the church, it's everybody coming together afterwards. If there's a God, and God wants church to look like something, that would be it. Flexible and moving, human and alive.

Elaine: Yeah, in Judaism, we believe you can pray anywhere. It's what you're saying to each other, rather than the church or the pastor. It was being there with each other.

Emma: Yeah, that was so important. To be with everyone was the most important thing.

Peg: If we wanted to move with the church being in your home, especially in your room, the symbols don't have to be a cross we hang up. They could be the pictures you have on the wall.

We talked about the fact that in ancient times, fragments of saints' bodies were saved and are, to this day, kept and revered. Relics such as these are visible reminders of an invisible God. We also talked about the cross as being like a photograph of the scene of Jesus' crucifixion, and thus a type of icon. The community of the first Christians, gathered together for support at a time of grief, held onto the symbol of the cross as a reminder of the friend and rabbi they had lost. The symbol took on meaning beyond loss, as resurrection became part of the ongoing story. Emma appreciated the connections.

> *Emma:* I like what she was saying about the picture and all the little scraps of paper we save after someone we love has died. Because I kind of did that, too. I have a little clay jar she made me. I keep that. I actually have a lot of her clothes. I didn't think of this when I got up; I'm wearing her shoes right now. They're little things, but they're important.
>
> *Dori:* They have sacred significance?
>
> *Emma:* It's a way I have of taking her with me.

As the church has icons — ways of taking God with us — so Emma has Rachel's shoes on her feet. Like a religious icon, they are a visible reminder of a relationship — this one begun on a playground — that yearns to express itself even beyond death.

Going Forth

The final step of the method is to name any changes that the story and conversation might cause. Often in this portion, I also ask participants what title they would give the story or if they agree with a title I have given it.

Peg spoke first. She said her professional life as a minister would be shaped by Emma's story. "I will always have this image of you if a family comes to me and says my son or daughter committed suicide," she said. Reflecting the mutuality of this teaching model, Peg said this image would remind her to avoid the insensitivity of the priest whose service did not reflect Rachel's life.

Elaine said the story reminds her to appreciate her own mental health. "The fact that we have the support of each other and that we can work through the bad times." Emma agreed. "I have this extra little bit of strength now. I know that I will never do what she did."

Finally, I asked if I could call this story "Will You Be My Friend?" because of a Godlike image that had stayed with me throughout our conversation.

> *Dori:* I saw God in one place especially in your story. I saw God on the playground, when Rachel came up to you and said, "Will you be my friend?" For me, that's a beautiful image of the holy or the divine because there, she's her genuine self. Rachel was a role in the play, on stage, but there is the real Rachel on the playground, and you have that particular memory.

> *Emma:* It was so honest. I didn't even question it. "Will you be my friend?" My answer was yes.

Echoes of Feminist Theology and Assertions of Girlfriend Theology

The motif of community lifted up and called *minyan* by Elaine reflects a prominent theme in feminist theology. Rosemary Radford Ruether wrote about the nurturing exodus community she called "women-church."[3] In women-church, women step outside male-dominated institutions and experience redemptive community. In such communities, cultural critique can take shape.

One goal of women-church is to deconstruct "symbols in their alienating form and reconstruct them in a form that reconnects with original blessing and authentic life."[4] In naming "church" as the group of friends gathered for genuine support and in redefining *minyan* to fit their own understanding, the participants were taking part in the creative reconstruction of symbols such as that which Ruether describes. Living a moment of women-church, they freed a symbol from its patriarchal roots, giving it new, redemptive meaning.

Rebecca Chopp writes about a new *ecclesia* that allows women to name the holy in ways that fit their experiences. The creative adaptation of tradition practiced by my collaborators reflects Chopp's underlying assumption that tradition is a "living object liable to growth and change." In this light, girlfriend theology becomes a playful space where "symbols and narratives...change and continually transform themselves if they are to be meaningful."[5]

As the participants played with the images of covenant, *minyan,* and icon, they were doing the "saving work" of theology that Chopp advocates.[6] This is work that enlists skills of critical thinking — naming the dichotomies between tradition and experience. Chopp writes, "women challenge the church as to whether or not it is really true to the Christian message and credible to contemporary human experience."[7] In naming the true church as the community of faithful who gathered after the tragedy to console each other and make a promise, the participants were acknowledging new definitions of church and synagogue that critique long-standing tradition. Their assertions reflect Alice Walker's words:

> Have you ever found God in Church? I never did. I just found a bunch of folks hoping for him to show. Any God I ever found in church I brought with me. And I think all the other folks did, too.[8]

Thus, out of this story theology session grew two of the seven preliminary assertions of girlfriend theology: (5) We go to church to "*share* God, but not find God." Religious institutions can affirm our hunches about God, but do not usually introduce us to God for the first time. (7) Church, at its best, is a community of compassion, a resource in our healing and a potential agent of change in the world.

A final connection between "Will You Be My Friend?" and feminist theology is the issue of Rachel's body image. Emma referred to Rachel feeling like a "big, fat pig" when she weighed in at ninety-eight pounds. Rachel's skewed body image could have spurred a lengthy reflection, but it didn't. It was dropped in favor of another line of thinking. Unfortunately, those lost moments occur during story theology.

As the facilitator, I mourned this lost opportunity to listen to adolescents talk about their bodies and to integrate their ideas with the wealth of mature feminist thinking on the topic of female bodies. At the same time, I remembered that the topic probably will surface again. I made a mental note to refer back to Emma's comments about Rachel's body image if the topic arose in a later session. In this instance, I never got the chance to revisit the issue with this group of girls. However, girls' bodies do become central in the next story under analysis.

This next story reflects the first of these two assertions, while introducing two others: (3) We have direct access to God through our bodies; and (4) our lives are like "fifth gospels." Our life stories are sacred texts, where God continues to reveal God's self.

Story #2: Tomorrow, Then

Cathy, a sixteen-year-old girl from a small town in the Southeast, told the next story to a group consisting of myself, an adult collaborator, and four other sixteen- and seventeen-year-old girls: Kim, Mary, Holly, and Tina. They were from Roman Catholic, Eastern Orthodox, and Protestant faith communities. The girls, who were from the South and Midwest, had gathered at a university campus as part of an intensive summer institute about theology. They volunteered to take part in these sessions during their free time in the afternoon on five consecutive days. Sarah, my adult collaborator, was raised in a fundamentalist Christian home and trained in a United Methodist seminary. At the time of this session, she described herself as "in between" religious affiliations.

Again, I had asked all of the participants to be prepared to share a story. On the previous day, we had heard a story about a friendship between a girl with an eating disorder and a boy who had been physically abused. The conversation focused on the pervasiveness of evil and produced an image of God as "the eyes which see the pain of the world." The sadness of the previous day's session was still with us as we gathered. For our second session, Cathy read aloud this story, which she had written the night before in her spiral notebook.

TOMORROW, THEN

We rode our bikes down the crunchy, sun-baked path. I was in the lead, and I didn't prefer to be, because I was feeling out of control, but I led anyway. Leah was close behind me and I could hear her breathing fast and unsteady.

"Leah, you okay?"

She did not answer, and in my obliviousness it did not occur to me that maybe she wasn't as used to traveling along these overgrown paths as I was.

We stopped our bikes at the dusty shore of Lake Jackson. Wow.

The trees encircled us. Before us lay a crystal lake. Looking into the shallow part, I could even see the polished stones at the bottom. The air seemed clearer — sweetened with the freshness of summer. There was a magic around me I couldn't quite put my finger on. Looking into Leah's eyes, I knew she saw it too.

"Here, you can blow these up." Leah handed me two inflatable rafts. One was blue, the other red. I sat upon the shore and began to heave out what little air was left in my lungs.

"You know, we're not supposed to swim here."

I was still breathing, my cheeks puffed out like a blowfish, but I questioned her with my eyes.

"Lake Jackson is the drinking water for Shawnee."

I paused for a moment, taking a breath that seemed to make my whole body float.

"Well, would it be totally weird if I peed in Shawnee's drinking water? Because I'm about to burst."

She made a face. "I guess not. I don't want to think about it."

She flipped her straw-colored hair from her eyes. "I need sunscreen."

I looked at the rough, sandy bank stretching around us. "You know, these are the types of places where Bigfoot is sighted."

Leah's eyes widened. "Yeah, I can see it now: Two girls abducted by Bigfoot in the deep woods of Shawnee, Mississippi."

"Eek," I squirmed. "Let's talk about something else." But a part of me would have been very happy to see Bigfoot.

We sailed across the water, enjoying the thought that those flimsy Super D rafts could take us anywhere. The cool shade of the tulip poplar trees mixed with the light breeze to make an unsummer-like pleasantness. I laid on my back and locked eyes with the big cloudless sky. Spreading out my arms and legs, I offered myself to whoever might be watching me up there.

"You know what would make this perfect?" Leah interrupted my trailing thoughts, and I successfully managed to roll on my side and look at her.

"What?"

"Margaritas."

I thought for a moment, chewing on my thumbnail. "No, blue margaritas."

"But don't you have to go to Mexico to get those?"

"Maybe." The wheels in my cooped-up summer mind began to turn. "Hey, we could go there!"

Leah jumped right in. "Yeah! We could take the Greyhound bus and fly over the border. I've got money in my bank account."

"Me, too. And we could sit on the beach and watch the sunset like they do in the movies — "

" — and listen to a Spanish guy with a big gut and a sombrero play one of those little guitars."

"Wow, we really could do it."

"I know. We could." Maybe we were reassuring ourselves.

"Let's do it." I bit my lip in excitement.

"All right." Leah wistfully dangled her hand in the glossy water. "But hey, Cathy?"

"Mmm?" My mind was with the fat Spanish guy and his little guitar.

"Why don't we wait?"

I bent my eyebrow in thought, staring at the stripes on Leah's swimsuit. "Okay. I actually think I'm pretty happy right here, too."

"Yeah, we'll go tomorrow."

"Okay. Tomorrow, then."

Doing Story Theology with "Tomorrow, Then"

Experience Near: Feelings, Emotions, and Associations

As Cathy concluded her story, smiles spread across all of our faces. During her story, there were several nods and laughs. All of the participants jumped in to share feelings, emotions, and associations ranging from fear to joy.

> *Mary:* You're riding your bike, and the sun is behind you, and Leah's breathing that way and, okay, some big tragedy is going

to happen. I'm expecting an asthma attack or something. But then it turns out that it's just one little moment in life when you're reassured that everything is okay.

Holly: I love those kind of moments. You can always look back at them and say, even though I have the most hectic life, I do have these moments. As you get older, you may not be able to have those moments as much.

Often, during this part of the discussion, a participant will ask the storyteller to clarify or provide additional detail. However, Cathy provided more detail on her own accord, spurring another participant to share an associated memory and raising what would become a prominent theme:

Cathy: That's two years ago. I don't know, I guess you probably noticed the voice is young in that story. That was my voice then. But, like, we still talk about that day. We knew it was a good day, you know. It was a pretty perfect moment.

Mary: It reminds me of the time when, it was like spring break. In Minnesota, that's a time when there's still snow on the ground. My friends and I went to the beach and, of course, the lake was frozen over. There was a park bench out there, and the snow was up to the seat. We just walked out and sat there on the bench. And everything was fine, you know. We still talk about it.

Throughout the "experience near" discussion, participants expressed memories of feeling directly connected to God and memories of naive innocence. They juxtaposed those with feelings of fear. Bigfoot lurked in the woods, and all-too-prevalent news accounts of real-life abductions lurked in our minds.

Experience Distant: Images, Symbols, and God

Kim turned the conversation toward images:

Kim: To me, everything in the story was shiny. The rocks, the water, the sky, the eyes, and the raft — it was all like glistening back on you and reflecting the joy of the moment.

Cathy: It's like, the world is so imperfect, but that doesn't mean there's not perfection. It's very important to have eyes that see the imperfection, but there are also so many wonderful things.

Then, as the facilitator, I shared some comments about the process, so the participants would be mindful of the way the conversation had shifted.

Dori: We've moved toward images naturally, so let's carry the conversation away from feelings to name those images. We've talked about shining, reflective light, and also the image of beauty — the beauty which is the flip side of the pain of life. God sees terrible sadness, but at the same time, God is seeing these shiny, glorious moments. God's witnessing you lying there with your beautiful body, sprawled out.

Kim: I thought of that when you said, "I locked eyes with the cloudless sky." I thought that was the coolest image. That was like a connection with God right there. You're seeing each other there and keeping it.

Cathy: That is God. Being in church is godly, but it's not God. Here are these beautiful, beautiful trees and not a single white cloud in this blue, blue sky. That's what makes me believe. Not being in a church where someone's telling me this story about some woman at a well, which is a good story, but that's not what makes me believe. It's the true witness of this wonderful moment.

After Cathy introduced the biblical story of the woman at the well, I jumped in with an interpretation, connecting the bright, shiny image of epiphany with the refrain "And we still talk about it."

Dori: There's a metaphor I like. Our lives are like a "fifth gospel."

I went on to briefly explain the concept of a fifth gospel, as developed by Judith Siqueira, the editor of the journal *In God's Image*. She uses the metaphor to describe the contextualization of feminist theologies, particularly those from third-world countries.[9] I went on to adapt the metaphor to the current context.

> *Dori:* So, when I think about the story of the woman at the well, I think how it's been handed down through the tradition through the centuries with layer upon layer of interpretation. I think it must have been something like this that happened at the well that day — some inbreaking of the holy into the ordinary. She must have had feelings like yours, feelings that made that story be one worth telling again and again. Somebody made the story of the woman at the well the community's story. And this moment for you is like your own personal scripture. Your fifth gospel. It's how you know, in a deep, dark, despairing moment, that God exists. You go back to that snapshot in your mind. You hold that. Just like we hold those scriptural stories as a community.

God-Talk: Water, Bigfoot, and Breathing

The theological language spilled forth in this conversation, which was typical of the sessions with this group of girls. Sometimes during "experience distant," participants focused on a single image of God and explored its depths. Instead, in this session, a wide-ranging free flow of images ensued. Eventually, a shared concern regarding bodies emerged, but only after this fluid, meandering God-talk.

The participants agreed with the image of our lives as fifth gospels, and added to this interpretation remembering and sharing stories that need telling again and again among the communities of which they are part.

We talked about "floating on the raft" moments as little epiphanies and Sabbath time. We talked about the times, such as the gospel account of the Transfiguration, where we see glimpses of what heaven might be like. We receive "foretastes of glory divine."

We also talked about the significance of water in many different religions. After sharing a story about a family ritual that takes place on a lake, Kim focused on the image of water. Just as the nameless woman in John's Gospel experienced God's presence at an ancient well, Cathy and her friend tasted of the holy at a reservoir, the modern equivalent of a well.

Kim: It's weird how much of it often has to do with water.

Cathy: The image of water . . . I forget, there's something somewhere in my brain. Someone somewhere told me that the image of water had something to do with rebirth and being clean. But I'm not sure what. I'm wanting to say it's the Buddhist tradition that says that water is the source of pureness that cleans people.

Kim: In the Hindu religion, they wash so many times a day.

Dori: Like baptism?

Cathy: Right! Right!

Kim: Oh, that's it! Baptism! (Laughter.)

Dori: The United Methodists have a prayer in our hymnal before the baptism. It's my favorite prayer because it talks about the waters of the womb as being connected to the waters of the flood and the waters that baptized Jesus. All of the places that water shows up in our lives and in scripture are pulled together in this moment right before we use water as an acknowledgment of coming into God's community.

The conversation eventually returned and stayed focused on Bigfoot and the danger lurking in the woods. The girls voiced anger about the struggles they encounter as they balance their parents' (and more seldom their own) fear over the safety of their bodies with their need to be free "to float on a raft on a crystal clear lake in the middle of the wood" without fear.

Holly: My mom's always like, "Don't do this, because you'll get hurt here. Don't do that, because you'll do this." It's like, if every time I have to think about all the terrible, horrible things that could happen. Sometimes I want to put all those bad things behind me and just do, just do what I want to do.

Kim: I run in the morning. And my dad's always like, you know, "Don't run alone, you're gonna get mugged, you're gonna get raped while you're running." But to run for forty minutes within the view of this dorm? You'd be like a rat, just going around. So this morning, my jogging partner forgot to wake up. I was like, "Hey, forget this, I'm just gonna go." And so I just went all around campus. It was so liberating. I got to look at people's faces. There are people who are smiling, and some frowning, on their way to work.

Here, using voice inflection and body language, Kim interjected a bit of sarcasm:

Kim: In my moment, I had forgotten that I was going to be assaulted, (laughter) and I was breathing. When you can break out of that, that's when it's the good times.

Cathy: It's really dangerous to have this feeling, because when you do, it weighs so much more than the chance of getting assaulted. That's good and dangerous. My mom thinks it's dangerous, and I think it's good.

Kim: (Laughter.)

Cathy: We cross a lot on that.

Kim: Me and my dad do, too.

Dori: And you know that risk is incredibly exciting and fulfilling and thrilling and liberating —

Holly: Not to your parents —

Dori: God is not in the parental moment there, I don't think. I think God is in that —

Sarah: God is in that risk.

Dori: God is in that jogging moment, breathing. You said it all when you said "breathing." That encapsulated the crux of five of the world's great religions in one. Breathe. Breathe. Be connected to the holy.

Going Forth

The final step of this method is to name any changes that the story and conversation might cause. In facilitating this session, I noticed it was time to ask that question while the God-talk was still going strong. I opted to introduce it later, with only a few moments left, rather than interrupt an energized conversation. I did this, not because I deem the final step of less importance, but rather I knew this group would have other occasions to talk about the future actions inspired by this story/conversation. Sarah, who on the previous day had shared the story about a girl with anorexia and a boy who had been physically abused, expressed this final thought.

> *Sarah:* I'm reminded, with your story, that a lot of us spend so much of our lives trying to get to those kind of moments and we often use so many other things to try to get there, whether it's addictions or other relationships. But it's really not about the substances. It's about those moments. And they're free. The lake was free. It's incredibly hard to get there, but it's also incredibly simple. You just got on your bike and went there. I wish I could take that story and tell it to some of my friends who are trying to sober up.

Echoes of Feminist Theology and Assertions of Girlfriend Theology

Three assertions of girlfriend theology surfaced in this session. First, participants directly echoed Alice Walker's character Shug in *The Color Purple,* stating the belief that we *bring* God to church. Cathy's story and the ensuing conversation underline this assertion, which also arose during discussion of the previous story, "Will You Be My Friend?" Our experiences of God, according to these adolescent girls, most often originate outside religion's official institutions. We look for church to affirm these original visions of God.

Two other assertions of girlfriend theology — our life stories as "fifth gospels" and our bodies as sites of access to the divine — emerged in this session. Both of these are strong currents in feminist theology.

In introducing the image of fifth gospels, I was directly translating a piece of emancipatory theology I encountered in my study of third-world feminist theology. Pui Lan Kwok, a Chinese feminist theologian, critiques traditional Western theology for its focus on a narrow and mystified view of the Bible. While acknowledging the power and authority of the stories found there, she asserts that "our religious imagination cannot be based on the Bible alone, which often excludes women's experiences."[10]

Confining religious imagination to the narrow cultural boundaries of the stories of scripture excludes the metaphors and traditions and life realities that arise from the many cultures into which Christianity has been transplanted. In order for Christianity to take root in its transplanted home, it must be reshaped and transformed by the soil in which it now grows. This entails an occasional shift of attention away from the Bible and the tradition of people in the Ancient Near East two thousand years ago, to contemporary people's stories, which likewise embody culturally conditioned images and metaphors.

Sadly, the image of Bigfoot lurking in the woods — interpreted more starkly as the real fear of rape or abduction — is written into the cultural script of what it means to be an adolescent girl in the United States today. To experience a transcendent moment of connection to God in the midst of that pervasive reality constitutes a story worth retelling. In this moment, the adolescent participants were connecting their experiences of oppression with a particular glimpse of potential liberation. Remembering and retelling this story, and others like it, is a powerful act of cultural critique that, to echo Kwok, includes the stories, metaphors, cultural traditions, and life realities of a unique substrata of American culture — namely, female adolescence.

Kwok's perspective is given the metaphor fifth gospel by Judith Siqueira, who writes, "God's story is revealed in our story in myriad and mysterious ways, in content and in form. Each of us is the pen with which God writes a fifth gospel. God's self-revelation to each of us through daily life and experience are our faith stories as fifth gospels. Hence, there are innumerable fifth gospels all over the world."[11]

My introduction of this idea was an explicit teaching moment. It differed vastly from a didactic lecture on third-world feminism, because its springboard was Cathy's story and the common chord it struck with her peers. In this way, girlfriend theology allows for teaching moments to be offered as suggestions, which can be accepted, rebuffed, adapted, discarded, or owned. As a method of theological reflection, it is conversational, encouraging a shift in the power dynamics of the adult/adolescent relationship. It is a kind of "real talk" that reflects a constructivist way of knowing and draws on the analytical abilities of each participant.[12]

Connected to the assertions that "we bring God to church" and "our lives are like fifth gospels" is the assertion that our bodies provide us direct access to God. Feminist theologian Carter Heyward best expresses this theme. She argues that traditional Christian spirituality trivializes and denies "bodyselves," thus damaging the self-image of those who are shaped within it. She offers an alternative: embodied spirituality. After telling a story rich with sensual details, she writes:

> If we learn to trust our senses, our capacities to touch, taste, smell, hear, see, and thereby know, they can teach us what is good and what is bad, what is real and what is false, for us in relation to one another and to the earth and cosmos. I say to myself, as I return to campus from my outing with my dogs, that sensuality is a foundation for our authority.[13]

Cathy, an exceptional writer adept with nuances of the language, beautifully imbues her story with sensual details. We hear about full bladders, chewed thumbnails, heavy breathing, straw-colored hair, and striped bathing suits in a fashion consistent with Heyward's notions of embodied spirituality:

> Our feelings are evoked and strengthened sensually by touching, tasting, hearing, seeing, and smelling with one another. Our senses and the feelings that are generated by them become primary spiritual resources. In knowing one another through our senses, feelings, and intelligence — and intuition is a form of intelligence — we come to know God.[14]

Cathy and her companion — along with the participants in this session who resoundingly recalled similar moments in their own lives — counteracted notions of dominant culture that say girls' concerns over their bodies are trivial. Here we see girls' bodies portrayed as central to a way of knowing God. Naming this embodied knowing is an act that resists dominant norms of behavior and contributes to a refashioning of the Christian tradition.

In their final sequence of God-talk, the participants echoed feminist theology, while carrying it a step further into the unique particularities of their adolescent world. Bigfoot lurking in the woods became a metaphor for a specific type of oppression that they find infused in their everyday lives. An act as simple as choosing a jogging path is, for female adolescents, imbued with the knowledge that women's bodies are often treated deplorably. The metaphor of breathing, relaxing into the jog and "forgetting I was about to be abducted," reveals a fully sensual connection to an alternative reality. Indeed, it is a "foretaste of glory divine."

God-Talk across Religious Borders

In this chapter, I've given thick descriptions of two girlfriend theology sessions. The voices of the girls spoke first through their stories, then through their group conversations, and finally through my analysis of the sessions. In that analysis, I connected the images, metaphors, and recurring themes I heard girls voicing with the images, metaphors, and recurring themes in contemporary theology. The result is a meeting place — a site where adult women's emancipatory theologies inform and may potentially be informed by the voices of adolescent girls.

I chose to group these two sessions together because they shared one thing in common: interfaith dialogue. In both of these sessions, the story theology model threw a wide net, creating an atmosphere that provided entrée to God-talk across religious borders.

Explicit interreligious dialogue took place in the first story session. The religious diversity of the group, which included a devout Jew, three devout Christians, and an eclectically influenced religious seeker, offered resources for expanding theological imagination. The interfaith group claimed ownership of the concepts of covenant, *minyan*, and icon as girls and women engaged in reciprocal dialogue around their respective traditions.

In the second story session, the ecumenical group brought to the table questions about water symbolism in Hinduism, Buddhism, and Christianity. Had this been an interfaith context, this moment could have provided an entrance into deeper discussion of the differences and particularities of water symbolism across the cultural and religious spheres represented by the three traditions.

As a Christian theologian, I focus primarily on my own faith community. However, ministry in a postmodern era invites — perhaps even requires — dialogue across religious borders. This is especially important in ministering to youth — especially those who, for both developmental and cultural reasons, may be testing or adapting inherited faith traditions. Developmental psychologists hold that a primary marker of adolescence, formal operational thinking, makes it a prime time for religious seeking. Adolescents often try on different identities, testing their parents' beliefs against those of their peers in an effort to come to ownership of their own unique identity.[15] Scholars of contemporary youth culture hold that tolerance of religious diversity is a hallmark of the generations born after the Baby Boomers. Generation X and the postmoderns — those born after the late 1960s — are multireligous generations whose distrust for universal narratives encourages questioning of faith traditions. In this milieu, writes Tom Beaudoin, "people of various religious traditions (or none at all!) need each other in a dialogue about the religious."[16] The playfulness and open-endedness of the story theology model invites this crucial border crossing.

Girlfriend theology requires more than religious border crossing. In order to understand the world of adolescent girls, adult women must know what it means to cross borders of ethnicity, race, and class. I have identified two key sources that provide guides in crossing those boundaries: women's autobiographies and women's emancipatory theologies.

In the next two chapters, I will turn to these sources, continuing the process of unveiling the biases that inform my practice of girlfriend theology. I began that unveiling in chapter 2, by sharing a piece of my adolescent journey and some resulting choices about methods of theology, education, and research. The next chapter also will begin autobiographically. Experiencing the misogyny of contemporary culture reminds me of the importance of celebrating women whose voice — be it in the form of political action or creative expression — has survived. Collecting and sharing these voices becomes central to an educational model by which adult women might mentor adolescent girls. I will share three such examples of women's voice — autobiographical accounts of women mentoring adolescent girls. Gleaned from the autobiographies of two black women and one white woman, these stories also will widen the conversation to include issues of race.

Chapter Four

Collecting Sea Glass
Building and Sharing the Usable Past

Someone in her life, or at least, very powerfully, in her imaginative life, must give her reason to rejoice that she is a woman.

—Carol Lee Flinders, *At the Root of This Longing: Reconciling a Spiritual Hunger and a Feminist Thirst*

I am not a football fan. I just happened to be in the room with my two daughters one Saturday afternoon in the fall of 1999 as my husband, sister, and brother-in-law sat deeply engrossed in the University of Florida vs. University of Tennessee game. During a break in the action, my eyes and the eyes of my four-year-old daughter automatically drifted toward the television. What we saw appalled us both. A young woman, bound and gagged, lay tied to railroad tracks in the snow-covered Colorado Rockies. Her assailant stepped away from the tracks, smiling to himself as a train approached.

"Mommy, why did that boy do that?" asked Erin, her eyes riveted to the screen as she walked over to share my lap with her baby sister. I couldn't formulate a response, so I drew my arms to encircle her. In a state of shock, I watched as the drama progressed. The engineer, seeing the woman, brought the train to a screeching halt.

I breathed a sigh of relief, and so did Erin. Then, the engineer peered out the window of his train at the bundle of woman and rope lying on the tracks in front of him. Making eye contact with the assailant, he smiled and said, "Nice knot." Someone popped open a Coors Light, and the commercial was over.

Adrenaline surged through my veins in a visceral reaction to that thirty-second segment of mainstream American culture. I do not live in a cocoon. I assume a general awareness of popular culture. But every once in a while, I am caught off guard. I forget how very poisonous this culture is to girls.[1] When the football game resumed, Erin's questions persisted. "Why was that boy being mean to that girl?" I didn't try to explain away what we had just witnessed. The only response I knew how to make in that crucial moment of parenting was to endorse her instinct that something was terribly wrong. I let Erin know it was very right to be angry. At the same time, I found myself sadly wishing Erin could share a little longer in her baby sister's obliviousness.

I was also caught off guard during a late-night sports broadcast in Chicago. I had been lying in bed with an open book. My husband, lying beside me, was catching the last of the news. We were both half-listening in that state of sleepiness just before turning the lights out. "The Bears acted like a bunch of *women* out there on that field today," sportscaster Mark Giangreco said to one of his colleagues in the newsroom. Needless to say, he was not complimenting them on their Amazon-like conquest of the Green Bay Packers. For days, in an angry fog of disbelief, I told this story to everyone I knew. In private moments, I alternately whispered and shouted the mantra, "Woman *is not* a derogatory term."

Regardless of my efforts to convince myself otherwise, the word "woman" and its synonyms are often used derogatorily. A history of the English language shows this "semantic derogation."[2] Positive or neutral terms for the female gender accrue negative connotations over time. The words "harlot," "hussy," "spinster," "prude," "tart," "wench," and "trollop" all degenerated from neutral or positive connotations to decidedly negative ones. I have noticed this process in my life: I sometimes cringe when my youngest daughter refers to her sibling as "sissy." Although I acknowledge that it is a much easier word for her to pronounce, I chafe at the negative connotations attached to calling someone a sissy. Sadly, the process of semantic derogation remains in full swing today, as Katie Haegele's example from cyberspace demonstrates:

Recently I launched an Internet search to do some initial work on a piece I was writing on women in the media. It soon became apparent to me that, no matter which word denoting "woman" and which other search word I chose to combine it with, I would be overwhelmed by a deluge of pornography.[3]

As people with a feminist consciousness, we readily see evidence of women's progress since the second wave of feminism in the 1970s. My biological sisters — one a veterinarian and one a physician — are constant reminders to me that my daughters have role models who were not as readily available one generation ago. Those of us who in these "backlash" and "postfeminist" days still proudly call ourselves feminists have much for which to thank our foremothers.[4]

However, as these examples from television and cyberspace show, we need not look far for reminders of the dominant culture's resistance to feminism's demands. As a daughter of the feminist revolution in the 1970s, I try to take my Coors Light anger out of the family room and my Mark Giangreco anger out of the bedroom. Armed with this anger, I move beyond the private realm, crafting an educational response aimed toward the granddaughters of that feminist revolution. In order for girlfriend theology to be such a response, it must be fortified not just with the anger spurred by a misogynist culture but with the hope engendered by what feminist scholars call a "usable past." A usable past refers to the ever-growing body of texts — both contemporary and those retrieved from the past — that provides an alternative to the predominant, androcentric worldview.[5]

In this chapter, I will argue that building and sharing our usable past is a necessary step in the feminist education of adolescents. After further defining the concept of a usable past, I will narrate three stories that I consider part of my own usable past. These are stories in which adult women remind adolescent girls of their inherent value and worth. After each story, I will reflect on ways in which these stories might enter an educational process such as girlfriend theology. This strategy seeks to provide an example of the interplay between stories — both personal and shared — that is central to the method I am describing. Before relating the stories, however, I need to define the term "natural education," a phrase I adapt from the field of developmental theory.

Natural Education as a Model
for Feminist Education

A natural education toward feminist consciousness points to potential moments in a girl's life. These are moments when one of the myriad influences surrounding a girl — ranging from the small circle of family members to ever-widening circles that include neighborhood, school, church, the media, etc. — functions to remind her that she is a person worthy of dignity and respect.[6] If we can observe such moments happening naturally, they might provide a key to the construction of feminist models of religious education.

Constructive-developmental psychologist Robert Kegan argues that developmental theory has a long-standing appreciation of nature. The best therapeutic processes are rooted not in theory but in nature. When a person seeks therapy, Kegan suggests, it is because the natural facilitation of development has broken down for some reason. Often, a therapist's best guide in nurturing a client toward psychological health is a careful simulation of this "natural therapy."[7]

Natural therapies are thus defined as "those relations and human contexts that spontaneously support people through the sometimes difficult process of growth and change." Exposing the details of those natural interactions is the key to building successful therapeutic models. Those details include the presence of "holding environments," which function to "keep buoyant the life project" of their guest. For the infant, the holding environment is quite literally the "mothering one," or, to make Kegan's term more gender inclusive, a "parenting one." For the adolescent girl, the holding environment may exist in the school, the family, the peer group, or the faith community.[8]

Natural education is an especially useful concept in examining female lives, because, as Gilligan and others have shown, broad-scope developmental models reflect masculine lives almost exclusively.[9] Female patterns of moving across the life span differ from those "norms." Mary Catherine Bateson describes the differences using the metaphor of improvisation. Like a jazz composition, women's lives often take unexpected turns, rather than following the Homeric quest so prevalent in male life narratives. Rather than seeing interrupted lives as deviant, she reframes the goal:

We see achievement as purposeful and monolithic, like the sculpting of a massive tree trunk that has first to be brought from the forest and then shaped by long labor to assert the artist's vision, rather than something crafted from odds and ends, like a patchwork quilt, and lovingly used to warm different nights and bodies.[10]

Women's lives provide examples of these patchwork quilts, examples that other women can use as guides to affirm their own improvisational acts.

I borrow the concept of natural therapy, transporting it to the realm of education. In perusing my usable past, I looked for evidence of women's natural education toward wholeness. I define wholeness as a sense of self-worth, a sense of moral agency, and possession of a voice with which to enter public discourse. Moments like this include girls' memories of resisting dominant culture's norms regarding women. These are moments in which girls experience holding environments that keep buoyant their life projects. With the goal of glimpsing moments of natural education, I turn to women's autobiographies, which are key sources in a feminist usable past.

The Usable Past and Dangerous Memory

Carol Flinders writes that, as an indirect response to her awareness of deeply ingrained misogyny, she began to pull together for herself a "body of evidence and imagery" to support her belief in feminine strength and dignity.[11] This process echoes my life experience and the experience of many of my peers. Like Flinders, we devoured books in an effort to sustain our belief in ourselves, despite the negative voices we heard around us. This process borders on a religious quest, as girls deprived of relevant faith traditions find in literature an "adequate substitute for religion."[12] Flinders writes:

[This reading was] reading not just for myself at all, but on behalf of the young girl I had been once, who would have given anything for these narratives of feminine courage and creativity, and, yes, unabashed feminine sensuality — a girl who might well have found the courage to speak and write her own truths much sooner if she'd had them.[13]

This act of gleaning results in the "usable past." As individual women, we have our own usable pasts; as communities of feminists in solidarity with one another, we have a collective usable past.

The concept of a usable past intersects with the term "dangerous memory," which Sharon Welch uses to describe acts of resistance found within communities practicing liberation theology. According to Welch, oppressed communities can move toward acts of resistance only after recovering their dangerous memory. Dangerous memory has two dimensions: the memory of suffering, conflict, and exclusion — and the memory of hope, freedom, and resistance.[14] Scholars have adapted dangerous memory from liberation theology to feminist theology.[15] When we recognize how our culture continues to be poisoning to girls and women, we own feelings of exclusion and oppression. In recounting the disturbing television commercial, in recounting the sportscaster's gender slur, and in naming the phenomena of semantic denigration, I connected with that anger-inducing part of my dangerous memory. In collecting and celebrating our usable past, we recall the "hope, freedom, and resistance" that forms the other part of dangerous memory.

Each woman of feminist consciousness has a usable past. Some of it is individual and particular, and some of it is shared among communities of mutuality and support. Our usable past is a body of evidence and imagery, gleaned from poetry, fiction, theater, art, quilts, dance, and other sources. It is this body of evidence that girlfriend theology invites into the conversation with adolescent girls. The first part of the girlfriend theology session stays close to the lived experiences of individual participants. It focuses on feelings, memories, and real-life encounters. The second part, however, turns directly toward stories and images. As adults entering conversations with adolescent girls, we are not silent partners. We have something to offer, something adolescent girls badly need, but for which they may not know how to ask. We have warehouses of images and stories that give us "reason to rejoice" that we are women. Our usable past becomes an essential resource in the education of girls.

Whose Usable Past?
Acknowledging Voices of Difference

I continually construct my usable past from many sources. Primary among them are women's autobiographies, women's emancipatory theologies, and feminist biblical studies. In this chapter, I share some of that body of evidence and imagery, particularly from autobiography. I argue that this source provides unique windows into the ways in which some girls experienced a natural education toward wholeness and voice and away from internalizing our culture's negative messages about women. These windows become especially important if we are to acknowledge differences of race, ethnicity, and class.

Three glimpses of adult women meeting girls at the crossroads of adolescence emerge in the stories I will share. These are not neutral stories.[16] They are stories that combat an androcentric worldview shaped by long traditions of white, Eurocentric values. Two of the stories surface from the lives of African American women; one is from a white woman.

These stories depict girls learning notions of healthy resistance. In them, we see girls soaking up mother wit, learning unctuousness as a virtue, and finding ways to love themselves.[17] We also see the presence of "mothering ones" — people who create environments that nurture young souls engaged in the task of sorting through what it means to be a girl, a woman, a survivor, and a force to be reckoned with.[18] They are isolated examples, slices of the lives of girls who found ways to hold onto the memory of being created in the image of God. These stories bear testimony to a girl's power to know that the holy resides within her, despite dominant culture's devaluing and denigration of women's lives and experiences.

Women's autobiographies reveal stories such as these — stories in which we see adult women educating girls in everyday places, like sidewalks, kitchens, and bathtubs. These are everyday lives reflecting difference: difference in race, in class, and in privilege. These differences are lived out in various levels of oppression, from subtle to enormous. For just as we live in a deeply misogynist culture, we also live in a deeply racist culture. Any discussion of women's lives and the resistance women muster to cultural oppression definitions must take into account those differences.

Until now, I have limited my discussion of oppressive forces to those I have resisted personally as a white female. However, I am mindful that oppressions are multiplied many times over for women of color. By choosing two stories of African American women, and by using the writing of womanist scholars to interpret these stories, I widen the conversation to include issues of race. Later chapters will widen the conversation further by engaging the voices of Asian and Hispanic women.

By incorporating stories of women of color into my usable past, I am borrowing from a community that is not my own. As a white feminist, I know it is not the burden of women of color to educate me about racism.[19] That is why, in addition to personal relationships of mutual support and accountability, I highly value the written record of women of color. This record — in both autobiographical and analytical forms — helps me begin to understand the triple oppression of gender, class, and race facing many women of color. It enables me to acknowledge white privilege, and it provides a starting point for me to begin the dismantling of racism.[20] Therefore, attention to the writings of women of color is essential for feminists who hope to provide a welcoming space in which all girls — regardless of the oppressive forces they face — may be heard to speech.

"Not Blossoms, but Blooming": Three Stories of Girls Shaping Identity

Story One: Saved from Silence

African American educator and poet Maya Angelou tells a story, which I have entitled "Saved from Silence," in her autobiography, *I Know Why the Caged Bird Sings.* The young Angelou, a victim of rape, testified in court against her abuser. Laden with shame over her history of abuse, the girl stopped talking to everyone but her brother Bailey. For a year, she lived in morose silence, sopping around the house "like an old biscuit, dirty and inedible" until she met a woman who threw her a "lifeline."

Mrs. Bertha Flowers, a wealthy black aristocrat, singles out the young Angelou, whose name as a child was Marguerite, for special attention. As they are walking, Mrs. Flowers initiates the following conversation:

She said, without turning her head, to me, "I hear you're doing very good school work, Marguerite, but that it's all written. The teachers report that they have trouble getting you to speak in class." We passed the triangular farm on our left and the path widened to allow us to walk together. I hung back in the separate unasked and unanswerable questions.

"Come and walk along with me, Marguerite." I couldn't have refused even if I wanted to. She pronounced my name so nicely. Or more correctly, she spoke each word with such clarity that I was certain a foreigner who didn't understand English could have understood her.

"Now, no one is going to make you talk — possibly no one can. But bear in mind, language is man's way of communicating with his fellow man and it is language alone which separates him from the lower animals." That was a totally new idea to me, and I would need time to think about it.

"Your grandmother says you read a lot. Every chance you get. That's good, but not good enough. Words mean more than what is set down on paper. It takes the human voice to infuse them with the shades of deeper meaning."

I memorized the part about the human voice infusing words. It seemed so valid and poetic.

She said she was going to give me some books and that I not only must read them, I must read them aloud. She suggested that I try to make a sentence sound in as many different ways as possible.

"I'll accept no excuse if you return a book to me that has been badly handled." My imagination boggled at the punishment I would deserve if in fact I did abuse a book of Mrs. Flowers'. Death would be too kind and brief.

The odors in the house surprised me. Somehow, I had never connected Mrs. Flowers with food or eating or any other common experience of common people. There must have been an outhouse, too, but my mind never recorded it.

The sweet scent of vanilla had met us as she opened the door.

"I made tea cookies this morning. You see, I had planned to invite you for cookies and lemonade so we could have this little chat. The lemonade is in the icebox."

It followed that Mrs. Flowers would have ice on an ordinary day, when most families in our town bought ice late on Saturdays only a few times during the summer to be used in the wooden ice-cream freezers.

She took the bags from me and disappeared through the kitchen door. I looked around the room that I had never in my wildest fantasies imagined I would see. Browned photographs leered or threatened from the walls and the white, freshly done curtains pushed against themselves and against the wind. I wanted to gobble up the room entire and take it to Bailey, who would help me analyze and enjoy it.

"Have a seat, Marguerite. Over there by the table." She carried a platter covered with a tea towel. Although she warned that she hadn't tried her hand at baking sweets for some time, I was certain that like everything else about her the cookies would be perfect....

As I ate, she began the first of what we later called "my lessons in living." She said that I must always be intolerant of ignorance, but understanding of illiteracy. That some people, unable to go to school, were more educated and even more intelligent than college professors. She encouraged me to listen carefully to what country people called mother wit. That in those homely sayings was couched the collective wisdom of generations.

When I finished the cookies, she brushed off the table and brought a thick, small book from the bookcase. I had read *A Tale of Two Cities* and found it up to my standards as a romantic novel. She opened the first page and I heard poetry for the first time in my life.

"It was the best of times and the worst of times...." Her voice slid in and curved down through and over the words. She was nearly singing. I wanted to look at the pages. Were they the same that I had read? Or were there notes, music, lined on the pages, as in a hymn book? Her sounds began cascading gently. I knew from listening to a thousand preachers that she was nearing the end of her reading, and I hadn't really heard, heard to understand, a single word.

"How do you like that?"

It occurred to me that she expected a response. The sweet vanilla flavor was still on my tongue and her reading was a wonder in my ears. I had to speak.

I said, "Yes, ma'am." It was the least I could do, but it was the most also.

"There's one more thing. Take this book of poems and memorize one for me. Next time you pay me a visit, I want you to recite...."

On that first day, I ran down the hill and into the road (few cars ever came along it) and had the good sense to stop running before I reached the Store.

I was liked, and what a difference it made. I was respected not as Mrs. Henderson's grandchild or Bailey's sister, but for just being Marguerite Johnson.[21]

A Womanist-Informed Reflection

This story can be read as one woman's attempt to integrate a pivotal event into the overall picture of her life. The story of Mrs. Flowers's intervention forms a bridge between parts of the girl's life — silence and speech, sparseness and beauty. It paints, like Van Gogh, "not blossoms, but blooming."[22] We do not see the finished product but a girl on the way to inventing her adult identity. We see the young Angelou in a moment of transformation. In telling this story, a woman makes meaning out of the everyday events of life that shaped her emerging, multidimensional identity. As such, this story provides a glimpse of part of one woman's natural education toward liberation. She learns healthy resistance to the evil she has experienced.

"Homeplace" is one womanist theme that helps bring this story into conversation with the larger historical realities facing African American women involved in identity formation.[23] In the essay

"Homeplace: A Site of Resistance," bell hooks argues that African American women have always honored spaces such as those in Mrs. Flowers's house: a kitchen out of which flows the sweet smell of vanilla, a living room lined with books, a table at which a girl sits for her lessons in life. These are spaces, she argues, where "resistance means opposition to being invaded, occupied, assaulted, and destroyed by the system." These are spaces where the injured turn for help in healing themselves. In hooks's treatment, sites of homeplace take on different forms, depending on issues of economics and class. Clearly, Mrs. Flowers's residence represents a relatively privileged version of homeplace. Equally compelling in their power to instruct are depictions of homeplace that include slave shacks with dirt floors and morning scenes in which girls and mothers struggle through hair-combing rituals.[24]

It was these kinds of spaces, bell hooks argues, "where all that truly mattered in life took place — the warmth and comfort of shelter, the feeding of our bodies, the nurturing of our souls. There we learned dignity, integrity of being; there we learned to have faith."[25] In spite of racist and sexist notions that made it the African American woman's lot in life to keep house — the white person's house all day long and then, at day's end and beginning, her own home — she nonetheless acted subversively, using her power as an educator and liberator within the domestic sphere. In honoring this history of service, womanists acknowledge the systems of oppression that underlie it, while at the same time celebrating the ways their foremothers resisted.

> It does not matter that sexism assigned them this role. It is more important that they took this conventional role and expanded it to include caring for one another, for children, for black men, in ways that elevated our spirits, that kept us from despair, that taught us to be revolutionaries able to struggle for freedom.[26]

Angelou certainly became a revolutionary able to struggle for freedom. Having been "occupied, assaulted, and destroyed by the system" — which allowed the sexual victimization of a young girl and the further victimization of a pain-inflicting judiciary proceeding — the girl hungered for a means to resist. Self-chosen silence was one such means of resistance. But by throwing her a lifeline, Mrs. Flowers provided an alternative, a healthier means of resistance. By the time Angelou graduated from eighth grade, she was the head of her class.[27] Mrs. Flowers used the homeplace she had created to reach out to what some might consider a stranger. The young girl had no connection to the higher-class matron, other than that of awe-struck admirer. Mrs. Flowers responded to Marguerite out of some deep calling of her own, claiming her responsibility to the community by offering herself as a resource in the healing of one girl.

Implications for the Religious Education of Girls

What does this story, and its analysis in light of a womanist theme, bring to a method of religious education of girls? That question must be explored on various levels.

First, if some adolescent girls lose voice in part due to the internalization of the advice of adult women in their life, as Gilligan and Brown maintain, this story provides an alternative. Angelou was, quite literally, "heard to speech." Interpreting this moment as a pivotal one in Angelou's life, we can understand the hearing provided by Mrs. Flowers as the kind of hearing that Nelle Morton describes, a hearing which "evokes speech — new speech that has never been spoken before."[28] This story serves as one piece of evidence supporting the potential of adult women in communities of faith to respond to the plight of some adolescent girls by listening and providing lifelines.

Second, if, as Robinson and Ward argue, having found voice, African American girls often translate their autonomy and self-esteem into *unhealthy* forms of resistance, this story describes a way of inspiring *healthy* resistance.[29] It emerges from a community of mentors who claim responsibility for girls' difficulties in wading through oppressive culture. Mrs. Flowers is an example of the community of "other-mothers" who reach out from domestic circles to ever-widening spheres of influence, seeking to shape the society that inflicts racist and sexist wounds.[30] This story provides further encouragement for communities of faith to take an ethical stance in support of adolescent girls. In the absence of a natural community of mothering ones, faith communities can create spaces where other-mothers could interact intentionally with adolescent girls, empowering them to integrate healthy forms of resistance into their emerging identities.

Most important, this story shows the construction of identity and meaning from the stuff of everyday life. Not all girls are gifted with the instinct toward self-reflection that Angelou has honed into a skill for storytelling and used to aid in the narrative construction of identity. But many girls might respond to an invitation to tell their stories. A method of religious education in which "hearing is a direct transitive verb that evokes speech" would incorporate "mothering ones" — those who empower girls to name their own realities and engage in healthy resistance — into the life of the church's educational mission.

What outcomes might emerge from such a model of religious education? If the experiences of diverse communities of women become the starting point for thinking about theology and ethics, new images of God will appear. Might not the girls, through their own theological instincts or through the nudging of a conversation partner, find meaning in the image of God reflected in a Mrs. Flowers? Does that image not have points of connection to scripture and faith tradition? In this way, those images — which have been historically submerged but more recently retrieved from invisibility — might enter into the identity-forming and meaning-making space of young girls. I suggest this method has the power to enable girls to rename their reality, to participate in a form of engaged pedagogy that has the potential to liberate their bodies, souls, and minds from the oppressive constructs that shape their thinking about God, self, and community.[31]

Story Two: The Mother of God Revisited

The second story also comes from the life of an African American girl. Here, poet and essayist Audre Lorde self-consciously reflects upon the women who "mothered" her into identity, seeking to answer the question:

> To whom do I owe the power behind my voice, what strength I have become, yeasting up like sudden blood from under the bruised skin's blister? My father leaves his psychic print upon me, silent, intense, and unforgiving. But his is a distant lightning.

Images of women flaming like torches adorn and define the borders of my journey, stand like dykes between me and the chaos. It is the images of women, kind and cruel, that lead me home.[32]

She continues to answer her rhetorical question with a series of stories, one of which follows.

DeLois lived up the block on 142nd Street and never had her hair done, and all the neighborhood women sucked their teeth as she walked by. Her crispy hair twinkled in the summer sun as her big proud stomach moved her on down the block while I watched, not caring whether or not she was a poem. Even though I tied my shoes and tried to peep under her blouse as she passed by, I never spoke to DeLois, because my mother didn't. But I loved her, because she moved like she felt she was somebody special, like she was somebody I'd like to know someday. She moved like how I thought god's mother must have moved, and my mother, once upon a time, and someday maybe me.

Hot noon threw a ring of sunlight like a halo on top of Delois' stomach, like a spotlight, making me sorry that I was so flat and could only feel the sun on my head and shoulders. I'd have to lie down on my back before the sun could shine down like that on my belly.

I loved DeLois because she was big and Black and special and seemed to laugh all over. I was scared of DeLois for those very same reasons. One day I watched DeLois step off the curb of 142nd Street against the light, slow and deliberate. A high yaller dude in a white Cadillac passed by and leaned out and yelled at her, "hurry up, you flat-footed, nappy headed, funny-looking bitch!" The car almost knocking her down. DeLois kept right on about her leisurely business and never so much as looked around.[33]

A Womanist-Informed Reflection

From this story we glimpse one woman's attempt to integrate an alternative figure of authority and power into a cast of more conventional figures telling her how women should be. For the young Lorde, the

person of DeLois lifts up a form of beauty that resists the white standard of beauty, which glorifies thin figures and light skin. It also resists
the black female standard of beauty that internalizes white racism and
makes straight hair somehow better than kinky hair.[34] As in the story
before, we see a glimpse of "not blossoms, but blooming" in the depiction of the young Lorde trying to peep at the woman's large bosom
and, by comparison, reflecting on her own body as lacking enough
space for the sun's warmth to shine upon. As Lorde reflects upon the
process of a girl inventing her adult identity, we see her choosing to
admire and emulate a woman who "loves herself, regardless."[35] In
telling the story, Lorde makes meaning out of the everyday events of
life that shaped her emerging, multidimensional identity. As such, this
story provides a glimpse of part of one woman's natural education
toward healthy resistance.

The womanist theme of "unctuousness as a virtue," explored by
Katie Cannon through the life and writings of Zora Neale Hurston,
helps to make connections between Lorde's story and the larger canon
of stories surrounding the historical, social, and cultural experiences
of African American women.

Cannon lifts up the term "unctuousness," as used by Alice Walker,
to refer to a black woman's ability to consistently "act sincere in the
most insincere situations."[36] Unctuousness emerges in the lives of
African American women who "maintain a feistiness about life that
nobody can wipe out, no matter how hard they try." Forged out of
the historical realities of sexism and racism, unctuousness is a survival
strategy often adopted to resist evil and respond to suffering "which
is the normal state of affairs."[37] In the life of Hurston, unctuousness
included embodying the "mama says" phrases that told her to

> "jump at de sun" so that she would not "turn out to be a mealy
> mouthed rag doll" with a squinched spirit by the time she was
> grown. "We might not land on the sun, but at least we would
> get off the ground."[38]

In such a way, Hurston lived into healthy resistance inherited from
her mother, rather than internalizing the voice of her father who re-
peatedly admonished her to adopt a "spirit of docile complacency."[39]
In the story of DeLois, Lorde provides an image of unctuousness

embodied. This unctuousness is witnessed by and incorporated into the emerging identity of the girl, who sees in DeLois's prideful walk echoes of the woman her mother once was and an image of womanhood to which she aspires. In her refusal to seek the approval of the neighborhood women, in her comfortable acceptance of dark skin and an ample carriage, in her refusal to acknowledge the demeaning taunts of a passerby, DeLois keeps right on moving, "like how I thought god's mother must have moved."

Regina Austin critiques the use of role models that do not adequately respond to material conditions that limit choices of young black women. The figure of DeLois is the kind of role model Austin calls a Sapphire. These are the "host of nonelite black women who everyday mount local, small-scale resistance grounded in indigenous cultural values, values whose real political potential is often hidden even from those whose lives they govern."[40] The image of a Sapphire is of a woman who testifies on her own behalf and does not muffle her indignation.

Implications for the Religious Education of Girls

Like Angelou's story, this story adds to the evidence supporting the need for a model of religious education that engages girls in theological reflection of their own life stories. To paraphrase Alice Walker, women must scrape the white man off our eyeballs before even trying to get a glimpse of God.[41] Out of this story, new glimpses of God emerge. These new images can function to break through the stereotypes of God so embedded in our minds that they seem glued to our eyeballs. A story like this, incorporated into the storehouse of narratives available to an adult facilitator, could prove useful in leading girls through theological reflection of their own life stories. It could provide a link, allowing girls to realize that they too may someday move with the self-assurance of a DeLois and may incorporate virtues such as unctuousness into their identities. Through telling the story of a DeLois or Mrs. Flowers in her own life, and making connections to larger stories, a girl could begin to learn what it means to resist the internalized voices that operate to belittle, demean, and negate self-worth.

Story Three: She Believed I Could Fly

The final story comes from the experience of a white woman. In *An American Childhood*, author Annie Dillard remembers a moment in which she learned to resist conventional norms of behavior, while finding the source of sublime joy within her body. This story differs from the two that came before. This story does not arise out of the complex web of oppressions facing Maya Angelou, Audre Lorde, Alice Walker, bell hooks, Katie Cannon, and Ntozake Shange. It springs out of the experience of a girl born into privilege by virtue of her skin color, class, and economic status.

Stories of resistance take on a different character in the lives of white girls, who, although oppressed by sexism, do not bear the double burden suffered by black girls in a racist society. However, stories of white women's natural education toward resistance do exist. When brought into conversation with womanist-informed feminist theology, these stories also can provide a resource for the liberatory education of adolescent girls.

This story follows the stories of African American women, because I believe it reflects an overlapping issue confronting all women, regardless of race. Across cultures, many secular and religious traditions continue to perpetuate dichotomies between the body and the spirit, between rationality and sensuality. This story serves to break down those dichotomies, inviting the interplay between these two connected ways of knowing.

In the following story, Dillard is running down the sidewalk, "revving up for an act of faith."

> I was conscious and self-conscious. I knew well that people could not fly — as well as anyone knows it — but I also knew the kicker: that, as the books put it, with faith all things are possible.
>
> Just once I wanted a task that required all the joy I had. Day after day, I had noticed that if I waited long enough, my strong unexpressed joy would dwindle and dissipate inside me, over many hours, like a fire subsiding, and I would at last calm down. Just this once I wanted to let it rip. Flying rather

famously required the extra energy of belief, and this, too, I had in superabundance. . . .

I ran the sidewalk full tilt. I waved my arms ever higher and faster; blood balled in my fingertips. I knew I was foolish. I knew I was too old really to believe in this as a child would, out of ignorance; instead, I was experimenting as a scientist would, testing both the thing itself and the limits of my own courage in trying it, miserably self-conscious in full view of the whole world. You can't test courage cautiously, so I ran hard and waved my arms hard, happy. . . .

Up ahead I saw a business-suited pedestrian. He was coming stiffly toward me down the walk. Who could ever forget this first test, this stranger, this thin young man appalled? I banished the temptation to straighten up and walk right. He flattened himself against a brick wall as I passed flailing — although I had left him plenty of room. He had refused to meet my exultant eye. He looked away, evidently embarrassed. How surprisingly easy it was to ignore him! What I was letting rip, in fact, was my willingness to look foolish, in his eyes and in my own. Having chosen this foolishness, I was a free being. How could the world ever stop me, how could I betray myself, if I was not afraid?

I was flying. My shoulders loosened, my stride opened, my heart banged the base of my throat. I crossed Carnegie and ran up the block waving my arms. I crossed Lexington and ran up the block waving my arms.

A linen-suited woman in her fifties did meet my exultant eye. She looked exultant herself, seeing me from far up the block. Her face was thin and tanned. We converged. Her warm, intelligent glance said she knew what I was doing — not because she herself had been a child, but because she herself took a few loose aerial turns around her apartment every night for the hell of it, and by day played along with the rest of the world and took the streetcar. So, Teresa of Avila checked her unseemly joy and hung on to the altar rail to hold herself down. The woman's smiling, deep glance seemed to read my own awareness from my face, so we passed on the sidewalk — a beautifully upright woman walking in her tan linen suit, a kid running and flapping her arms. We passed on the sidewalk with the look of accomplices who share a humor just beyond irony. What's a heart for?

I crossed Homewood and ran up the block. The joy multiplied as I ran — I ran never actually quite leaving the ground — and multiplied still as I felt my stride begin to fumble and my knees begin to quiver and stall. The joy multiplied even as I slowed bumping to a walk. I was all but splitting, all but shooting sparks. Blood coursed free inside my lungs and bones, a light-shot stream like air. I couldn't feel the pavement at all.

I was too aware to do this, and had done it anyway. What could touch me now? For what were the people on Penn Avenue to me, or what was I to myself, really, but a witness to any boldness I could muster, or any cowardice, if it came to that, any giving up on heaven for the sake of dignity on earth? I had not seen a great deal accomplished in the name of dignity, ever.[42]

A Womanist-Informed Reflection

In this story, we see one woman's attempt to incorporate a moment of embodied ecstasy into her identity as a woman who relies on her own internal compass to determine appropriate behavior. Reading this story, we hear echoes of the dramatist's line, "I found God within myself and loved her. I loved her fiercely."[43] Once again, Alice Walker's words ring true: this girl is learning to love herself, regardless.[44] Once again, we see a glimpse of "not blossoms, but blooming" as the young Dillard recounts a moment, a slice of life, later remembered as part of her natural education toward healthy resistance. The girl chooses which external voices to internalize, deciding that the embarrassed reaction of the businessman need not, at least in this moment, shape the contours of her inner life.

The young Dillard is experiencing a moment akin to the one my adolescent collaborator Cathy related in her story, "Tomorrow, Then," discussed in chapter 3. Dillard, like Cathy, was learning to trust her senses, to feel the blood coursing through her veins and know that her body is one reliable source of knowing God. Dillard does not trivialize or deny her body, running full tilt and finding joy in this particular form of self-expression. Senses and intuition are the source of her intelligence, as she intuits from the linen-suited woman all she needs to know to confirm the reliability of her internal compass. She senses a moment of connection; real or imagined, it propels her. She finds authority in the trueness of her sensory experiences of feet on pavement, breath pounding, arms flapping. This authority gives her the strength to look foolish in the eyes of the world in order to remain true to the voices within her telling her she can fly.

Implications for the Religious Education of Girls

Like the two stories that precede it, Dillard's story adds evidence to the call for a model of religious education that encourages girls to reflect theologically about their own life stories. In reflecting on a story with themes similar to "She Believed I Could Fly," we can imagine a girl bringing to voice the intuitive knowledge that God is both within us and outside of us, as near as the next breath yet constantly being affirmed in the deep glance of an understanding other. If this story is part of a body of evidence and imagery possessed by an adult facilitator, it could help counteract notions of dominant culture that say girls' concerns about their bodies are trivial. Here we see bodies portrayed as central to a way of knowing God that resists dominant norms of behavior.

Discussion of sensuality can open a conversation about sexuality — a topic of dire importance to adolescent girls. Girls, bombarded at an early age with decisions about sexual choices, deserve an opportunity to tell stories about their bodies and their relationships in a zone of concern and safety. By asking questions such as "Where is God in this story?" in the midst of a reflection about bodies and relationships, girls might come to articulate an awareness that God is a part of our nature as sexual beings, and not standing in judgment of it, as many traditional portrayals of Christianity would lead them to believe. As in the previous examples — which showed promise for surfacing feminine images of God — a story that echoed themes of Dillard's story might bring forward new ways of thinking about relational images for God. Those images, which have been historically submerged but recently freed to enter into God-talk more regularly could become a resource in the identity-forming and meaning-making of girls at a critical time in their lives, before the damaging effects of narrow, wounding views of bodies, sensuality, and sexuality become permanently glued to young eyeballs.

Autobiography's Place in the Usable Past

In these three stories, autobiographical writings afforded windows through which to view powerful moments of natural education. These moments, in turn, inform the educational method that is girlfriend theology.

Elements of a usable past in our feminist warehouse include much more than autobiography. Women's history of achievements in all fields has a place within that collection. Autobiography, however, makes a unique contribution because of its status as "the most democratic form of American letters."[45] Whereas other literary genres threw up barriers of exclusion across lines of race, class, and education, autobiography was accessible to any literate person and, through oral tradition, to preliterate persons as well. As early as 1836, Jarena Lee began a long tradition of black women's autobiographical writing with her text *The Life and Religious Experiences of Jarena Lee, A Coloured Lady, Giving Account of Her Call to Preach the Gospel. Revised and Corrected from the Original Manuscript, Written by Herself.* This was followed by slave narratives and spiritual autobiographies, in which black women used their religious faith to gain selfhood in the face of a society depriving them of all rights.[46]

The writing of an autobiography constitutes a literary construction of self. For women, the act of writing and the creation of self are often simultaneous.[47] In the act of writing an autobiography, women make meaning out of events that shaped their perceptions of the world. Marginalized voices appear in autobiographies, thus making them "frontier sites where private issues enter public discourse."[48] Although coming from widely different backgrounds and speaking with diverse voices, black women autobiographers "are joined together by their awareness of the impact that race and gender have had on their lives." This common ground accounts for "a strain of radical resistance that runs through even the least overtly political" of black women's autobiographies.[49] For these reasons, women's auto-biographies are invaluable pieces in the construction of a usable past that is inclusive of difference. Thus, autobiography is a key resource in the practice of girlfriend theology.

Sea Glass

During the long hot summer of 1997, I spent a lot of time along the shores of Lake Michigan with my daughter Erin, then two and a half, and our friends. I was hugely pregnant, so I received that clear, cold water and the company of other moms as welcome tonic each afternoon.

Between building sand castles, munching on cheese crackers, and splashing in the waves, Erin and I started collecting tiny pieces of sea glass. Although the smooth pebblelike fragments also wash up in white and brown, our favorites were Mountain Dew green. Oddly shaped and shockingly green, the fragments kept surfacing all summer long as I unpacked sandy pockets, picnic baskets, and beach towels. Our collection grew to fill a small bowl.

When that summer ended, so did my pregnancy. Our baby Sophia was stillborn from an unknown cause in late August. During the course of my intense grieving, I found many ways to name the life-giving presence of Sophia, despite the overwhelming sadness of our loss. Somehow, I knew those pieces of sea glass would become important.

Now, two years later, Erin and her new sister, Olivia, are my daily companions. Landlocked in southwestern Virginia, far from those refreshing Lake Michigan shores and our equally refreshing Evanston companions, I find vast comfort in those pieces of sea glass. They escaped the bowl that sought to contain them. Three sit on my desk, hastily taped up in a moment when I needed inspiration. Arranged in a circle, a dozen of them adorn a scrapbook holding memories of Sophia. Two hang in a window, encased in a beaded purse created for that purpose by a dear friend. Those pieces of sea glass are constant reminders of a physical and personal community that upheld and supported me. They are reminders that the time we spent creating Sophia was not wasted time.

Like the sea glass in my collection, the stories that make up our usable past represent hard but necessary pieces of our life. Strategically placed, they can provide comfort and sustenance in the midst of our daily battles with the ever-present remnants of patriarchal culture. Audre Lorde reminds us that "for women, then, Poetry is not a luxury." She goes on to write, "The farthest horizons of our hopes and fears are cobbled by our poems, carved from the rock experiences of our daily lives."[50] An empowered woman's usable past represents the difficult and necessary work of resisting dominant culture. Our dangerous memories of hope and resistance energize us. We transform angry moments when we feel misogyny's slap into artistic expression, carved from our daily lives. We find glittering fragments of women's stories scattered among the refuse of the literary and artistic paths we walk. Together, that collection sustains the very personal, yet highly political act of finding and maintaining voice, power, and agency. It reminds us of our potential for wholeness that can birth a "belief in the self far greater than anyone's disbelief."[51] This belief lets us know ourselves as moral agents able to voice our truest convictions and able to effect change. Girlfriend theology is one method that encourages the very vulnerable act of sharing that collection, our dangerous memories as potential resources in young women's futures.

Chapter Five

God-Talk in the Midst of Violence and Death

To work magic, we begin by making new metaphors.
— Starhawk, *Dreaming the Dark*

Where is God when the gun goes off? Or when a father becomes abusive? Or when a girl becomes hospitalized because her body is wasting away? Adolescents today experience violence, both real and vicarious, on a daily basis. Girls suffer directly from multiple forms of violence, including sexual assault, domestic violence, and eating disorders.[1] Murder and suicide are the second- and third-leading causes of death for persons between the ages of fifteen and twenty-four. For every violent death, there are at least another hundred nonfatal injuries caused by violence.[2] The adolescents who experience this violence, and their sisters, cousins, friends, and lovers, carry a heavy grief that seems to have few outlets.

When given the opportunity to share a story of importance in their lives, my collaborators often used the occasion to speak out loud these stories of violence.[3] In chapter 3, Emma shared the story of her close friend's suicide. The two stories I have chosen for this chapter return to a place of tragic pain. The first one, "No Way Out," is a seventeen-year-old's story about the gang-related death of her cousin. The second, "Then, One Day, I Saw," is about a friendship between a girl who suffers from anorexia nervosa and a boy who bears the physical scars of his father's abuse.

Story #3: No Way Out

Hannah, a seventeen-year-old girl from Chicago, told the following story to a group including me, an adult collaborator, and two other girls, Katie and Elaine. Meeting for a weekend at the home of Elaine, this group was a mix of religious, ethnic, and economic backgrounds: Hannah is a white Roman Catholic; Elaine is a white Conservative Jew engaged in critiquing her tradition; Peg and I are both white ordained United Methodist ministers; and Katie is an African American who describes herself as religiously unaffiliated but is a frequent visitor at Roman Catholic and Pentecostal churches. Elaine, Peg, and I are all middle-class and lived in a city near Chicago at the time. Hannah comes from a middle-class family and lives in the city of Chicago. Katie, born into a low-income family, left her home of origin at the age of thirteen to live in a group home for girls. When we met, she was working several jobs to help pay her mother's rent.

Hannah told this story on our second day together. We had already shared in several deeply moving story sessions. At this point in the weekend, despite the fact that one girl had left and another had taken her place, common themes were beginning to surface among the stories. Hannah, who had converted to Roman Catholicism in the third grade, was quite active in the life of her parish, having trained and served as a eucharistic minister. Her parents dropped her off on Friday night and whisked her away to figure skating practice shortly after this story session ended. Here is Hannah's story:

NO WAY OUT

This story happened when I was in sixth grade. So it happened about five years ago. I left out names because it was in the news, and it's just easier for me to talk that way. So I refer to him only as my cousin.

My cousin messed up in his life. He dropped out of school and had kids too young. The worst part, especially having kids, was his involvement with a gang. He was never home. When he was, his girlfriend would often throw him out because he was drunk or high.

A couple of years went by. His son was four years old, and his daughter was two years old. I don't believe I'll ever know why, but one night he came home and stayed home. Of course it was not as simple as that. He flipped back and forth for a while from being a gang member to being a dad. I guess it was his son that provided him with the strength to reach for something better. He got into a drug rehab program. He also attempted to dispel the bonds between him and gang members. I've always heard that you can get out of the gang for finding religion, but I guess finding yourself is not a permissible excuse.

His girlfriend had kicked him out and was not ready to live with him again. For the past year, he had spent his nights crashing at friends' homes or on the street. His parents knew that he was still being harassed by the gangs, so they let him move into the basement. On July 4 his girlfriend decided to bring the kids over. Things went so well. My cousin proved to his girlfriend and his parents that he was finally clean. By this time, his parents had helped him pay off debts he owed to gang members. You could see this story as a true miracle. A life was changed around and a family was reunited. He had been given a new lease on life.

I'd like to end this story here with this inspirational conclusion and the knowledge that you can always change, but I can't. Although the offenders were never apprehended, we know who they were. On July 6, the gang got my cousin out. They threw a Molotov cocktail through his parents' first-floor window. His parents had both left the house, but as they must have known, my cousin was in the basement. The only exit out was now engulfed in flames. What the gang did not know was that his girlfriend and two kids were still there from the long weekend.

One of the hardest things I've ever had to do in my life is walk into that funeral home and see those two pure white coffins and a pint-sized one in the middle. You may wonder why there were only three coffins. That's the miracle in this story. In his last moments, my cousin saved his daughter. Firemen found her lying unconscious under her dead father. He had shielded her from the poisonous gas and melting flames.

I don't know where exactly they got that priest from at the funeral. I know my aunt was ready to get up and sit him down. He preached to a church that was full of teens. He preached to us about the travesty of gangs and drugs and not to get involved with them. Well, we didn't need him to lecture us on that. The two-year-old girl who stood by the three holes in the ground was all the lecture we needed.

Doing Story Theology with "No Way Out"

Experience Near: Feelings, Emotions, and Associations

As Hannah concluded her story, raw emotion showed on the faces around the circle. I felt my heart pounding and noticed other visceral reactions, such as heavy sighs and tears. It took several moments before anyone felt ready to break the silence.

> *Elaine:* It made me so mad. It *makes* me so mad. The senselessness of the murders, and then, on top of that, the pain of the funeral.

Other participants named feelings of anger and sadness. Then Katie, who had told us of her childhood in a notoriously violent Chicago housing project, shared close associations with Hannah's story.

> *Katie:* The whole situation is upsetting. It probably was a bottle with alcohol in it. I can honestly imagine someone throwing that bottle in that window. I can understand how you feel because that has happened in my family, so much. That's why we don't have any males in my family. Because they have all been killed senselessly. A lot of them have been gang-related. This was a tragedy. Even if there had just been one death, it would have been a tragedy.

> *Elaine:* The two-year-old is going to grow up knowing that her father died shielding her. She's going to live with that forever.

From pain, the conversation returned to anger, focusing on the religious service that failed to console or "wake up" the congregation, made up mostly of teenagers. Hannah added further details:

> *Hannah:* It was unbelievable. It was all teenagers. You saw rival gang members. A lot of people respected him because he was trying to get out. That's how it got labeled, that he finally got out. They were saying "He was ours. We took him back. We let him out."

Experience Distant: Images, Symbols, and God

Acknowledging many feelings of anger and sadness, I turned the conversation to the second part of the method, asking, "Do you see any symbols or images in this story? Is there any meaning for us here?" The conversation focused on the lingering smoke after a fire and the image of a father protecting his daughter.

> *Elaine:* I can't get the smoke out of my mind. And how he was trying to protect his daughter. The smoke still lingers, like the lingering effects of a smoky fire five years ago. And it's not going to go away. It's almost like, after the smoke clears, it's still here.

> *Katie:* I also have this other image that stands out, of him protecting her, you know, covering her up. It's like he's not even just protecting her from the smoke and from immediate danger, but almost from the world.

The longer we played with these images, the more they came into focus, carrying the discussion from personal loss to critical social analysis. The lingering smoke was the grief that Hannah still works through. The lingering smoke also includes the little girl, whose life is forever maimed by the loss of her family. It is the ongoing reality of gangs who entice young boys to join, yet will not let young men out. And it includes a society in which gangs flourish because they provide some cohesiveness in the midst of widespread poverty and institutionalized racism. The church, represented by a white priest addressing a hall crowded with mostly black and Hispanic teenagers, seemed to have nothing to bring to this lingering tragedy.

> *Elaine:* Do you think the lingering effect, that it hurt a lot of people, is going to stop them from doing it again?

> *Peg:* Certainly the priest didn't help. He was at a loss to help them see the lingering effects.

> *Katie:* If you're a member of a gang, you don't want to hear him at this point.

> *Elaine:* I'm visualizing an old guy who has no concept of what's going on. They're not going to listen.

After we had named many connections between the lingering smoke and the evil present in the story, I said, "I keep wishing there was an image of water. It just feels overwhelmingly smoky, and water would be an image of God for me here."

God-Talk: A Bent-Over Father Crying Tears of Life

When I asked where God was in this story, two related stories from scripture surfaced. Peg said she was reminded of the parable of the prodigal son. The parents welcomed back the ex–gang member in a demonstration of unconditional love and forgiveness. Elaine said the little girl's survival against all odds reminded her of Moses' birth narrative. "She must have survived for a special purpose," Elaine said.

Katie identified with Elaine's interpretation. Although Katie had actively taken part in the conversation up until this point, now her involvement intensified. She claimed a space everyone honored. She offered a striking contrast to the image of the out-of-touch priest: God was more like the bent-over father who saved his daughter.

> *Katie:* You might say God really wasn't there. But I think he came late. He was present, because this little girl was saved. It's amazing that he was able to save her. I think that your cousin was playing the God role by protecting her and saving her.

> *Peg:* And with that, with your cousin trying to be the shield for his daughter, it was like his parents were trying to be a shield for him. They provided a sanctuary for him in the basement. It's conflictual for me that one dad can be the God-like shield, and the other dad couldn't shield his children.

Katie wasn't interested in discussing the contrasting images of God and, with an authoritative voice, dismissed Peg's comment as an interruption to her train of thought. She became very animated as she completed her portrait of God as an ex-gang-member father, crying life-giving tears:

> *Katie:* You have to think that he's sheltering this girl. He's got to be crying. There are tears. That's the water that counteracts all this lingering smoke. If you think of it, that's probably what

saved her. There's got to be a lot of smoke in there, but she's getting wet. The tears are evaporating and turning into air for her to breathe. I'm quite sure he was holding her and crying —

Dori: Her father, the tears —

Katie: He had to be thinking, "my child, my child." The water is the tears.

Quite touched by Katie's depiction of God, Peg moved beyond her initial connection to embrace and affirm Katie's interpretation.

Peg: My belief about God is that God's crying, too. God is watching this thing happen. God is at this funeral....

Katie: God is crying over the priest who is screwing it up. Crying for all these lives that are gathered, but just don't get it.

Peg: Crying and crying and crying. It's those tears that hopefully serve some purpose. We don't think of tears as productive. People think they're a waste of time. But here, the tears are God's tears.

The dynamic between Peg and Katie well illustrates the adult facilitator's role. She introduces ideas, which sometimes connect with the girls' experiences and sometimes do not. Here, Peg realized the need to let Katie's speech flow after an early interruption. Later, she supported Katie's interpretation, authentically sharing points of connection between it and her own beliefs.

Going Forth

As our time grew short, I moved into the final stage of the method by asking if anything in this story moved us toward a new way of being or acting in the world. Hannah responded, sharing her reasons for bringing this particular story to the group: recently, she had begun dating someone with a history of gang involvement. They had broken up after he accused her of "being a white girl in khakis" who couldn't understand his experience as a Hispanic male. "I had tried to put the death of my cousin behind me, but when I went out with Juan it all came back. That's what I have to deal with, and that's why I have to get this out." Although we had come to the end of our formal discussion, the girls in the group had much to say to Hannah about her relationship with Juan and about the complexities of cross-cultural relationships in general. That conversation took place as we ate vegan sandwiches on the back deck.

Echoes of Feminist Theology and Assertions of Girlfriend Theology

To speak of God as a loving father bent over his daughter crying tears of life is a powerful metaphor. In this instance, girlfriend theology exemplifies the best of hermeneutic tradition by bringing a fresh, new interpretation to the ancient metaphor of God as a father. The result is a fusion of horizons that offers vitality to a metaphor in danger of slipping into irrelevance, at best, or repudiation, at worst.[4]

Feminists have closely dissected the image of God as father with many fruitful results. When women look "beyond God the father," a multitude of life-giving images flourish. Often retrieving imagery found in the writings of medieval mystics, feminist scholars of the Bible and theology depict God as a nursing mother, as a mother eagle, as a midwife, and as a woman giving birth, to name only a few.[5] For me, and many of the women I know, these images of God and others like them rescued a faith tradition that seemed so laden with patriarchy that it could not survive.

Although these nonmasculine images of God still remain invisible within many churches, they might never have reached the light of day in contemporary times without serious reflection on the nature of metaphor, spurred in part by naming the oppression women experience when God is depicted only as male. In Mary Daly's words:

> The biblical and popular image of God as a great patriarch in heaven, rewarding and punishing according to his mysterious and seemingly arbitrary will, has dominated the imagination of millions for thousands of years. The symbol of the Father God, spawned in the human imagination and sustained as plausible

by patriarchy, has, in turn, rendered service to this type of society by making its mechanisms for the oppression of women appear right and fitting. If God in "his" heaven is a father ruling "his" people, then it is in the nature of things and according to divine plan and the order of the universe that society be male-dominated.[6]

To briefly summarize the lengthy critique around the image of God as father, I turn to the work of liturgical theologian Ruth Duck, biblical scholar Elisabeth Schüssler-Fiorenza, and theologian Sallie McFague.

Duck, in her book *Gender and the Name of God,* argues that exclusively masculine names for God need to be understood in light of social context. In contemporary U.S. culture, that means taking into account the fact that many fathers abuse their children physically, sexually, and emotionally.[7] Turning exclusively to images of God as mother does not suffice. There, too, we see evidence of troubling and abusive human relationships. Duck has worked to loosen the tight hold on patriarchal imagery for God, introducing hymns and prayers into liturgy that reflect the wide spectrum of human experience.

Schüssler-Fiorenza's feminist hermeneutic of suspicion aids Duck in this task by supporting a critical reading of the Bible, which foregrounds the feminist quest for women's power, freedom, and independence. Schüssler-Fiorenza, although sympathetic to the feminist precaution against using exclusively male imagery for God, nonetheless makes a distinction between patriarchal and nonpatriarchal male imagery for God. In her vision, masculine imagery freed from patriarchy can bear life-giving connections with biblical sources. As an example, she cites the fatherhood of God elaborated in the Jesus traditions as reflecting "the gracious goodness usually associated with a mother."[8] Rosemary Radford Ruether offers a similar position, arguing that Jesus' references to God as father are nonhierarchical and function to overthrow patriarchal imagery that equates fathers with rulers.[9]

Breaking down essentialist categories of male and female subjectivity is an ongoing task of feminist scholarship.[10] Naming as "father-like" characteristics usually attributed to mothers, and vice versa, assists in this task. By imagining a provider-mother or a nurturer-father, feminists defy the tendency of ascribing certain stereotypical roles to men and women, thus countering essentialist categories.[11]

Critique of father-God imagery, at its most basic level, centers around the nature of metaphor, a topic explored in depth by Sallie McFague. McFague argues that literal interpretations of metaphorical language constitute idolatry. When the Bible is interpreted literally, it becomes an idol and stands in danger of losing its relevance.

> When a model becomes an idol, the hypothetical character of the model is forgotten and what ought to be seen as *one* way to understand our relationship with God has become identified as *the* way. In fact, as happens when a model becomes an idol, the distance between the image and the reality collapses: "father" becomes God's "name" and patriarchy becomes the proper description of governing relationships on many levels.[12]

In contrast to this idolatry, McFague argues for thinking about God metaphorically. Thinking metaphorically involves "spotting a thread of similarity between two dissimilar objects ... one of which is better known than the other, and using the better-known one as a way of speaking about the lesser known." Metaphorical theology thus emphasizes personal and relational language about God, but not necessarily as the Christian tradition has interpreted these categories.[13] She cites as an example a suppressed strain of feminine imagery within the Judeo-Christian paradigm. "Masculine imagery in this suppressed tradition gives credence not to a patriarchal, but to a parental model, with shared characteristics of motherhood and fatherhood."[14]

Katie's image of God as a bent-over father crying tears of life exemplifies this kind of metaphorical thinking, rescuing the image of God as father from idolatry. Katie has known gang members. She told of one in particular, an uncle. Within him she saw violence and human failure, but she also saw something redemptive, something that bears a thread of similarity to what God must be like. The fatherly God she depicts is not Peg's image of the upstairs father, who graciously welcomes back the prodigal son and offers sanctuary in a distant basement. Rather it is the prodigal son himself: the ex–gang member, a Hispanic father-God, holds his daughter close enough to feel his last breath and be drenched by his tears. This is not an all-powerful, faraway God, but one well acquainted with human limitations, suffering, and pain.[15]

The tears of this God offer life, not death. Contrary to some traditional depictions of God as a father requiring the sacrificial death of his son, we see a God who provides life-giving sanctuary. It is a relationship bearing resemblance to the one between God and Jesus depicted in Matthew's Gospel, where we find a God who says, "This is my beloved child, in whom I am well pleased," and a God with whom Jesus shares tender, pain-filled conversation in the Garden of Gethsemane hours before his execution.

From this session, two closely related assertions of girlfriend theology surface: (1) God is mysteriously omnipresent, but not magically omnipotent. Although we cannot explain it, God *is* at work within human tragedies to create healing potential. God may not fix things, but neither does God abandon us; and (2) God feels our pain and cries with us. Although I have drawn connections between these assertions and feminist theology, they also resonate with depictions of God in process and liberation theology. As John Cobb writes, "Process theologians do not accept the view that God has at every moment the capacity to set things right, but never does so. . . . God does not stand by idly observing the suffering. God is present and active in every event seeking to bring out of it what good can be obtained."[16] In the language of the liberation theologian Gustavo Gutiérrez: "The Biblical God is close to human beings, a God of communion with and commitment to human beings. The active presence of God in the midst of the people is a part of the oldest and most enduring Biblical promises."[17]

Thus, girlfriend theology can offer a nonpatriarchal male image for God that feminist, womanist, liberation, and process theologians might all endorse. The source of this imagery is historically and culturally situated in the real-life experience of contemporary girls who, unfortunately, have front-row seats to life's violent side.

The next story session also depicts fathers and revolves around violence. It affirms the assertion that God is a constant presence who feels our pain, brings healing potential to the suffering, and shares our tears. However, it carries this line of thinking a step further by introducing human volition as participating with God's action in the world. This brings to the foreground an additional assertion of girl-friend theology: (6) God is most fully alive in us (incarnated) when our eyes are open to the pain of others.

Story #4: Then, One Day, I Saw

Sarah, twenty-six, told this story. I recruited Sarah to be a second adult female participant in this group, which met every day for a week as part of the Youth Theology Institute (YTI).[18] This group included five sixteen- and seventeen-year-old girls: Cathy, Kim, Mary, Holly, and Tina. They were from Roman Catholic, Eastern Orthodox, and Protestant faith communities. As participants in YTI, they were all exceptionally bright, ambitious, and theologically articulate. They all came from middle- to upper-middle-income families.

I knew little about Sarah before this first session. She had come highly recommended by a colleague who knew I was looking for a seminary graduate with a feminist commitment to help with my research project. We spoke on the phone a few times to clarify her role and briefly share our views of feminist theology. A graduate of a United Methodist seminary, Sarah described herself as being between religious affiliations. In introducing herself to the group, Sarah said she struggled with the patriarchy she witnessed in the fundamentalist Christian home where she was raised. Going to seminary was a way to answer her questions about God and faith that had been stifled during her formative years.

Following the pattern I established in each of my research contexts, I asked my adult collaborator to be the first storyteller. In this way, an adult was able to model appropriate self-disclosure, while taking on the vulnerable position of being the first to share. By making sure my adolescent collaborators were fully aware of the process before bringing their own autobiographies, I attempted to adjust the adult/adolescent power dynamic. Sarah told this story at the group's first session together:

THEN, ONE DAY, I SAW

Chris was the bane of my existence in ninth grade. I was the stereotypical perfect principal's daughter at a small Christian school, and Chris was the stereotypical bad boy of the class — of the entire school, actually. He was smart, had a quick wit, and was, politically, very astute. And he was critical of — well, of everything and everyone (except for Lydia Warren, who was the prettiest girl in the class). Since Chris was constantly getting into trouble for everything from drinking to talking too much in class, he and my dad, who was the principal, got to know each other really well. I think my dad spent more time with Chris than he did with me, in fact.

The problem was that Chris was every principal's nightmare. He was smart enough to attract a following of admiring peers. He was wild enough to take risks he probably shouldn't take. And he was savvy enough to succeed or get away with most of them. I think my dad probably secretly hated Chris, or hated the anxiety and stress that Chris caused him. But of course he never said as much, because hate was a sin. But Dad sure would be glum and very rigidly calm after those days when he'd had to deal with Chris.

Now obviously, Chris didn't like my dad much either. But he knew that if he took his rage out directly on my dad he'd be expelled. So, after being punished by my father — who would often paddle Chris, and ask him to repent of his sins and think about what Jesus would have done — Chris would come back into English class or science class and take things out on me. One day he would make fun of my red hair. The next day he would call me fat. The next day he would call me ugly. The next day he would laugh at my father in front of my face. And the next day he would call me a nerd who was going to be a nun her whole life.

Looking back on Chris's words now, I want to laugh, to shrug him off like the annoying little pest he was. But during ninth grade, when I was all awkward angles and insecurities and hopes and fears, Chris was more than a pest: he was a nightmare. And the way he saw or treated me would determine how I felt about myself for the remainder of the day — even the week.

And then one day, I saw the marks on his arm where it looked like somebody had beaten him with a belt buckle. And I overheard him telling one of his friends that his dad had gotten pissed at him the night before. And I started to wonder if Chris was really as tough and uncaring as he wanted me to think. I wondered if he was as lonely inside as I was, just in a different way. I wondered what it felt like to have your dad, not ignore you — like mine was doing — but rather, pay too much attention to you, and not a good attention either, but kind of a painful attention.

And then other things started to happen. I grew a little bit older, I went into the tenth grade. I went to a different school and started feeling depressed. Started feeling anxious and lonely. And I started to lose weight. By the time I turned sixteen and was getting ready to be in the eleventh grade, I had gone from 115 pounds, which was already pretty thin, to 90 pounds. I was anorexic. Everything in my life began to revolve around food or avoiding food, around exercise, and around the scale in the bathroom. I stopped talking to my friends. I stopped going out. I stopped all social activity, and people started to draw away from me. They were afraid. They didn't know what to say or do. Everybody, that is, except for Chris.

I don't know why he didn't run away like the other ones did. But he somehow stayed around. He talked to me. He no longer made fun of me. He treated me like a friend. He was a friend. Why? Perhaps something in his rebellious angry side sensed that I, too, was a little bit angry — that I was pretty miserable, like him, even though I was outwardly the perfect principal's daughter: never sinning, being unkind, or making anything less than an "A." Maybe, like me, parts of him were starving inside, and he knew what it felt like to have no control over your life except what you do with or to your body.

So after all the tension and anxiety over Chris in the ninth grade, I found myself becoming friends with him in the eleventh grade. It's strange, isn't it, thinking about it now — was it me who changed or him? Maybe we both did. Maybe he had grown up enough to recognize that the world was not going to change simply if he got angry and hurt people. And maybe I had grown up enough to realize that life was not going to be good simply if I was always good.

But instead of attacking the world or other people, like Chris had done, I did what lots of women tend to do, I attacked myself. I punished myself for the sins of the world, or of myself. I starved myself down until I almost disappeared, almost as if I were saying I don't deserve or want to be here.

One other thought: maybe Chris and I became friends because at the core of things we were both just hurting kids. We were both sort of disenchanted with life the way we had been taught. I was no longer eager to be perfect. And Chris was no longer eager to be bad. And somewhere between that middle way, between rebellious guy and starving perfect girl, we saw some commonality and we became friends.

It's been a number of years since I heard from Chris. I heard a while back that his parents had sent him into the Marine Corps to shape him up and put some of the "fear of God" into him. I don't know if it would have worked.

And as for me, well, I slowly recovered from my anorexia. It took me a good two years to get my weight back up to a healthy level and then another two years to start addressing my own rage and depression and the reasons why I starved myself. But I still kind of carry the weight of it around with me. And I imagine Chris might carry the weight of his own years of being a rebel and being beaten by his father. I wonder if he is as confused about God's love, about grace, and about redemption today as I still am. Maybe not. I miss him. And sometimes I think I miss God, too.

Doing Story Theology with "Then, One Day, I Saw"

Experience Near: Feelings, Emotions, and Associations

When Sarah finished her story, all participants joined easily into the conversation. They connected at a deep emotional level with the fact that Sarah had suffered from an eating disorder. They shared feelings of self-consciousness, especially regarding their body images and a tendency they notice in themselves and their friends to direct pain inward, rather than outward.

Cathy: This made me feel sad, because with girls, I guess it's a generalization, but we seem to push things inside. Chris, when he was angry, he acted out. But girls tend to say, "Something's wrong with me, because this is hurting." And so, Chris acted out and did things to other people with his anger. He didn't go inside himself. Doesn't it seem like that, you all? I mean, the girls I know do that. I know *I* do that. I don't automatically think, "What's wrong here?"

Sarah: Yeah, I think you're right that it implodes instead of exploding.

Kim: Yeah, when someone says something, even if you know the guy's a jerk, it just shatters. It shakes you to your core, and you just feel like sludge.

Holly: And sometimes you tend to believe the bad stuff about yourself instead of believing the good stuff. Like, if someone pays me a compliment, it's hard for me to believe it. But if someone tells me something bad, it sticks. It's easy to find a lot of fault in myself.

All of the participants shared similar experiences, connecting them to aspirations of perfection. However, the talk centered on what it feels like to be singled out or ostracized. The girls acknowledged this happening for both negative and positive reasons, such as appearing to "have it all together."

Kim: Every girl I talk to seems to feel incredibly isolated. Like they don't necessarily fit in.... They float from group to group.

Cathy: I was talking to a friend who said, "That just means you have more things figured out than a lot of people around you...."

Kim: I've been told that.

Cathy: But that doesn't do any good. I still feel isolated.

Kim: So, I'm still a social outcast who has a lot of things figured out —

Mary: I feel that way sometimes, like I have so many different aspects of my life that I can't really be categorized. That's isolating.

Tina: It sounds like we're all floaters.

Cathy: Yeah...I'm like that. It has to do with transcending social boundaries. I understand the boundaries, but I don't necessarily see them.

Kim: You never feel like you really fit into the group.

Cathy: Kind of like on the outside, looking in, a social outcast.

I sensed the talk moving toward images, so I stepped into the role of facilitator, summarizing what I had been hearing and moving the conversation on toward the second step of the method. But as I often do, especially during initial sessions with a group, I reminded them that any lingering feelings could still be brought into the conversation.

Dori: I want to isolate a few words that seem to encapsulate some of what we're talking about. Let's remember and go back to this idea of transcending social boundaries. I think it's very connected to our feelings about this story. But before we get too far away from the experience of hearing the story, is there anything else that you felt in your body or memories or associations before we move out of the feeling realm? Once we've moved out of the feeling realm and you identify a feeling you can always jump back. This is a very fluid method, so feel free to do that.

When Cathy subsequently started talking, I was glad I had put out one more call for feelings. We stayed in an in-between place, still connected to feelings, yet beginning to move toward images.

Cathy: When you were talking about having to be perfect, I was feeling sick to my stomach. I've never had an eating disorder, but I do worry about my weight, like any American girl. But

I've always had this compulsion for perfection. No matter what I've accomplished, it's never good enough. For me, there's always that next achievement that I have to get to. . . .

Other participants shared this compulsion for perfection, saying that it didn't come from their parents, at least not on the surface.

Mary: I know what you mean. The pressure doesn't come from my parents. It's something inside.

Cathy: I don't know how it got planted or embodied in us. You all say it's not your parents. *I* think it's *my* parents. (Laughter) Who makes us think that we need to do this and this and this?

Kim then took us to the second part of the method, answering Cathy's rhetorical question by alluding to the Bible.

Kim: Because it's certainly not there biblically, remember? It's like you're perfect in who you are, a child of God.

Dori: Just be.

Kim: Exist.

Dori: When I was hearing you, Cathy, I remembered the feeling of almost being like an arm of my father, an extension. Whatever the arm did that was good made him look good. Sometimes I just wanted to sever it. I think that's what I did when I moved two thousand miles away from home. It was my way of saying, "I am not your arm." As much as it was his love that made him want me to excel, I needed to have my achievements be my own, not his.

Cathy: That's a lot of how I feel. I can remember being younger and really, I think, believing to some certain extent that what I didn't do right was going to be reflected in how much my dad loved me. You know what I mean? That felt horrible. That's a bad feeling. That's not a healthy way to envision how you should be, or your perfection.

Experience Distant: Images, Symbols, and God

After this very animated discussion of feelings and emotions, we moved on to images.

> *Dori:* Is there a guiding metaphor or an image that comes to you? We've talked about this idea of transcending social boundaries and the link to the story is the bad boy and the good girl meeting someplace in the middle. What images, as you think back to the story, seem significant?

> *Mary:* For me, it's like the understanding that everyone has problems in their own life. I remember when I realized that we all carry things with us. That was a big thing for me: other people have struggles.

> *Kim:* I think there's something like a revelation that comes at some point in high school that not everyone's family is the way yours is. There is no normal. And I hear about these people who have been abused or whatever, and it's all they've known. And they think it's normal, and I think my life is normal. But there isn't a set normality.

> *Cathy:* And also I think that you start to develop a different kind of relationship with your friends in high school at a deeper level. You begin to see the mechanics of their family functions. And it's true there is no perfect thing. It is weird to see all the different perspectives. In terms of an image or a related story, I thought immediately of *The Breakfast Club*. I thought of you as that girl and him as that guy.

We talked for several moments about the movie *The Breakfast Club*, a cult classic that celebrates an unlikely coalition of high school friends.

> *Sarah:* I actually just watched it a month ago. It made me cry again because of the feelings of all these kids. They're all estranged and alienated from each other. Once they finally sit down and start opening up, they finally start to realize how each person is just human. The hard part is then going back to school and figuring out how you're going to deal with it now.

I always wanted them to make a sequel to the movie to see if they actually continued talking or if they just drifted.

Holly: You cried when you saw that?

Sarah: Uh-huh. I cry at movies. Did you cry?

Holly: I don't cry at movies. What was it that made you cry?

Sarah: The last little speech. It was the ending scene when I realized Judd Nelson's character was getting in touch with the fact that he was human and could be taken care of by somebody — and that he was lonely, and that it was okay to admit that. That sort of broke it open. It made me cry, both because I thought it was really cool and because I wondered what in his life is going to help him sustain that. You know, he has an abusive father and all that sort of stuff. Is he going to be able to stay alive and stay passionate about things?

From the movie, Kim brought us back to scripture, where images of God began to emerge from the story.

God-Talk: Seeing the Scars

Two stories from Jesus' life, one of which had been discussed in a YTI class earlier in the day, surfaced.

Kim: I thought of the woman who touches the hem of Jesus' garment. I have the idea that with anorexia and eating disorders, I would want to be healed. If there was just one thing that would make me all whole and better again —

Sarah: Yeah, a healing touch. That's a great image.

Mary: I'm thinking about Jesus being at the well. We were talking about this story this morning — how Jesus talked to this woman who he was never supposed to talk to, because she was in this category. He was not even supposed to talk to women, and especially not her. It wasn't right for the perfect kid to be friends with the rebel. The social boundaries get crossed.

At this point, I affirmed the connections the girls were making. "With these stories in mind," I asked, "how do you see God in this story?" Cathy became very animated.

> *Cathy:* Well, the spirit of God was definitely inside of you when you saw the scars on Chris's arm and you thought, "What is this?" You could've overlooked them. Many people would have just dismissed them or thought he deserved them. But that perception...God was in that perception.

> *Dori:* I like that idea. God is present in the compassion, in being able to see the scars.

> *Sarah:* Just like in *The Breakfast Club.* That's what allowed them to transcend social boundaries.

> *Cathy:* Their common element, their wound, brings them together.

When this engaging banter came to a pause, Sarah rolled her eyes, leaned back in her seat, and exhaled deeply.

> *Sarah:* This is fascinating to me. When I wrote this, I was thinking about who God was for me, and because of my issues with God, I would have said God was the distant or unreachable father here. Either my father or Chris's father. I'm used to seeing things in a more negative or pessimistic way. To hear you all immediately point to God as being in me, the spirit that was able to see the scars — I hadn't thought of it like that before. It's just a completely different way of seeing it, and it's helpful.

> *Cathy:* Well, I think God is in the scars.

> *Dori:* God is in the scars?

> *Kim:* And your eyes, that you see them.

Going Forth

When I noted the time and asked the girls to move into the final part of the session, they were a little resistant. There was a strong feeling of celebration in the air, which, I think, had to do with Sarah, as an adult, expressing genuine appreciation to the girls for giving her new insight. It also had to do with a form of emotional catharsis. These girls had been together in a group of sixty young men and women for two weeks, discussing topics of faith. This was the first time they had met together in an exclusively female space. In the previous ninety minutes, they had shared extensively on emotional and spiritual levels. When we finally came to "going forth," Kim had this to offer:

> *Kim:* I think what sticks with me most is that your friendship, later on, was based on this thing that had hurt you both and made you so uncomfortable. Your pain becomes the basis of an important friendship.
>
> *Cathy:* So many times we don't see the scars —
>
> *Dori:* The scars become the source of healing, the hem of the garment. When we find a way to see the scars, Chris no longer is the bane. He turns out to be the balm.

After the time for this session was up, the girls did not want to leave. We spent the rest of their free time reflecting on what had just occurred and getting to know each other better. Cathy mentioned how good it felt to be in the company of other girls. The others agreed. "Some talks you can only have with your girlfriends," someone said. It was from that comment and later discussion with this group that I came to understand the work we were about as "girlfriend theology."

Echoes of Feminist Theology and Assertions of Girlfriend Theology

In naming the way their actions would change because of this story, the girls spoke of solidarity, although they did not call it that. In identifying God in the moment of perceiving another's oppression, they were echoing a major theme of liberation and *mujerista* theology.[19] In the next chapter, I will discuss a major tenet of *mujerista* theology as defined by Ada María Isasi-Díaz. She calls for North American churches to move from an ethic of charity to an ethic of solidarity and mutuality in their treatment of Latin Americans and other oppressed peoples. The first step toward such a move, Isasi-Díaz writes, is crossing borders and making friendships. In this story session, the social-historical setting was not one of racial and ethnic boundaries, such as the boundaries of which Isasi-Díaz speaks. However, "transcending social boundaries" became a dominant theme. As Cathy mentioned, it is common to assume a person deserves the scars he or she wears. Modeling Jesus' compassion, Sarah chose not to blame the victim, but to see the scars as a sign of common suffering and an invitation to relationship. The girls affirmed God's presence in the compassion felt toward another person's wounds. In doing so, they were understanding the dynamics of solidarity and mutuality as part of their Christian vocation.

Connected to the issue of solidarity is the theological theme of sacrament. In this story, our conversation danced around the fringe of an affirmation: that is, God is present not only in our compassion, but in the scars themselves. To see God's presence in the everyday is to experience an inbreaking of the holy into the profane. This is a sacramental moment in which "we have eyes to see and ears to hear."[20] Significantly, it is a wound, an image deeply ingrained in Christian symbolism, that provides impetus for this sacramental moment.

A third theological theme that surfaced in this story points back to McFague's work on metaphorical theology and father-God imagery. The fathers in this story — one distant and aloof, the other physically abusive — illustrate the argument of many feminist scholars that father language for God should be altogether abandoned. Too many women, they argue, bring to the metaphor of father painful memories of hierarchy, subordination, and patriarchal authoritarianism. As Roberta Bondi poignantly summarizes:

The primary and earliest place we do learn about fatherhood, human and divine, is from our own fathers, but the fatherhood we learn about is not unfallen fatherhood. In the world of experience, because our own fathers were wounded, even when they long to, they never do perfectly image God's fatherhood.

Without even meaning to, and sometimes even trying very hard not to, they have wounded us, their children, by the way they were fathers, just as we wound our own children, and so, without intending to, our fathers pass on a wounded image of God's fatherhood as well.[21]

Although we have seen how the image of God as father can be salvaged and invested with nonpatriarchal meaning, painful memories of earthly fathers point to the need — recognized by so many feminist scholars — for alternative ways of naming and imagining God. Although fully developing the alternative metaphor of God as friend, McFague points to numerous other generative images and their relational nature. The potential metaphors for God, she writes:

are too various to enumerate: liberator, comrade, creator, mother, friend, rock, father, thunder, lover, brother, teacher, sister, light, fire, defender, sustainer, nurturer, advocate, and so on. The images which tumble from the mouths of those experiencing the liberating love of God are not meant *to describe God* so much as *to suggest the new quality of relationship* being offered them. Hence, religious metaphors and the models that emerge from them are not pictures of God, but images of a relationship; as such, they are nonrestrictive and highly particular.[22]

As Jesus identifies with the suffering of others through his life and death, Sarah identified with the suffering of another. In seeing the scars, Sarah was, like Jesus, transcending social boundaries and entering into solidarity with another. Thus, "the eyes that see the scars" can enter McFague's litany of "nonrestrictive and highly particular" metaphors for God.

In fleshing out her model of God as friend, McFague draws attention to the imminent nature of God, echoing both Hannah's and Sarah's story sessions. She writes, "Rather than stressing the protection, comfort, and redemption of individuals *apart from* others and the world, the friendship model emphasizes sacrifice, support, and solidarity *with* others and the world. God is our friend who suffers with us as we work to bring about a better existence for suffering humanity."[23] Thus, this story session begins to make connections between four assertions of girlfriend theology: (2) God feels our pain and cries with us; (6) God is most fully alive (incarnated) in us when our eyes are open to the pain of others; (1) God is mysteriously omnipresent, but not magically omnipotent. Although we cannot explain it, God *is* at work within human tragedies to create healing potential. God may not fix things, but neither does God abandon us; and (7) church, at its best, is a community of compassion, a resource in our healing, and a potential agent of change in the world.

God-Talk in the Midst of Violence and Death

In this chapter, I have given thick descriptions of two more girlfriend theology sessions. The voices of girls spoke through the stories themselves, through their group conversations, and through my analysis of the sessions. In that analysis, I connected the images, metaphors, and recurring themes I heard girls voicing with tenets of contemporary theology. The result was a meeting place — a site where adult women's theological meaning-making both informed and was informed by the voices of girls.

Both of these story sessions dealt with violence. In the first session, the death of three people left a lingering smoke. In the second session, a boy's physical abuse and a girl's anorexia, both connected to looming father figures, left lingering scars long after the initial infliction of pain. In both of these sessions, but especially in the second, I see adult women making available their usable past as potential resources in the lives of young women who deal with violence. This usable past slips out of tidy categories, such as literary or biblical. It lapses momentarily into the therapeutic and the very personal. Taken together, perhaps it is best termed a "spiritual" usable past, because our spiritual selves are able to bring together various resources — literary, personal, therapeutic, and biblical — to aid in our "whole-making."[24] Sarah entered the storytelling space vulnerably, bringing part of her intimate struggle with a crippling disease. As is often the case as we deal with the effects of grief, violence, or addictive behavior, we recover in bits and pieces, not all at once. Sarah, in sharing part of her process of recovery, met girls at the crossroads where adolescence and adulthood overlap. She did so with utter appropriateness, never allowing the focus to center on her, but allowing the conversation to be about all of us, engaged together in God-talk among girlfriends.

Sometimes it seems as if only a miracle can counteract the centuries of androcentric bias within Judaism and Christianity. Many women who enter into serious reflection on these traditions decide they are best abandoned: the hurtful history is too much to overcome. One such person is Starhawk, a practicing Wiccan of Jewish lineage. She writes, "To work *magic*, we begin by making new metaphors."[25] As a feminist reformer rather than a revolutionary, I paraphrase Starhawk, affirming that to work *miracles* we begin by making new metaphors.[26] Transforming a tradition laden with a patriarchal bias requires new metaphors. Girlfriend theology offers us these: God as a bent-over father crying tears of life and God as imminently present in the moment when our eyes are opened to another's scars.

In the process of coming to these metaphors, girls and women did much more than create two new metaphors: they learned *how* to create them communally, from life experience, in a safe place where doubt and critique of tradition become steps toward transforming and embracing tradition. Frequently as we engaged in this playful, creative process, a discomfort would arise. Is *any* metaphor for God okay? Are there limits we want to place on the ways we name God through this method? In our research circles we found that erring on the side of inclusion always worked best. That way, people did not censor ideas for fear of being disregarded. Occasionally, an idea about God would be voiced with which others disagreed. We would talk through the nuances of the different interpretations, reminding participants that we do not all have to leave with the same conclusions. A standard measure for us became this: Did the image or idea grow out of or connect to any long-held truths — either obvious or hidden — that exist within our faith traditions? In other words, did the theological image or metaphor we were creating connect to the Bible stories, even little-known ones? Did it surface an element of Judeo-Christian tradition and teaching? Could we see reflected in it some experiences common to human life? Did the image meaningfully intersect with the long history of human philosophy, thought, and reason? These four sources — scripture, tradition, experience, and reason — known to historians of theology as John Wesley's quadrilateral, provided a yardstick by which to measure our thoughts, ideas, and beliefs. Other theological methods that use the yardstick of scripture, reason, experience, and tradition enter into conversation with girlfriend theology in the next chapter.

Chapter Six

Slipping through
the Barbed Wire Fence

Crossing the Borders of Women's
Emancipatory Theologies

[The school] was a machine for condensing souls into the smallest possible area. I have seen souls so compressed that they would have filled a small thimble.

— Olive Schreiner, *The Story of an African Farm*

I come from a land of strawberries, oranges, and adolescent awakenings.

I am thirteen years old, lying on a single bed a few inches away from a screen window, opening onto a dark spring night. As I lie awake, strains of music float across the yard, the garden, the pasture, and the pond, tracing a path I know well in daylight. I sit up and look out the window, straining in the darkness to see the source of this music — this lively, thumping guitar music, accentuated every few minutes with a loud shout and an outbreak of applause. I see only faintly the lights of the party, dimly piercing the darkness. I lie back down and listen to the music, slipping through the window in my mind, bare feet first collecting dew from the yard, then deep rich soil from the garden. I slip between two pieces of barbed wire and jump over the drainage ditch, following the light and the music across the wide pastures and around the edge of the pond to the other world that lies about a quarter-mile from my bed.

My fantasy trip to this other world takes me across a border — the border between white girls lying in bed and brown bodies, dancing, singing, and entering space not seen by an overseer. The first world is mine. The second belongs to the Mexican migrant workers whose labor transforms the bright red strawberries growing low to the ground into the cash that fills the bank accounts of the white farmers who occupy the pews of the First Baptist Church of Dover.

Eventually, on that spring night, I fell asleep, imagining the party and the bodies swaying in the night to the rhythms of a place far away.

At school the next Monday, and every weekday throughout junior high school, my girlfriends and I flirt with the boys from the migrant camps. We know this is something our parents would not like and something for which popular girls cast glances of disdain our way. In the afternoons when our homework is done, we tear off on bicycles, our mechanisms of freedom. We ride to Johnson Road — a forbidden realm where we meet our friends. Here the mutual exploration of the borders of our lives continues. We learn that some of our friends truly are Mexican, but most of them are Texan. We learn their names and the names of their little sisters, who smile when they see us coming.

Late one night, camping out in a tent in a pasture behind Cindy's house, we write the anthem of our resistance in the key of bluegrass: "Mama don't allow no riding down Johnson Road. Mama don't allow no riding down Johnson Road. We don't care what Mama don't allow, we're gonna do it anyhow, we're gonna have some fun before they leave."

It is all about young sexuality, forbidden fruits, and budding questions that crop up in the space between childhood and adolescence. In junior high, we are learning subtle ways to resist oppressive authority: we study Spanish harder than we study English, and we keep our bicycle tires full. In high school, we forget our friends. Many of them don't come back. A few of them stay year-round. But we have outgrown our bicycles and lost interest in that border crossing.

Now I am eighteen. It is a cold February night. A bitter, record-breaking frost has hit in the peak of strawberry season. It is my first day on the job as a college intern at a metropolitan newspaper forty-five minutes from my home. My first assignment is to cover the frost. I follow journalistic procedure, calling the farm bureau spokesperson and getting the estimated losses and the sad stories of woe, well-rehearsed by the wealthy landowners. Then, I get in my car and go to the community center less than a mile from my parents' home, where the workers have called a meeting. They are gathering, organizing, and politicizing. Here, the impact of the freeze is different. I learn — in what Spanish I remember — about heat being turned off in the trailers where families huddle together under a few blankets. I learn that the workers are being told to "go home" — there will be no berries to pick, no work, no pay. It does not matter that there is nowhere else to go, or that the workers had committed to stay through the berry season. It does not matter that the oranges have all been picked and the next known paychecks will not come for many more months, when Michigan's cherry season begins. There is a different story here, and I tell it: between the lines, I write my adolescent history of nights spent listening to guitar rhythms and days spent riding bicycles.

I am fourteen, fifteen, sixteen, living the life of a privileged middle-class girl. I am seventeen, eighteen, nineteen, and on the edges of my memory, there is an awareness of injustice, an awareness of arbitrary borders separating "us" and "them." It is during these years, through fits and starts of overheard conversations, books stumbled upon, and a subversive teacher or two, that I come into a space between two meanings. There is the meaning of childhood, which is cloaked in the private awareness of family and sheltered by views I do not know I can question, and the inchoate meaning of adulthood, which is filled with moments of awakening to political and spiritual realities and views other than my parents' and an awareness of the choice to question, to criticize, and to think for myself.

These memories of adolescent border crossings inform my practice as a white, feminist theologian. As a flirtatious middle-class adolescent, slipping through the barbed wire fence meant an excursion to an exotic world of difference, an escape from the mundane. As a young journalist with a budding critical conscience, slipping through the barbed wire fence meant beginning to acknowledge white privilege and its companion, white racism. Today, as a practical theologian envisioning new models of education, slipping through the barbed wire fence means the disciplined act of listening to the voices that speak on behalf of the marginalized and oppressed.

Barbed wire and border crossings speak of danger. But the danger is not to my life, as is frequently the case for those persons who cross real borders laced with razor-sharp wire.[1] A more appropriate word is risk. Sharon Welch argues that an "ethic of risk" is necessary if feminists from different cultural backgrounds are to build coalitions.[2] In our forays into other women's experiences, we risk saying the wrong thing or asking the wrong question, and thereby revealing unhealed parts of the racism and cultural imperialism embedded by years of socialization. This fear, although real, diminishes as we learn to cross borders as an act of friendship, walking humbly into unknown worlds and authentically seeking to own and to heal our pasts.

In chapter 4, I discussed women's autobiographies as a key source for the feminist education of adolescent girls. Interpreting autobiographies through the lens of womanist theology and ethics, I introduced a second key source: women's emancipatory theologies. I use "emancipatory" to refer to the wealth of theologies arising out of particular contexts of oppression around the world. In this chapter, I will introduce two additional emancipatory theologies: *mujerista* theology and Asian-feminist theology. In conjunction with womanist theology, these writings provide critical voices historically excluded from feminist theology.[3] After describing the context, theological method, biblical hermeneutic, and key concepts of the writings of *mujeristas*, Asian feminists, and womanists, I will show how these critical voices can add to the warehouse of stories and images that girlfriend theology invites into dialogue between adult women and adolescent girls.

Mujerista Theology: Its Roots, Methods, and Motifs

Hispanic politician and activist Maria Antonietta Berriozábal tells a story about her adolescence. She grew up in a Mexican American barrio in the southwestern United States. In this neighborhood, she experienced connection to her family, her God, and her wider community as a shawl, woven of many threads and wrapped around her. This shawl gave her life meaning and orientation. It helped her define her vocation as being in service to *la comunidad*. As she left junior high school and entered a high school outside of her neighborhood, she found many of the treasures her Mexican American upbringing had valued largely ignored in the wider culture. The resulting identity crisis caused her to question and doubt the dearly held beliefs that had given her life meaning.[4]

This story rings true to recent ethnographic research conducted by the American Association of University Women (AAUW). In a 1996 study, the AAUW identified girls, usually of Latina descent, whom they called "border crossers" because of the involuntary border crossing required of them. The success of these girls, as they wade through the difficult adolescent waters of junior high and high school, depends largely upon the similarities or differences between the school's culture and the girls' culture of origin. If the school culture values the "treasures" of her community, the girl will usually find a wide arena in which she can carve out a successful niche. If, however, the school culture values the dominant culture's norms to the exclusion of cultural differences, the girl might be labeled a troublemaker and will find successful avenues of achievement severely limited.[5]

In the following section, I will explore the context, theological method, and key themes of *mujerista* theology as it emerges primarily through the writings of Ada María Isasi-Díaz. I do so mindful of girls who, in the process of growing up, sometimes cross borders into hostile territory.

Historical Context of Mujerista Theology

Mujerista theology emerged during the 1970s and 1980s along with many other theologies unmasking the white, Western, androcentric bias of neo-orthodox theology by focusing on contexts of race, ethnicity, gender, social class, and sexual orientation. Acknowledging their roots in liberation theology, which grows out of Latin American base communities, Hispanic feminists in the United States began to express long-held feelings of marginalization within the largely white, middle-class circles of feminist theology. They began to voice their own theological method, visions of God and the church, and biblical hermeneutics. This movement included women primarily of Mexican, Puerto Rican, and Cuban descent and sought to claim a common identity among these groups while not erasing the differences each brought based on their nation of origin and other socioeconomic factors.

Isasi-Díaz, who migrated to the United States from Cuba as a teenager, became a primary enabler of this grassroots development. She led retreats of Hispanic women and articulated in her writings a vision of theology as a "liberatory praxis of Hispanic women oppressed by ethnic prejudice, sexism, and poverty in the United States."[6] This vision grew out of Isasi-Díaz's formative experiences as a Catholic nun serving among a community of the poor in Lima, Peru, for three years. Her liberatory praxis consists of the following: (1) enabling Latinas to understand the struggles of their daily lives within the context of the many structures that oppress them and stand in need of change; (2) helping Latinas to imagine and define their preferred future; and (3) challenging Latinas to understand how the prevailing oppressive systems in society — including organized religion — have internalized within them attitudes of self-effacement that contribute to their sense of powerlessness and lack of voice. This three-part analysis enables Latinas to engage communally in *la lucha,* the empowering struggle for the liberation of all people. *La lucha* becomes a source of hope as Latina women begin to challenge that which requires their servitude or self-abnegation. The result is a strong sense of moral agency accompanied by communal and individual self-worth.

In addition to this primary goal of empowering and enabling Latinas, *mujerista* theology has a secondary goal: to effect change, contributing to a refashioning of the mainline theologies that currently support the status quo in North American church and society.

Theological Method of Mujerista Theology

Mujerista theology uses techniques of qualitative research in order to place the lived experiences of Hispanic women at the center of the theological task. The qualitative research tools Isasi-Díaz draws upon are ethnography and meta-ethnography.

Ethnography refers to the gathering of the voices of grassroots women, primarily through intensive retreats and interviews. The retreats involve interconnected movements of storytelling, analysis, liturgy, and strategizing. The goal is to hear women articulate the events of and the meanings arising from their everyday lives — that which constitutes their common and shared reality. Often this process becomes a "hearing to speech," as it provides a forum for women to reflect upon their lives and discover meanings, thus developing their own voices.[7] In addition to retreats and interviews, *mujerista* theology uses other ethnographic techniques, such as the observation of and participation in popular religious rituals and practices occurring in the everyday lives of Hispanic women.

Meta-ethnography refers to the interpretation of these ethnographic accounts. As the theologian reviews the accounts of retreats and interviews, key metaphors and themes emerge. She notes commonalities and differences arising from the women's stories and process of meaning-making. These key themes become generative words that resonate with and express the life situations of Hispanic women. These words are then "translated" by the writer/theologian. As a central part of this task, the theologian returns these translations to the community to check their authenticity. In this way, the method stays rooted in the community, remaining in a dialogic tension between the professional theologian and the women to whom she is accountable. Isasi-Díaz calls this a "joint search for understanding and articulating meaning."

This method provides a critique to dominant theological norms by beginning with the lived experience of women, rather than with the understandings and practices that are considered to have important religious significance. Thus, *mujerista* theology becomes a subversive act, asking new theological questions. Isasi-Díaz provides a compelling example of this when she contrasts two Hispanic views of Jesus. Some male Hispanic theologians ask how Jesus can be presented so that he is more central and accessible to common folk. *Mujerista* theologians, on the other hand, are more inclined to ask why the majority of Hispanic women do not relate to Jesus. This causes them to focus their attention on the centrality of Mary within the popular religious lives of women. By asking a different question, new understandings about the presence of the divine in everyday life emerge.

Biblical Hermeneutics of Mujerista Theology

Isasi-Díaz approaches the Bible with the question "How can this enhance and enable the moral agency of Hispanic women?" making the struggle for liberation the lens through which to view the Bible. The Bible becomes a strategic tool for Latinas in defining their preferred future. Thus, in their interpretation and appropriation of the Bible, *mujerista* theologians seek stories that can serve as sources of hope. Biblical depictions of persons, including Jesus, who struggled for survival become the canon within the canon, helping Latinas define a heritage of resistance to domination and oppression.

Doing biblical exegesis is a communal task in which *la palabra de Dios* (the word of God) refers not to what is written in the text, but to how the stories and their applications aid in struggles for survival. Through continued resistance to traditional or fundamentalist interpretations of scripture, *mujeristas* discover the Bible as a wealth of "new information" providing stories that serve as interpretive keys in the struggle for liberation.[8] Literary and historical analysis of the text serves to uncover details of the biblical story that resonate with contemporary lives of Latinas. Shiphrah and Puah, the midwives who foreshadow the Exodus event, serve as models. They are risk-taking women whose defiance and resistance shed light on contemporary situations of oppressed women using their moral agency to shape the future of their people.

Key Themes of Mujerista Theology

In my reading of Isasi-Díaz, three key themes of *mujerista* theology emerge as badly needed correctives to the theology in North American churches. They include *lo cotidiano,* mutuality and solidarity, and a high anthropology.

Lo Cotidiano. *Lo cotidiano* refers to the starting point of *mujerista* theology — the lived experience of Hispanic women. As well as being a descriptive term, it refers to a hermeneutical task and sets up the epistemological stance of *mujerista* theology.

Descriptively, *lo cotidiano* refers not only to the daily chores associated with caring for families and maintaining households, but also to an analysis of all the systems of class, race, and gender oppression that affect to the daily lives of women. Relationships of family and community, systems of authority, and expressions of faith are part of this daily lived experience.

As part of the hermeneutical task, *lo cotidiano* refers to processes that shape Latina thought, interpretation, and action. These are necessarily subjective, as Latina women's perceptions of the world are not all the same. It is important to acknowledge these differences, rather than mask them. Thus, *lo cotidiano* is constantly shifting and changing — a transitory and subjective articulation of events as they occur close to home in the struggle to put food on the table, find jobs, move relatives across the border, and raise children. It is not an objective, removed, or abstract hermeneutical category.

Lastly, *lo cotidiano* is a way of knowing, an epistemology. It has to do with claiming women's daily experience, which is varied, complex, and infused with difference, as the starting point of shaping reality. This means "rescuing" what has been deemed unimportant in traditional theological systems. Daily lived experience, traditionally seen as a trivial and untrustworthy epistemological source, becomes the primary source of authentic relationship to the divine. This is a subversive act, making possible the reinterpretation of scripture and tradition from an admittedly subjective and provisional point of view.[9]

This theme provides especially important insight for girlfriend theology. Although the media and popular culture trivialize girls' activities in every dimension of life, here stands an alternative view. Girls' everyday lives are not trivial. The sexual innuendo on the bus, the hurtful racial slur, or the history of familial violence need not be hidden. Sharing such pieces of everyday life is the necessary first step in constructing an ongoing, living religious tradition. Like Hispanic women, teenage girls can become "organic intellectuals" who reflect critically on their everyday lives, finding moral agency and means of resistance to oppression.

Mutuality and Solidarity. Isasi-Díaz proposes a shift in the way mainstream theology approaches ethical behavior. Traditionally, the church has seen charity as the appropriate Christian ethical behavior. She proposes that, in order for mutuality to exist between the oppressed and the oppressors, this must change. The appropriate Christian ethical response must be solidarity — specifically, understanding the interconnections that exist between the rich and the poor, the oppressed and the oppressor. She defines solidarity as both a theory and a strategy.

As theory, solidarity is the understanding or worldview that allows us to see all of humanity as intrinsically linked, meaning the privileges of some are connected to the oppression of others. As strategy, solidarity implies forming relationships of mutuality between the oppressed and the oppressors. In these relationships, persons develop a critical awareness of the ways in which their own daily lives and actions contribute to the oppression and domination of others. As they listen to oppressed communities, the nonoppressed become "friends" who enter the struggle for liberation.

The shift from charity to solidarity is an example of one way *mujerista* theology seeks to alter theological categories outside of a Latina frame of reference. This shift is essential to dismantling the legacy of imperialism that Christianity bears. It is especially important, then, that religious educators in mainstream North American churches find ways to bring this corrective into our curricula. Understanding the ways in which *mujerista* theologians welcome the presence of "friends" who join in a community of solidarity enables white North American Christians to move from debilitating roles of guilt and/or sympathy to the empowering praxis of solidarity and mutuality.

High Anthropology. Isasi-Díaz articulates a high anthropology and a low Christology. She rejects the traditional Christian notion that Jesus' suffering was greater than all other human suffering. For *mujeristas*, suffering is not the central motif of the Christian story, but rather *la lucha*, the struggle against such suffering. The fiesta, occurring in the midst of *la lucha*, celebrates the struggle against suffering that is in process, not the suffering that has taken place. *La fiesta* celebrates the community of solidarity, that which energizes the ongoing struggle.

Isasi-Díaz uses the powerful phrase *permítanme hablar,* which means "allow me to speak," to articulate her high anthropology. Unless Hispanic women allow themselves to speak and be heard, the degradation of their humanity from the dominant structures continues. Unless Hispanic women value their own stories, their own voices, their own realities, and their own theological formulations, they will continue to internalize dominant culture's objectification of themselves. Thus, *mujerista* anthropology is "from within" and "from below" as it centers not on an abstract view of humanity but on a particularized context.

I share with Isasi-Díaz this high anthropology and lift up the importance of *"permítanme hablar"* in the lives of adolescent girls of all races, classes, and ethnicities. The story theology method prioritizes the voices of adolescent girls, making a claim that words of importance will emerge. As opposed to traditional religious education models, which begin with scripture and move toward life experience, girlfriend theology moves in the opposite direction. Thus, it is also "from below" and "from within."

Contributions to Girlfriend Theology

In making connections between *mujerista* theology and girlfriend theology, I keep two goals in mind. One goal is to create a method of religious education for female adolescents that is aware of, inclusive of, and helpful to girls from varying social and cultural contexts. Therefore, it must take into serious account the theologies arising from women of varying ethnicities, classes, and sexual orientations. My appropriation of *mujerista* theology attempts to contribute to a wider understanding of what it means to be a woman in contemporary American culture.

A second goal is to allow girls of inherited privilege to be able to critique the dominant culture in which they find themselves and to name this act as a necessary part of their Christian vocation. In order to critique dominant culture, they must be aware of alternative cultural forms that provide correctives to Western, white, patriarchal structures. I find *mujerista* theology replete with examples of alternative visions — visions that value everyday lives, stress the importance of community, lift up the potential of humans, and invite the formations of coalitions.

Adopting themes from *mujerista* theology entails relating its historical context. Purely transplanting the concept of *lo cotidiano,* for instance, into a middle-class North American context, without explaining its roots within an oppressed community, would constitute cultural looting. I will say more at the conclusion of this chapter about the standard guiding my borrowing across cultural borders.

Asian-Feminist Theology: Its Roots, Motifs, and Methods

When Asian-feminist theologians turn a critical eye toward Western theology, they name many of the same realities that feminists around the world expose in Eurocentric, neo-orthodox methods of speaking about God and humanity. But Asian feminists do so from a perspective that is "very Third World, very Asian, and very women."[10] Two central critiques include Western theology's exclusive reliance on biblical paradigms and its hegemony over the definitions of norms and categories of theology.

Historical Context of Asian-Feminist Theology

In the mid-1980s, Asian women began gathering to formulate critiques of Western theology and male-dominated Asian liberation theologies.[11] A leader in this movement, Korean theologian Hyun Kyung Chung identifies three major settings that were central to the emergence of a feminist, liberation-oriented theological consciousness among Asian women. Those settings were the Christian Conference of Asia, the Ecumenical Association of Third World Theologians (EATWOT) and the Asian women's theological journal, *In God's Image.*[12]

As is the case in most women's emancipatory theologies, an enormous amount of diversity exists within Asian-feminist writings. Although Western feminist theologians share a Judeo-Christian cultural and religious background, Asian-feminist theologians, "despite certain common cultural bases, have extremely diverse histories, religions, cultures, and traditions."[13] Rather than try to summarize this multifarious body of literature, I focus on two Asian-feminist critiques of Western biblical and theological norms before describing a theological method communally agreed upon by Asian feminists.

Asian-Feminist Theological Motifs: Two Critiques

Pui Lan Kwok, a Chinese feminist theologian, critiques traditional Western theology for its focus on a narrow and mystified view of the Bible.[14] Although acknowledging the power and authority of stories found there, she asserts that religious imagination based on the Bible alone is apt to exclude women's experiences. This perspective is shared by Judith Siqueira, who develops the metaphor of a "fifth gospel" to describe the contextualization of the Christian message.[15] Both of these women's perspectives entered the girlfriend theology process, as related in chapter 3.

Kwok continues her critique by focusing on the classic trappings of Christianity that missionaries brought with them to Asian cultures, which were, until recently, uncritically adopted. Among these trappings was the stress to study Hebrew, Greek, Latin, and German, while denying the importance of indigenous linguistic heritages. Further, the theologies of Augustine, Aquinas, Tillich, Barth, and other European men defined the norms of theology, setting the categories in which Asian theologians were trained to function. As Hyun Kyung Chung explains, her teachers, trained in Europe and North America, spent most of their time trying to understand a spiritual reality through concepts and symbols that did not resonate in the hearts and minds of her people. This passive reception of Western theology was a disservice to her people and the whole church, she maintains.

When integration between the indigenous and the transplanted takes place, Kwok argues, "there will be many theologies." A plurality of voices will replace the unified discourse of traditional theology. The norm of theology will become the praxis of communities within their particular struggles for liberation. Chung argues that women, especially, must reclaim their right to speak about God and generate new symbols from their own experience, thus participating fully in the process of myth- and symbol-making. To this end, she writes:

Only when we Asian women start to consider our everyday con-crete life experiences as the most important source for building the religious meaning structures for ourselves shall we be free from all imposed religious authority.[16]

Asian-Feminist Theological Method

In keeping with this mandate and in contrast to traditional neo-orthodox theology, Asian-feminist theologies grow out of stories—stories set in common, everyday experiences of life. This method of doing theology, although implicit in many liberation theologies from the third world, receives explicit articulation from Asian fem-inists. The clearest articulation of this methodology comes from the Women's Committee of the EATWOT. Chung describes this method as three circular steps: storytelling, critical social analysis, and theological reflection.[17]

Step One: Storytelling. Kwok writes that Indian, Burmese, Jap-anese, and Chinese women all have a "treasure chest" of lullabies, songs, myths, and stories that give them a sense of identity and a vision for the future. Opening this treasure chest is the first step to doing theology, she writes. At EATWOT gatherings and writings, the storytelling step begins with women from diverse backgrounds listen-ing carefully to one another as they relate the particularities of their lived experiences. Stories of family violence, political activism, sex-ual abuse, and cultural and religious imperialism, for example, serve as the starting point for asking questions about God's presence and activity in the world.

The power of these stories lies in their tangible nature. They reflect concrete life experience rather than abstract metaphysical concepts. Chung uses the term "embodied historiography" to refer to this story-telling methodology. It emerges from an understanding of history as a construct that leaves out the stories of the powerless. Behind the "objective truths" of written history lie hidden realities, which are exposed as Asian women tell their stories and move into acts of solidarity. This embodied historiography deals with the whole per-son immersed in the complex web of political, social, economic, and personal factors that determine her options in life.

Step Two: Critical Social Analysis. Sharing stories leads to the second step in this theological method: critical social analysis, which involves looking intently at the larger picture. What is going on politically, economically, and socially that shapes this story? In a story about sexual abuse, questions concerning patriarchal culture and its claims on women's bodies emerge. In the story of a woman whose exposure to Christian missionaries robbed her of her native spirituality, questions of cultural bias and hegemonic religious practices emerge. When the larger contexts of personal stories are examined, they reveal multiple layers of gender oppression, economic exploitation, and social discrimination. This step exposes the cultural and psychological patterns that perpetuate women's oppression. It is a process of conscientization, of bringing to awareness interlocking systems and enlarging the vision of women engaged in struggle at the grassroots level.

Step Three: Theological Reflection. After taking a critical look at the social influences that set the stage for the story, this method moves to theological reflection. Chung names four sources for Asian women's theological reflection: women's lived experience, "engaged subjective reason that takes sides," tradition, and scripture. The key to this is anthropology. God is not revealed outside of humanity, but rather within the Asian woman's experience of suffering and hope. The Bible is part of this step, but only as appropriated from the bottom up.

The goal is to bring Asian women's lives into dialogue with the tradition of Christianity. It is a practical theology, one that does not perpetuate the age-old interpretations of the Bible that are laden with Western assumptions, patriarchy, and colonialism. Rather, it selects the stories that give meaning to women's lives, critically examining inherited interpretations. Chung notes that this last step in the theological method is called *hyun jang* theology, which means it centers around the places where historically meaningful events are transpiring.

In this theological reflection, ethical commitments are necessarily intertwined. The litmus test of this method is whether it contributes to the authentic personhood of women, fosters just communities, and develops caring and respectful attitudes toward all of creation. Chung determines if a theology is "good theology" by discerning whether it untangles the Korean woman's *han* (the sin of internalized self-hatred) and thus liberates her from bondage. If it enables *han* to continue to accumulate, it is bad theology, regardless of what other purposes it might serve to the church or its traditions.[18]

Contributions to Girlfriend Theology

The three-step method of Asian-feminist theology as practiced by EATWOT shares significant points of connection with girlfriend theology. Just as Chung asks "Who is Jesus?" and "Who is Mary?" from an Asian woman's perspective, girlfriend theology asks questions such as these from the perspective of culturally situated youth. In both cases, the answers contribute to a refashioning of Christian symbols and images. The four-part method of story theology used in girlfriend theology shares many of the assumptions underlying Asian feminists' three-step circular process of storytelling, critical social analysis, and theological reflection. In order to reveal these connections, I will turn to three significant tenets of emancipatory theology that Asian-feminist theology exemplifies: (1) theology begins with sharing stories of lived experience; (2) theology is communal, rather than individual work; and (3) theology seeks to connect personal experiences of oppression with structural causes of oppression.

Theology Begins with Sharing Stories of Lived Experience

Just as "the Indians, the Burmese, the Japanese, and the Chinese all have stories that give meaning and orientation" to their lives, North American youth have stories, particular to their subcultures, that shape their approach to life. These stories, for both Asian women and marginalized youth, will most often be tales of struggle, pain, suffering, and oppression. Whereas in Asian cultures these themes arise within repositories such as lullabies and folktales, for American youth, these themes appear in various genres of popular culture such as hip-hop and rap music, subway graffiti, skateboard performance, street drama, and personal narratives. Unlocking these deeply textured, culturally imbued treasure chests of stories is the first step in helping youth understand the realities in which they live. A method of religious education that elicits these stories is in keeping with the emerging theological tradition of Asian feminists that values meaning-making from the bottom up and seeks to make visible hidden realities.

Theology Is Communal Rather Than Individual Work

Asian women view God not as an individual, but as a community. The image of God as "the community in relationship" allows women to move out of individualism into a stance of honoring their responsibility and connectedness to the community. A method of religious education that stresses the individual's ability to rely upon others as sources of meaning-making in their lives embodies this image of God as community in relationship.

This relational understanding calls upon wider images of God than those contained within traditional theology, encouraging youth to name images of God discerned in their concrete, everyday realities. As Chung writes, "In this image of God as the community in relationship, there is no place for only one solitary, all-powerful God who sits on the top of the hierarchical power pyramid and dominates all other living beings."[19] As youth appropriate this understanding of relationships and community, we could expect liberating images of God to emerge, adding to the creation of the "many theologies" Kwok celebrates within Asian theological contexts. As theology becomes the product of the whole community, rather than the elite, a new understanding of the word "theologian" emerges. Youth participating in a process of creating meaning out of their daily experiences might claim for themselves the role of theologian, coming to understand themselves as stakeholders in the emergence of new, life-giving forms of Christian tradition.

Theology Seeks to Connect Personal Experiences of Oppression with Structural Causes of Oppression

A theology stressing personal sin lays the blame for oppression on the victims themselves. By contrast, Asian-feminist and other liberatory theologies engage critical reasoning that takes sides, thus looking to the larger context of structural systems of oppression. These emancipatory theologies locate sin and evil in economic, political, and social realities that women come to identify as having oppressive effects in their lives. As Asian women come to name these systems, they can begin to mobilize themselves to change them, while at the same time freeing themselves from internalized oppression.

Adolescents are able to engage in formal operational thinking for the first time in their lives and are thus able to conceptualize abstractly. With the help of other critical thinkers, they are able to see the connections between their experiences and larger systems, thus forming the basis for active resistance to systems of oppression. This can accompany an increased capacity to shift from an emphasis on personal sin to an understanding of corporate sin. This theological shift allows individuals to name their participation in sinful structures and in internalizing oppression, while mobilizing them toward action.

Womanist Theology: Its Roots, Methods, and Motifs

Of the three women's emancipatory theologies I use as key sources for girlfriend theology, womanist theology is the one I have most thoroughly integrated into my educational theory and practice; gleanings from womanist theology appear in almost every chapter. Because I draw continuously from this source, my treatment of it here will be brief.

Historical Context of Womanist Theology

Linda Moody provides a helpful summary of the emergence of womanist theology, dating its articulation to Audre Lorde's 1979 letter to Mary Daly critiquing her for generalizing white, middle-class women's experience as normative for all women. At the same time that womanist theology has remained critical of white feminist thought that does not acknowledge the interconnectedness of race, class, and gender, it has critiqued black male theology for its androcentrism. Born in the gap between black male liberation theology and white female liberation theology, womanist theology has articulated distinct methodologies and biblical hermeneutics based on sources heretofore unacknowledged as authoritative (or altogether invisible) within Western theology. Those sources include black women's contemporary experiences, slave narratives, biographies of African American women, and African American spirituals.

A defining step in the historical emergence of womanist theology was Alice Walker's four-part definition of "womanist" in her 1983 book *In Search of Our Mothers' Gardens.* Based on this definition, to be a womanist means: (1) To act grown-up, responsible, and in charge; (2) to love other women, sexually and/or nonsexually and to be committed to the survival and wholeness of all people, male and female; (3) to love music, dance, the moon, the Spirit, food, roundness, struggle, the folk, and to love yourself, regardless; and (4) to be to feminist, as purple is to lavender. This evocative definition has provided a common point of reflection for women practicing womanist theology.[20]

Theological Method of Womanist Theology

Based on Walker's four-part definition, Delores Williams articulates four methodological principles of womanist theology. First, the methodology is intentionally dialogical, consciously seeking to remain in conversation with diverse communities while continuing to focus on those struggling against multiple layers of oppression, such as women of color and their children. Second, it is liturgically informed, using the ritual life of the black church as a source for theological reflection while critiquing the homophobia, sexism, and classism found there. Third, womanist theological methodology seeks to be didactic, reshaping the ethical and moral life of the church and society based on its critiques. Last, the methodology is committed to both reason and experience as sources of imagery and metaphor.

In addition, womanists believe that theology should be engaged in ethical praxis and that bifurcations between the sacred and the sexual should be rejected. Toinette Eugene articulates a methodological "praxis wheel" that illuminates these last two points. Experience is the starting point in the praxis wheel. It is followed by social and critical analysis, which leads to theological and ethical reflection. The last step in the wheel, which is where theology and ethics have traditionally broken off, is preparation for action in the world, otherwise known as praxis. Eugene's insistence that womanist theology and ethics complete the circle from experience to action contributes to her understanding of womanists as "transformative intellectuals," deeply engaged in the academic world of analysis and reflection and the everyday lived reality of "the folk."[21]

Biblical Hermeneutics of Womanist Theology

Womanist theologian Jacquelyn Grant approaches the Bible with the question, "Who do womanists say that Jesus Christ is?" For her, black women's own experience of oppression and God's witness as a liberator within that context provide the lens through which to read and interpret the Bible. In this way, womanists hold in tension two sources of revelation — the Bible and black women's experience. Through this hermeneutic, Jesus emerges as a highly personal manifestation of God, one who feels pain, knows of the struggle, and provides comfort in the midst of oppression.

For womanist Delores Williams, the liberatory acts of God must be seen alongside the biblical witness of times when God does not act as a liberator. The story of Hagar — a surrogate mother and slave who is banished to the wilderness — offers a paradigm of survival, not of liberation. Hagar's story provides a point of critique, acknowledging that God does not always liberate. Some people, most often the ones with whom the biblical writers *do not identify*, are left in subordinate positions — as is Hagar.

In this paradigm of struggle and survival in the wilderness, Williams sees many parallels both with black people's experiences, as reflected in slave narratives, and with black women, children, and men in contemporary American society, where oppression continues despite the promises of the civil rights movement. In light of these parallels, the tendency of black male theology to focus on the liberating God of the

Exodus falls short. Hagar encounters God in the wilderness, a place where one learns to survive and where one is transformed. Born of this critical biblical hermeneutic is the need for womanists to turn to extrabiblical sources — especially West African sources — to provide what Williams calls "woman-inclusive" correctives to nonliberating aspects of scripture and tradition.

Key Themes of Womanist Theology

Among the many generative themes within this body of literature, three arise as particularly crucial as I integrate womanist thought into a model of religious education for adolescent girls. Because I have discussed these three themes individually in previous chapters, I will summarize them briefly here.

The first is Alice Walker's insistence on acknowledging the presence of adolescent girls. Walker's definition of womanist, which describes the experience of girls as "acting womanish," serves as a badly needed corrective to white feminist theology and to normative theology in mainline white churches in North America.[22] For the most part, the experience of adolescent girls has been invisible in these realms.

The second is bell hooks's concept of homeplace as a site of resistance. White feminists often portray domestic life as a sphere of menial labor and drudgery. In contrast, hooks reminds us of the importance of homeplace: it is where survival skills are passed down from mothers to their offspring. By reframing domestic life as a position of power rather than subservience, black women create "a way outa no way" to ensure the survival of their people.[23]

The third is Katie Cannon's concept of "unctuousness as a virtue," drawn from the life and works of Zora Neale Hurston. Cannon builds upon Alice Walker's definition of unctuousness as "the ability to act sincere in the most insincere situations" and a "feistiness about life which no one can knock out" in her analysis of Hurston's life. Working during the Harlem Renaissance, Hurston was often forced to cater to the whims of the white patrons who funded her ethnographic research in her all-black central Florida hometown. There, Hurston gathered in rich detail the stories, songs, and survival strategies of her people. Using the unctuousness instilled in her by her mother,

Hurston was able to maneuver within systems of white oppression, carving out enough room to create a lasting cultural repository. Cannon sees Hurston's life as an example of what it means to live to one's full potential, despite the limiting factors of racism.[24]

These three themes arise from a dynamic tradition. Womanist theologians and ethicists do not operate out of the same historical context, theological method, or biblical hermeneutic. I have endeavored to show this by naming particular writers in connection with their ideas.

Guides for Border Crossing: Appropriation and Reciprocity

In her book *Mujerista Theology,* Isasi-Díaz tells of her sadness, anger, and frustration in trying to "plant her garden" in the soil of white feminism. Transformed by the women-church movement and naively entering into community with white feminists, Isasi-Díaz discovered racism inherent there. When she tried to plant her garden — replete with memories of her Cuban childhood and immigrant experience — she found it was not welcomed.[25] When told from the perspective of women of color, this has often been the experience of women seeking to engage in theological discourse across the boundaries of ethnicity, race, and economic status.

Out of this painful history grew academic discourse between some of the womanist, feminist, and *mujerista* theologians and ethicists who take part in the American Academy of Religion. One result of these conversations was naming the joined concept of "appropriation and reciprocity" as an ethical guide in theological border crossings.[26]

Appropriation refers to taking the stories, metaphors, concepts, or modes of discourse of one group or culture with the intent of converting them for one's own use. A history exists of white persons appropriating the cultural reserves of black persons without caring about the specific experiences out of which they grew, about whether interpretations retain integrity of meaning, or about giving something back. This constitutes misappropriation and breeds distrust.

Reciprocity moves toward restitution of this kind for misappropriation. It refers to entering into relationships of mutuality and accountability. It also means giving back to the community from which one borrows and caring about the communities from which the commodities and discourse arise.[27] An understanding of appropriation and reciprocity serves as an ethical guide for women engaging in shared theological reflection across borders of race, ethnicity, and class.

I draw connections between the writings of *mujeristas,* Asian feminists, and womanists with the goal of allowing these voices to take part in reshaping girls' religious lives. Although I acknowledge the critical differences between these theological perspectives, I nonetheless see similarities that hold great potential.

All of these theological expressions mark women's daily experiences as the starting point for reflection about God. They all share a high anthropology, believing and acting as if real lives and bodies matter and provide avenues toward knowing God. They all would agree with Chung's statement that women's spirituality is found "not in university desks, but in kitchens, laundries, fields, and factories."[28] Finally, they all believe theology must take sides with the poor and oppressed, opening possibilities for coalitions across borders of differences.

Adult women aware of the writings of *mujeristas,* Asian feminists, and womanists possess something of immense value to female adolescents: the knowledge of narratives spoken in native tongues. This knowledge is especially critical to girls of color, as this story from Gloria Anzaldúa shows:

> In the 1960s, I read my first Chicano novel. It was *City of Night* by John Rechy, a gay Texan, son of a Scottish father and a Mexican mother. For days I walked around in stunned amazement that a Chicano could write and get published.... When I saw poetry in Tex-Mex for the first time, a feeling of pure joy flashed through me. I felt like we really existed as a people.[29]

This flash of "pure joy" occurs when echoes of one's personal experience spoken in one's native tongue enter the public discourse. I see the potential for replicating this flash of "pure joy" if adult women of faith armed with their carefully collected usable pasts step forward to share them with adolescent girls. Girls of minority descent would discover an appreciation of their cultural heritage within their communities of faith. Seeing this appreciation might support a girl's inchoate yearnings beyond conventional expectations. This yearning — a common characteristic of adolescent female identity formation — often wanes, unnoticed and unsupported.[30] White girls might slip through the barbed wire fence, learning the ethical discipline of border crossing, which can lead toward the dismantling of racism. To invoke this chapter's epigraph, a community of faith might provide a *soul-expanding* alternative to the *soul-shrinking* learning environments that are prevalent in dominant culture.[31]

Chapter Seven

Breast-Feeding Women and Vegan Girls

Girlfriend Theology as Embodied Pedagogy

In February 1999, the following letter appeared in the *Evanston Review*, a weekly newspaper in a city just north of Chicago:

Dear Editor:

Is breast-feeding offensive?

As the mother of a two-month-old daughter, I spend much of my time breast-feeding. In between, I take part in everyday activities such as grocery shopping, visiting the library, and working out at the gym. Every once in a while, my infant daughter demands a feeding when I find myself away from my rocking chair, smack in the middle of a public place.

Recently, this happened at Northwestern University's Henry Crown Sports and Aquatics Center. After discreetly nursing my daughter in the most private of two seating areas, I was asked by a child-care worker to visit the facility director's office. There I was gently told that my action had offended another gym patron. I was told that, although the facility "does not have a policy against" breast-feeding, I would have to nurse in the women's dressing room or to cover myself with a blanket while nursing. Taken off guard, I nodded a quick assent and, after a few brief words, left the director's office.

Since that moment, I have become increasingly dismayed that I was asked to hide a perfectly natural, healthy act. I have also learned that Illinois law protects my right to breast-feed in public by stating that breast-feeding does not constitute indecent exposure. There is currently federal legislation pending to ensure nationwide standards supporting breast-feeding in the workplace and other public spaces.

Up until now, I have not felt the need to speak out about breast-feeding. I have never attended a La Leche League International meeting, although I support that organization's goal to decrease global health risks by increasing breast-feeding.

Now I see that breast-feeding is an act with very public implications.

If I choose to take the advice of the facility director, hiding while breast-feeding, I implicitly teach a new generation of parents that breast-feeding is somehow indecent, lewd, or offensive. The very act of throwing a blanket over my shoulder and my baby implies that we are participating in something indecent. If I enter the dressing room to nurse, I am left to sit on the floor or in a very uncomfortable position on a bench, teaching a new generation of parents that putting extra wear and tear on a mother's body is inconsequential. If I go one step further, expressing breast milk in private to bottle-feed my baby when we are in public, I teach a new generation of parents that increasing a mother's already heavy workload is acceptable. The last step would be to give up on breast-feeding altogether. Had I not been an experienced mother convinced of the benefits of breast-feeding, I might have chosen this step when confronted with the request not to nurse in public.

Breast-feeding is not a lifestyle choice. It is a significant medical choice for my baby. The American Academy of Pediatrics guidelines strongly endorse breast-feeding during the first year of life as the best way to ensure a child's long-term health.

Despite the obvious health benefits of breast-feeding, an anonymous gym patron has found my simple act of mothering offensive. In an era when young women succumb to eating disorders, in part due to society's ideal of feminine beauty, opportunities to be offended abound: a woman's breast serving its biological function should not be one of them. I believe the patron's complaint should not have been passed on to me. It should have stopped at the listening ear of the director, who could have explained my legal right and done a bit of breast-feeding education at the same time.

Despite laws, many obstacles — including embarrassment and lack of cultural affirmation — stand in the way of women breast-feeding. I hope our community will benefit from a positive public discussion of breast-feeding, thereby enabling and encouraging women to do what is best for their infants.

Sincerely,
Dori Baker

The day this letter appeared, my phone rang off the hook. I got calls from my midwife, my nurse practitioner, my older child's preschool director, and total strangers. "The same thing happened to me and I never nursed in public again," said the nurse practitioner. "I've always wanted to go back and change that." "You go, girl!" said Roberta, whom I had never met. She told me that for years she regretted shamefully retreating to the stall of a public restroom after being asked not to nurse in a restaurant. "I read the letter to my sons over dinner," said the preschool director. "They think it's no big deal to see a woman nurse in public." All of the women called specifically to thank me for responding in public to a very private affront. As my friend Sue empathically stated, "I'm sorry this happened to *you*. But I'm glad it happened to someone who knew how to respond."

On the day I nursed Olivia in the gym, I didn't *feel* particularly able to respond. On hiatus from my writing, research, and teaching because of my new baby, my days were spent in the foggy haze of repetitive tasks central to child-rearing. Going to a gym that provided child-care was a way of providing myself a brief respite from the constant needs of an infant and a preschooler. Not engaged in a teaching community of women and girls (*except* that of my own daughters), I was out of the habit of feminist consciousness. When confronted, I responded directly from my own veneer of "nice and kind," politely silencing my initial instinct to say, "This is *not* my problem."[1] For a moment, I felt shame and embarrassment. Maybe I *had* been wrong to nurse in public. Maybe I *had not* been as discreet as I intended to be. As I loaded my children into the car, my body helped me remember a feeling beyond shame and embarrassment—that of anger. As I drove home, my adrenaline began to flow and my heart rate increased as I began to find a voice for the anger. When I got home I phoned a friend for encouragement, sat down at the computer while my children napped, and figured out "how to respond."

Remembering this incident jolts me back to an awareness of the permeable borders between public and private, body and mind.[2] The personal is political, and my mind is "wreathed in flesh and warm."[3] Although I may lapse into the habit of compartmentalizing, the categories of public vs. private and body vs. mind are not separate entities. Nor are politics and theology easily separable. Giving voice to my indignation was a political act birthed by a profoundly theological instinct. The voice in me that speaks for myself, for women, and for children grows directly out of my connection with a God I have come to know through Hebrew and Christian scriptures, interpreted through many layers of experience, tradition, and reason. It is partly by naming myself as created in the divine image that I am able to embrace the image of a breast-feeding woman as being nuanced with holiness.

The letter did not address theology, but it did address pedagogy: I made the claim that breast-feeding teaches. Choices about where and how women nurse their babies are *shaped by culture,* but they also hold the potential to *reshape culture* in ways that are more life-affirming than the status quo. Voicing our dangerous memories can unleash change. Dangerous are the memories of shame, embarrassment, and anger I felt that day in the gym. Also dangerous are the memories of hope and solidarity I felt when friends and strangers called to celebrate my act of resistance.

At the outset of this project, my goal was to fashion a theological response to the psychological literature calling attention to the complex web of difficulties facing adolescent girls. I hoped this response would equip young women with a usable past, a connection to their faith story, and an ability to voice the dangerous memories that can bring about change. In the previous chapters, I have attempted to show that the biblical faith tradition, when widened to include the voices of formally marginalized women, has much to offer in repairing a tragically skewed vision of what it means to be created in the image of God. In chapter 8, I will return to theological language, constructing a model of God and humanity that grows out of girlfriend theology.

In this chapter, I turn from explicitly theological language to the language of educational theory, specifically that of critical pedagogy. Critical pedagogy is a field of study that examines teaching practices, acknowledging that no education is politically neutral. Borrowing from Brazilian educator Paulo Freire, critical educators build the case that teaching practices can empower subjects to become agents in the process of social change. The teacher becomes a "transformative intellectual" who critically engages culture with the aim of creating more just public spheres.[4]

In the language and concepts of critical pedagogy, breast-feeding teaches. Even though I was not engaged in a teaching community with the young women and men working out in the gym or the retired men and women walking the track, I was potentially informing their politics of parenting.

If breast-feeding teaches, so does veganism. Veganism refers to abstaining from eating or using animal by-products. A popular trend among adolescent girls today, veganism makes a political statement out of the very personal act of eating.[5] Like many of the ways girls speak through their bodies, it is an act of resistance with side effects that are potentially harmful.[6] But it also shows a positive face. Comparable to my choices regarding breast-feeding, girls' choices about veganism can reshape culture. Parents who wish to keep a sacred quality in shared family meals find ways to accommodate vegan girls around the dinner table. Web pages devoted to Jewish vegan recipes testify to this. When two of our teenage neighbors, with whom my family and I regularly shared meals, became vegan, we learned to eat eggless chocolate cake and to carefully read the labels on bread and pasta packages. Conversations with vegan friends widen my vision. Although I have not adopted their practice, I have tuned into the debate and read with newfound attention accounts of the conditions in our nation's meat, dairy, and egg industries. As practiced by my teenage friends, veganism teaches: it contributes to the creation of a culture more mindful of the need for ethical treatment of animals.

As I immersed myself in the world of girls, I learned to pay attention to veganism, as well as many other significant ways girls speak through their bodies. As symbols, these markers sometimes speak more than words say.[7] As I neared the conclusion of my research, I realized that "the body" was not *one* theme that frequently surfaced in girlfriend theology; rather, for historical and cultural reasons, bodies and consciousness of them *pervade* female adolescent life today. As Sara Shandler writes in an anthology of girls' voices called *Ophelia Speaks,* "I do not have a cute nose, perfect skin, long legs, a flat stomach, or long eyelashes. My awareness of these facts makes my body a backdrop for my everyday life.... My stomach, back, skin, knees, hair are always in my peripheral vision. Never my sole focus (I'm too healthy for that!), but always just tickling at my consciousness."[8] Joan Brumberg's historical study of girls' bodies echoes this first-person account, "Girls today make the body into an all-consuming project in ways young women of the past did not."[9] Henry Giroux makes a similar point about bodies from the perspective of working- and lower-class youth. He writes that, especially in the absence of hope for economic security, "one forever feels the primacy of the body."[10]

I began to see the multiple ways girlfriend theology engaged bodies as a significant source of knowing, teaching, and learning. As I thought about the thirteen story sessions I hosted, a picture of a classroom emerged. It was a classroom in which vegan teens and breast-feeding adults discussed body piercing, eating disorders, alcohol, suicide, drugs, dating, crying, and kick-boxing. This body-talk was part of our God-talk.

It became important to me to listen to what girls are saying in, through, and about their bodies. How are they reacting to and resisting dominant culture's standards of beauty? How are their spirits being diminished by the implicit expectations regarding thinness, whiteness, and the other culturally approved edicts of attractiveness? When Asian American women remember their adolescent bodies, they sometimes recall deep longings to change the shape of their eyes to look more Western. "I yearned in front of the mirror, wishing for a face that would save me from ridicule and shame. A white face would make others respect me, I wanted them to respect me. I knew that whiteness was part of what was required to have power in the United States," writes Hyo-Jung Kim.[11] Lanika, a girl writing in an anthology of African American girls' voices, remembers the tyranny of taking ballet lessons in a space clearly designed for white girls:

> Even the tights for ballet are not meant for black people. The tights are pink . . . and blend in with white girls' skin. But when I put those pink tights on, you can see my brown skin coming through. . . . I told my ballet teacher that I wasn't even tryin' to wear pink tights because they are not made for me. . . . And then there's the hip issue. Ballerinas are also supposed to be real petite, you know, with real small waists that curve in real slightly and then curve back out only a little bit more. But your hips are not supposed to stick out, and mine do. Sometimes my teacher will tell me to put my hip down, and I have to tell her that that is where it is, and it's not going anywhere, never mind down![12]

How might voices like these — if taken seriously by those who design educational spaces, methods, and environments — contribute to changing the way we teach? Might we design educational environments that truly welcome girls as they are, in a great variety of body shapes, sizes, and colors? Few educational spaces explicitly encourage diverse bodies. Even fewer educational spaces encourage thinking about the connections between body-talk and God-talk. I return to the girlfriend theology classrooms in order to name the ways I saw this fostered. I call this an embodied pedagogy because so many of the characteristics of the classroom point to the explicit welcoming and affirming of bodies. I draw links between the embodied pedagogy of girlfriend theology and the postmodern critique of education that grows out of the field of critical pedagogy.

Bodies Matter: The Postmodern Critique

Bodies and minds are connected. All teaching is political. All knowing is historically and socially situated, tinged through and through with relationships of power and social dynamics. Taking into account these various voices of postmodernity, the fields of critical pedagogy and cultural studies have, during the past two decades, chipped away at the ideal of an unbiased education formed from classics of the Western canon.[13] Critical educators call for a restructuring of educational institutions and processes so that they cease to privilege those in the West, the male, and the economically advantaged. In contrast to education as the reinforcement of domination, they posit "education as the practice of freedom."[14]

Although the critique aims at creating public educational spaces and methods that will make fully participatory democracy possible, it also provides a guide for the restructuring of religious educational spaces and methods. If religious education is to contribute to equipping persons to participate in public discourse, we must integrate a critical postmodern notion of resistance into our theory and practice. The writings of Henry Giroux, Peter McLaren, Mary Belenky and her co-authors, and bell hooks provide guides for religious educators who seek to engage in "education as the practice of freedom." After briefly defining critical postmodernism, I will explore the ways in which these writings inform religious education generally and girlfriend theology particularly.

Critical Postmodernism and Critical Pedagogy

Various and sometimes contradictory discourses fall under the banner of postmodernism. In my use of the term, I refer to four critiques classified as postmodern: (1) a rejection of modernism's meta-narratives; (2) a debunking of the authority of positivistic science; (3) an attack on the belief in a unified goal of history; and (4) deconstruction of the Enlightenment ideal of an autonomous self acting independently of history.[15] The effect of such critiques is to turn attention to the local, the specific, and the partial, with the resulting awareness that knowledge is socially constructed.

Tom Beaudoin adds texture to this definition. From his perspective as a member of the first generation to come to maturity during postmodernism, Beaudoin describes some of the cultural events that mark the social and political memory of his generational peers. These include the shifting views of family life as a result of an unprecedented divorce rate; a pervasive fear of nuclear annihilation, epitomized by the 1983 television broadcast of *The Day After;* and the 1986 explosion of the space shuttle *Challenger,* watched by schoolchildren across the country because a teacher was on board. Events such as these, coming as they did after the Vietnam War and the Watergate scandal, contributed to the "cultural crisis" inherited by the postmodern generation, alternatively known as Generation X.[16]

In the midst of political upheaval and competing discourses of truth, some define postmodernism as an era in which the quest for meaning is futile. Taking my lead from Giroux and McLaren, I make a distinction between *ludic* postmodernism — which tends toward nihilistic reflections on the heterogeneity of realities in which meaning is inevitably unascertainable — and *critical* postmodernism, which does not give up on finding meaning. Critical postmodernism aims at the creation of nonhegemonic public spheres in which different perspectives encounter one another and participate in mutual meaning-making.[17]

Border Pedagogy

For Giroux and McLaren, postmodern ideas about contingency and the loss of certainty are not harbingers of the triumph of nihilism. Rather, they represent a state of possibility. Given this stance of openness, Giroux constructs a "border pedagogy" which offers new possibilities for engaging the memories, histories, and stories of those who have been dominated.[18] The borders refer to the physical and cultural realms of meaning that are historically and socially constructed and that both limit and enable particular identities and social forms. Critical educators equip students to become border-crossers who realize that learning involves shifting parameters of place, identity, history, and power.

Specific implications of border pedagogy include: (1) The belief that curriculum can best inspire learning when it builds upon the tacit knowledge students already possess; (2) the view of the student and teacher as co-learners in a process of discovery in which students become the subjects, rather than merely the objects, of history; and (3) the acknowledgment that certain views of history have been excluded from the dominant discourse, leading to the need for digging up countermemories. This "digging" attempts to recover communities of memory and their stories of struggle that can provide a sense of meaning and identity to subordinated groups.

Engaged Pedagogy

bell hooks's ideas about teaching find good company among Giroux's. Influenced by Freire and the Buddhist monk Thich Nhat Hanh, hooks seeks to reform education so that it holistically engages the mind, body, and spirit. She advocates classrooms where passion has a place, and where students learn to think differently about gender, race, and privilege. This is knowledge that informs action, allowing students to lead transformed lives. hooks acknowledges that this kind of teaching can be frightening. She tells of the fear she felt when a black student, during the course of a class exploring internalized racism, announced to everyone her decision to stop straightening her hair. "Nothing about the way I was trained as a teacher really prepared me to witness my students transforming themselves," hooks writes.[19] In transforming herself, the student became the teacher, challenging hooks to continue to integrate her theory and practice.

Specific implications of hooks's engaged pedagogy include: (1) the assumption that teachers will address the connection between students' overall life experience and the knowledge they are acquiring in the classroom; (2) the view of the classroom as a communal place in which teachers strive to create participatory spaces for sharing knowledge; (3) the belief in teaching as a sacred vocation involving the sharing of not only information, but also the intellectual and spiritual growth of students; (4) the belief that there is no such thing as politically neutral education; and (5) the belief that honoring and respecting the reality and experiences of persons who are nonwhite requires new pedagogical processes and styles of teaching.[20]

Connected Teaching

Giroux's vision of border pedagogy and hooks's vision of engaged pedagogy echo the concept of "connected teaching" expressed in the 1986 collaborative effort *Women's Ways of Knowing*. Focusing specifically on methods of teaching and learning that empower women's public voice and action, Mary Belenky and her co-authors would agree with Giroux and hooks that education is never politically neutral.

Other specific implications of connected teaching include: (1) the image of teacher as midwife, collaborating with students to bring new knowledge to birth;[21] (2) the freedom for teachers to claim their own vulnerability, at times finding the courage to think out loud with students, rather than creating the illusion that knowledge is the already complete, private possession of the teacher; and (3) The welcoming of diversity of opinion, which involves looking at the subject of inquiry through the students' multiple viewpoints.[22]

Pedagogical Innovations and Religious Education

These critical educators envision radically transformed classrooms. Their vision is not utopian, but rather it engages in the quest for meaning in the midst of life's real struggles over power, wealth, and authority. Reverberations of these critiques echo in the field of religious education.[23] For just as the hegemonic Enlightenment worldview of rational science and pure, objective ways of knowing held sway in public education, it also seeped into the core of religious faith and became ingrained, handed down from generation to generation.[24] Churches often portray theology as a body of knowledge and doctrines and creeds to be ingested, rather than a process of meaning-making in which humans engage with each other and with God. Churches often view scripture as a literal source of unchanging truths, instead of as a story of particular people in specific historical settings that embodies particular truths. Religious education has often adopted a "banking model," in which teachers act as if students are empty vessels to be filled with correct understanding.[25]

Many religious educators use the ideas of critical postmodernism to nudge the church into claiming its role as an agent of change in the world.[26] Just as Giroux's goal for public education is the creation of "transformative intellectuals" equipped to participate in pluralistic democracies, the goal of these religious educators is to equip persons of faith to be "public theologians" engaging in ethical discourse shaped by their religious commitments.[27] This is not the hegemonic discourse of the religious right, which seeks to impose its theological interpretations on issues such as abortion rights, gay marriage, and prayer in the public schools. Rather, it is discourse akin to liberation theology, in which grassroots organizations learn to see the political realm as a locus of God's activity in the world and seek to bring God's justice to situations of racial oppression, unfair distribution of the world's resources, and military dictatorships.

Critical postmodernism proves fertile ground for reimagining education. It provides the connections between border pedagogy, engaged pedagogy, and connected teaching, and gives birth to numerous other pedagogical innovations. Megan Boler's pedagogy of discomfort, for instance, stands in the same tradition. In this model, students of varying race and class backgrounds learn to name their own privilege, or lack thereof, collectively engage in cultural critique, and "come out as allies without severe injury to any party."[28]

Cutting across all of these pedagogical innovations is an awareness that bodies matter, for it is as bodies that we experience the specifics of history and culture, as I did when breast-feeding Olivia in the sports center. With that in mind, I return to the classroom created in girlfriend theology to illustrate the specific emphasis on bodies that emerged there.

Embodied Pedagogy: The Girlfriend Theology Classroom

In describing my research method in chapter 2, I set the stage for girlfriend theology to take place within a "haven of hospitality."[29] I referred to the process as open-ended and flexible. I stated that the aim of this process is not grand conclusions, but rather to have each participant leave with her own awareness or set of conclusions, some of which may be mutually agreed upon, and some of which may be individually held.[30] I referred briefly to the disciplines of keeping confidentiality and honoring the silence.

As the research progressed, these initial guidelines evolved and new ones emerged. Often the girls suggested changes, informally structuring the space where transformative learning about God, self, and others could take place. Many times, I recognized these changes only in retrospect, naming and incorporating them into later instructions to a different group of girls. As I thought about these guidelines, I often heard echoes of women's writings within them. I have used footnotes to point to those writings when they provide further illumination. The guidelines for embodied pedagogy that emerged are:

1. Bodies, whenever possible, should be comfortable. We seek rooms with couches, armchairs, and carpet. Water bottles, Starbucks cups, and Coke cans sprinkle the scene. We welcome bathroom breaks, crossed legs, and bare feet.[31]

2. We pay attention to our physical surroundings as having potential effects on our moods and the content of our thoughts. For example, we might move outside on a warm day when the sun is shining. What we see and feel there might influence what we think and say.

3. If we meet over meals, we honor individuals' dietary choices without singling out persons as requiring special measures.

4. Different bodies have different stories to tell. We treasure differences of skin color, hair texture, and dialect and the different histories those features imply. No one should ever feel that her differences are merely tolerated or lumped into an undifferentiated category of "other."

5. Emotions are explicitly welcomed. One part of the story session deals specifically with the articulation of emotions, but emotions also emerge unbidden at other moments. We pay attention to the emotions released through our bodies in the form of tears, adrenaline surges, increased heart rates, the impulse to reach out to touch someone, or the feeling of being "sick to my stomach."

All of these are clues to emotional terrain that may be either too difficult or impossible to articulate.

6. Disagreement and conflicting interpretations are welcome. Although a common understanding often emerges, we try not to ignore differences of opinion in favor of a facile consensus. When disagreement occurs, we notice raised voices or defensive body language. We remain present with both sides of the exchange, modeling the ability to disagree without harming one another.[32]

7. We acknowledge the fluidity of our emotional/cognitive selves. Although we are often able to structure our participation, talking about feelings at one point and saving ideas for another, we recognize the connectedness of our emotional and intellectual ways of knowing. We remind ourselves that "the method is flexible" and always choose to compromise the method, rather than silence a person.

8. We honor the occasional need to maintain confidentiality. But, because action is a desired outcome, we do not offer blanket confidentiality. Often, the action that emerges is a new behavior resulting from a new way of thinking about God, self, and others. These new ways of thinking may warrant sharing them with our circle of friends or our faith community. Blanket confidentiality would confine the learning to the story session. Requested confidentiality protects participants from leakage of sensitive information while affirming the ongoing process of communal meaning-making outside of the story session.

9. Silence is holy. When chosen, silence is a way of honoring one another's deep sharing. Being silenced degrades us. We do not hush, gloss over, or ignore one another.[33]

10. Interruptions, usually considered rude in group settings, happen all the time. They are the hallmark of a community making meaning together. In the flow of thinking, we usually do not stop to say, "excuse me." However, we encourage participants who contribute frequently to step back when those more hesitant to speak take the floor.

11. Often, a participant claims her authority and begins to speak boldly, even prophetically, seemingly unaware of those around her. We honor that moment as one in which she has been "heard to speech." We entertain the possibility that God may be choosing to be present among us in the form of her prophetic utterance.[34]

12. As adults and adolescents, we journey together. For adults, girl-friend theology can provide a privileged glimpse into adolescent lives and as experienced travelers, adult women have much to offer. Along with that experience and age comes a power dif-ferential. Adults practice the discipline of not saying too much, especially avoiding the instinct to judge or provide remedies for perceived adolescent problems.

These twelve guidelines form part of the introduction I provide before beginning girlfriend theology with a new group. By sharing these guidelines, I affirm at the outset that bodies will be treated with honor and respect. In keeping with the pedagogical innovations cited earlier in this chapter, embodied pedagogy acknowledges po-litical commitments. The primary political commitment of girlfriend theology is to the feminist principle that bodies and minds are in-tegrated, not split. This underlies the accompanying conviction that theology is not a disembodied process, but rather a way of knowing that can and should engage the body, mind, and spirit. This con-tributes to an understanding of honoring bodies as a shared practice of the Christian faith.[35]

In such a classroom as this, body-talk can inform God-talk, and vice versa. The clearest example of this was in chapter 3: Emma, somewhat surprised, realized she was wearing Rachel's shoes, just as we finished talking about Rachel's suicide. Wearing the shoes of a deceased friend came to be seen as a way of honoring the dead and keeping her memory alive. Emma's shoes and the instinct to wear them helped to make sense of the church's age-old tradition of pre-serving relics, such as the remains of a saint's fingertip. The image of the saint's fingertip, in turn, helped us understand the sacred qual-ity of the shoes on Emma's feet. We named connections between our bodies and ancient traditions, reinvesting each with new meaning.

Another example of body-talk informing God-talk occurred in chapter 5, when Katie talked about the ex-gang-member father bending over his daughter in the midst of smoke and flames. As Katie vividly imagined the posture of the father and the daughter, she named his tears as the source of her survival. In his crying, the father revealed an aspect of God for us. We named connections between an ancient image and a contemporary body, replacing machismo with the ability to cry and reinvesting each image with new significance.

Why Girls and Women Need Embodied Pedagogy

In describing embodied pedagogy, I have envisioned a classroom where learning takes place on many levels. In such classrooms, the content of women's emancipatory theologies, women's usable past, and the Christian faith travel through processes that engage bodies, minds, and spirits. Thus, the teaching becomes a form of praxis, an activity seeking emancipation and transformation.[36] Creating such learning contexts is critically important at this juncture of history and culture, because many educational experiences — both formal and informal — operate to damage the integrity of body, mind, and soul.

When my friend, whom I will call Lisa, was a teenager, her parents took her to a psychiatrist because she exhibited "lesbian tendencies." The doctor said she was going through a stage that would pass. Lisa tried to abide by this "diagnosis." But her body would not let her. Whenever Lisa was in the presence of a certain girl to whom she was attracted, she had to leave the room to vomit. Lisa experienced confusion of body, mind, and spirit during adolescence and well into her early adult years. A deeply religious person, she tried her best to adopt the behavior her church, parents, psychiatrist, and culture deemed appropriate. Her body stores many memories of those years of repression.[37]

Many female bodies store memories of old wounds.[38] They bear testimony to the fact that cultural norms, which can become embedded in family systems, often have pernicious effects on female bodies across the spectrum of race, class, and ethnicity. Some girls become dangerously thin; some become dangerously overweight. Some turn to drugs and alcohol for escape; some turn to sex for affirmation. Some girls cut themselves in order to feel something, and some girls become pregnant as an act of resistance. Their bodies are their voices, and they are shouting loudly. I will examine two of these forms of voice: diet and self-mutilation.

Theorists believe one factor causing the life-threatening disorders of anorexia nervosa and bulimia is white culture's standard of thinness as epitomizing beauty. Carol Lakey Hess points to eating disorders as resistance to the demand to enter the "cult of femininity" and calls anorexia "the underground prophet in our midst." Recalling three incidents of anorexia in her own adolescence and young adulthood, she writes, "I now believe I was making a political statement, but it was not a conscious one. At the time, I felt shame more than agency."[39] Becky Wangsgaard Thompson bolsters the opinion that girls' bodies suffer cultural wounds. In her study of black, Latina, and white girls with eating disorders, she discovered a wide range of traumas out of which problem eating behaviors grew. The list included racism, sexual abuse, poverty, sexism, emotional abuse, heterosexism, class injuries, and acculturation.[40]

Eating disorders that promote extreme thinness affect mostly affluent populations. As dangerous as these disorders are, they pale statistically in comparison to diets that result in dangerous obesity.[41] Clinicians note a significant increase in the rate of life-threatening obesity among poor female adolescents. Lack of nutritional education, combined with the intense marketing of fast-food restaurants in poor communities, results in the high consumption of empty calories among the poor. Limited resources for girls' recreational exercise, especially in urban areas, and the use of food to pacify anger and frustration contribute to this rise in obesity among poor girls.[42] The long-term health risks of obesity, including hypertension and diabetes, are complicated by a lack of adequate public health care.

In addition to diet, girls are using knives and razors to voice their pain. Self-mutilation, defined as slashing, cutting, or burning without conscious suicidal intent, is an increasingly prevalent teenage phenomenon that has gained attention only recently.[43] Jennifer Egan, in an investigative report for the *New York Times Magazine,* followed one adolescent girl during several months of treatment for self-injury. Egan describes the life of sixteen-year-old Jill McArdle (a pseudonym) as full of self-scrutiny. When she was fourteen, a boy spread rumors about her sexual behavior. Depressed and worried, Jill cut herself with a wallpaper knife to relieve her anxiety. She found that by cutting herself she could temporarily ease her emotional distress. Soon, cutting became a habit.[44] Researchers who study self-mutilation conclude that it begins as a coping mechanism. As Egan writes: "People harm themselves because it makes them feel better; they use physical pain to obfuscate a deeper, more intolerable psychic pain associated with feelings of anger, sadness, or abandonment.... It can also jolt people out of states of numbness and emptiness — it can make them feel alive."[45] The behavior, similar to eating disorders and substance abuse, becomes a compulsion, tending to eclipse all other thoughts and actions.

Dusty Miller provides a provocative image of the scope of women's self-inflicted wounds:

> Imagine a long, black marble wall, inscribed with names, reaching far into the distance. Imagine a quilt, covered with names and images of loved ones who have died, stretching over acres of land. But instead of war casualties and AIDS victims, the names on this wall and this quilt are those of women who died by their own hand. They died from alcoholism, drug addiction, anorexia, bulimia, excessive dieting, self-inflicted burns and slashing, and a hundred other ways of harming one's own body.[46]

Miller, a therapist who specializes in the treatment of women who hurt themselves, theorizes that, in most cases, women's self-inflicted wounds stem from incidents of childhood abuse, particularly sexual abuse. This behavior, which is predominately a female problem and usually begins in adolescence, came to awareness at the same time as a rise in tattooing, piercing, scarification, and branding among adolescents. "While experts disagree on the relationship between the behaviors, the increasing popularity of body modification among teen-agers, coupled with the two million people injuring in secret, begins to make us look like a nation obsessed with cutting," Egan concludes.[47]

During adolescence, girls begin using their bodies to respond and to resist, as these two examples of diet and self-mutilation show. These examples of physical harm point to the untold internal pain girls undergo in their journey to adulthood. Contemporary American girls inherit and embody many diverse cultures, ethnicities, and economic realities; common to them all are the multiple conflicting messages about the value of girls' and women's body/selves.[48] Sometimes girls find healthy paths of resistance and manage to grow into womanhood spiritually, physically, and emotionally intact. But sometimes girls find only damaging ways to resist, and these behaviors often continue into adulthood. Thus, it is the female body that provides the most direct link between girls and women.

Gilligan's hope to see girls and women dancing at the crossroads of female development stems from a feminist vision that "one day, the underground knowledge women have stored inside themselves since girlhood will cease to be merely psychologically corrosive and become, instead, a public resistance that will remake the world."[49] As Behar notes, such a vision is utopian. But linked to transformative social action, utopian visions can become seeds of change. Any remaking of the world will require multiple paths of resistance. One such path involves the creation of alternative spaces in which to heal the bodies, minds, and spirits of girls and women. An embodied pedagogy provides clues toward the creation of such spaces.

Chapter Eight

God-Talk at the Crossroads of Souls

Some women will just "happen" to Race through these fields and pick up Messages of an Other and better world.... Such ... women will hear ripples of merriment, echoes of distant yet familiar raindrops, sunbeams. We will experience "coincidences," syn-Crone-icities, meetings at crossroads of species, of souls. We'll Race and Race and leap with deer and hop with rabbits. With ladybugs we'll climb tall stalks of grass. With barnacles we'll hug the rocks of seashores. With snakes we'll glide through gardens. Like butterflies we'll skit from flower to flower. Our Hour will come. It has already.

—Mary Daly, *Pure Lust: Elemental Feminist Philosophy*

As I neared the end of writing the dissertation from which this book is derived, I learned that my maternal grandmother was dying. Years of chain-smoking brought emphysema to her body, already brittle and shrinking from osteoporosis. In November, Grandma Jean became too frail to live by herself. She moved in with my parents. In February, after taking a fall that made it impossible for her to walk, she moved to a nursing home. During her brief stay there, she spent her time in ways we would expect: she learned the names of all the aides and housekeepers so that she could greet them when they entered her room, and she continued her practice of striking yoga poses when restless leg syndrome kept her awake at night. On a Saturday afternoon, my sister and brother-in-law brought her boiled shrimp with spicy cocktail sauce and fresh strawberry shortcake for dessert. She savored the food and relished the company. On Sunday, she contracted pneumonia.

I flew to Florida to be with her. When I arrived, I found her no longer able to eat or drink. It was clear that she was relinquishing control, joining the process of her body's letting go. We had expected this as well. My grandmother had obtained, signed, and forced us all to read a living will when they were introduced in the 1970s. Knowing my grandmother's feelings, my mother made sure to sign a "Do Not Resuscitate" order so Grandma Jean's life would not be painfully and needlessly prolonged. The only thing to do now was accompany her across the border between life and death. At one point during the evening, I crawled into bed beside my grandmother. Nestled there, I recited the names of our beloved ancestors who waited to welcome her. I drifted off to sleep and awoke later to the sound of her labored breathing. She died quietly a few hours later, my mother at her side.

After celebrating my grandmother's life and beginning to mourn her death, I returned to the routine of my home life. A few days later, I halted my morning jog in the parking lot of the preschool to hear the story of another graceful and grace-filled death. A friend of mine, Edie, had recently cared for her mother-in-law, Phyllis, during the months preceding her death from breast cancer. Phyllis had come to live with Edie, her husband, and their three-year-old daughter Mackenzie when she became ill. During that time Edie received the gift of learning about Phyllis's rich spiritual life, which included early morning Bible reading and time away in her prayer closet. She kept a book in which she collected names, photographs, and notes about people she had met years ago and for whom she continued to pray. If it had not been for those days of dwelling in the same home together, Edie would never have learned of these disciplined habits which bore fruit in Phyllis's warm and loving spirit.

When Phyllis's death became imminent, the family decided she would remain at home instead of seeking further medical treatment. One day Mackenzie and Edie heard Phyllis make an unusual sound and saw a strange look on her face. They ran to her side and found her unresponsive. They called her name and began to cry. Thinking she had died, they stepped away for a moment. Mackenzie remembered a dream from a few months before, of angels in shimmery white gowns coming down to earth to take her family to be with Jesus. Edie used that imagery to explain to Mackenzie what was happening to Phyllis. "Maybe the angels have come, and MeeMaw is going to heaven," Edie told her daughter. They went back to Phyllis's side to say good-bye. Mackenzie took Phyllis's hands and said, "I love you MeeMaw." Phyllis, who had not died but had been experiencing a stroke, squeezed Mackenzie's hand and roused in response to her voice. She was treated for stroke and died a few days later.

It takes courage to stay present in life's frightening moments. Daughters and granddaughters accompany their mothers and grandmothers at the border between life and death, just as friends, husbands, lovers, mothers, and midwives accompany newborns on the journey into life. Reaching out across generations to accompany one another through life's transitions is not easy. It is an uncharted path that is sometimes painful. Nevertheless, it is richly rewarding. Mackenzie, Edie, and I testify to that reality.

Between birth and death, we navigate multiple uncharted transitions. One of the most treacherous is adolescence. Girls at this transition need companions, midwives who are willing to deal with the messiness of life and to celebrate the clear, shining moments as they come. Throughout this project, I have attempted to outline a path developing such relationships within the context of faith communities. In this final chapter, I will describe the relationships women and girls formed in girlfriend theology. Out of such relationships grew a particular vision of God, which I will describe as a meeting at the crossroads *of souls*. I will argue that the church possesses a strong, albeit hidden, tradition of creating such crossroad spaces in the lives of women. These women's spaces *within the church* have been crucial for the development of feminist consciousness *outside the church*. In this way they have transformed society.[1] I conclude with this question: how might the contemporary church, through female clusters such as those envisioned in girlfriend theology, play a role in this ongoing tradition, transforming society in such a way that both women and men more fully reflect the image of God?

A Resounding Cry for Mentors

In much of the literature regarding contemporary American adolescence, especially female adolescence, one conclusion is pervasive: adolescents need adults who are willing to enter into relationships with them. This resounding cry for mentors echoes across academic disciplines.

Two recent sociological studies of male and female adolescence point to the importance of adult role models. In looking at resilient youth, those young people who are "invulnerable, successful-despite-the-odds," Joy G. Dryfoos cites the importance of youth having an attachment to a caring adult. She writes, "The best documented fact in the extensive U.S. literature on youth is the importance of social bonding between a young person and an adult." She points to the development of "safe havens" within communities as providing "safe passage" in a landscape otherwise devoid of traditional rites of passage from childhood to adulthood.[2]

Patricia Hersch titled her ethnographic study of high school students *A Tribe Apart,* referring to the sheer amount of time contemporary adolescents spend outside the presence of adults. "The teen-ager has been classified as a remote being," wrote one of her adolescent collaborators. "There is an unspeakable distance between youth and the grown-up world."[3] Hersch concludes her study with this plea:

> What kids need most from adults is not just rides, pizza, chaperones, and discipline. They need the telling of stories, the close ongoing contact so that they can learn and be accepted. If nobody is there to talk to, it is difficult to get the lessons of your own life so that you are adequately prepared to do the next thing. Without a link across generations, kids will only hear from their peers.[4]

Joan Jacobs Brumberg's research on the adolescent female body reaches a similar conclusion, but from a historical perspective. Today, girls' bodies are maturing sexually at a younger age. This is happening at a time when cultural mores regarding sexual behavior are in flux. The result of this convergence, Brumberg writes, is that girls need help making "sense of their own emotions, as well as the social pressures that are part of the postvirginal world." Calling for women to enter relationships with girls, she writes:

> I think that most girls desire and profit from connection with their mothers, their aunts, their women teachers, and even their friends, and that individual autonomy has been oversold as a model for female development and for social life in general.... As we prepare girls for the 21st century, we need to initiate a larger multigenerational dialogue that speaks to the reality of earlier maturation.[5]

Writing at the overlap of adolescent development and feminist theology, Joyce Mercer agrees. In looking for ways to promote "wholeness and thriving" among adolescent girls, Mercer lifts up five categories of social practice that seem to benefit girls in educational, religious, and clinical settings. One such category is "practices of education and care that invite sustained, in-depth conversation between a girl and an adult mentor, or a group of girls and one or more adults." She writes that these relationships support the vitality and well-being of adolescent girls.

> Girls communicated how infrequently they find opportunities to talk about their thoughts, feelings, ideas, and concerns in a substantive way with adults. They expressed a hunger for in-depth conversation about ethical issues, theology, family relationships, romance, friendship, the future, and much more. Girls affirmed the value of simply being listened to for an extended period of time.[6]

This echoes the thought of Carol Lee Flinders who writes, "One of the subtler aspects of the debate over 'voice' and 'silence' is that there is an immense difference between having permission to speak and enjoying the hope that *someone might actually listen to you.*"[7]

Mentoring relationships are reciprocal. Throughout her work, Hersch comments on the mutuality of the friendships she formed with adolescents. Glimpsing their worlds changed her world in positive, life-affirming ways. Gilligan and Brown also note this phenomenon, taking it from the personal to the political realm; not only do adult-adolescent relationships have the power to help girls, they have the power to transform society:

> When women and girls meet at the crossroads of adolescence, the intergenerational seam of a patriarchal culture opens. If women and girls together resist giving up relationship for the sake of "relationships," then this meeting holds the potential for societal and cultural change.[8]

The tradition of "other-mothers" in the lives of African American females exemplifies this dynamic in a mentoring relationship. Other-mothers, whose origins can be traced to West African cultures, are those women in the community who share child-rearing responsibilities with blood mothers.[9] Through other-mothering, the lives of women and girls intersect to transcend private realms and to have public impact. Beverly Jean Smith describes the effect of a community of other-mothers who looked after her, her sisters, and female cousins while growing up. Smith writes, "Surrounded by a large group of women: family, friends, and neighbors, I have always felt connected while acting alone ... I entered the world with a voice, and all of these women have helped me sing."[10]

A woman's sustained involvement with a girl other than her own daughter is unusual today, unless the relationship is the result of a professional role as teacher, professor, nurse, doctor, nutritionist, psychologist, social worker, or pastor.[11] These professionals sometimes step beyond their job descriptions, throwing the lifelines girls use to pull themselves through difficult times. These women are the Mrs. Bertha Flowers, the DeLois, and the "linen-suited business woman in her fifties" of girls' *natural* educations as discussed in chapter 4. But girls need intentional, explicit education that leads toward wholeness. The cry for mentors resounds, and girlfriend theology provides one way of answering the call.

From Solo to Community:
Mentoring Circles

Sondra Higgins Matthaei modifies the term "mentor" to characterize a specific relationship within the faith community. She defines a "faith mentor" as a "co-creator with God who, as a living representative of God's grace, participates in the relational, vocational, and spiritual growth of others."[12] I widen Matthaei's definition to the image of a faith-mentoring circle and add the element of feminist consciousness to describe the relationships that girlfriend theology seeks to create.

Throughout the literature on mentoring, one-on-one relationships are usually in focus. Yet several barriers make such relationships risky to both adults and adolescents. First, women often feel intimidated by the prospect of getting to know adolescent girls, who often present attitudes of insouciance. Second, often burdened with responsibilities of professional and family life, women fear creating close relationships that hold the potential for long-term responsibility. Third, without some common bond through which to initiate the mentoring relationship, women wonder, "What are we going to talk about?" and girls wonder, "What about me does she want to fix?" Lastly, no matter what safeguards are in place, one-on-one relationships run the risk of leading to the abuse of power. Sadly, many women report being emotionally and sexually abused by their pastors, counselors, and therapists. This potential exists whether the adult is male or female. The threat of such abuse and the fear of false accusations of abuse both contribute to an air of risk surrounding one-on-one mentoring relationships. With these risks under consideration, the image of a "mentoring circle" creates a path through some of these barriers.

In the research I conducted for this book, I created mentoring circles: groups composed of two adult women and between two and four adolescent girls. For the purposes of my research, the groups were necessarily short in duration. Although significant mentoring occurred in these short periods of time, ideally I envision girlfriend theology happening at a slower pace that allows for long-term relationships to develop and grow. In such mentoring circles, one woman alone is not fully responsible. Adults share responsibility with each other and with the girls for the relationships that form and the content of the sessions. Mentoring circles are mutual and reciprocal, acknowledging that women need the companionship and insight of girls as much as girls need the companionship and insight of women. The life story that each participant brings determines the content of the conversations. As girls and women take turns bringing the story, they take turns setting the agenda. In mentoring circles, adults are not trying to fix adolescent problems. Instead, they are willing to open the texts of their lives as potential resources to adolescents.

When the element of feminist consciousness is added to such mentoring circles, the vision of girlfriend theology is complete. Gerda Lerner defines "feminist consciousness" as:

> (1) the awareness of women that they belong to a subordinate group and that, as members of such a group, they have suffered wrongs; (2) the recognition that their condition of subordination is not natural, but societally determined; (3) the development of a sense of sisterhood; (4) the autonomous definition by women of their goals and strategies for changing their conditions; and (5) the development of an alternative vision of the future.[13]

As adult women and adolescent girls bring and find commitment to feminist ideals within mentoring circles, they join in an ancient chorus of voices that has worked throughout history *within the church* to create the very elements of feminist consciousness Lerner describes.

Female Clusters:
Reviving an Ancient Tradition

Lerner uses the phrase "female clusters, female networks, and social spaces" to refer to the pockets of history where women's intellectual activity flourished, despite patriarchy. In the absence of such groups, "individual women had to think their way out of patriarchal gender definitions and their constraining impact as though each of them were a lonely Robinson Crusoe on a desert island, reinventing civilization."[14] Biographies that focus on such exemplary female lives "explain only themselves." They serve the political purpose of affirming notions of the heroic, but they do not challenge official histories.[15] However, when the female subject is located in her political and social context, alternative histories sometimes emerge.

Lerner provides this kind of structural analyses of the societies in which women's thought gained momentum. She examines clusters of learned women, trying to determine what supported their existence. Throughout history, groups of religious women often provided the "cultural prodding" necessary for women to advance intellectually and educationally. For women to think, to write, and to enter the marketplace of ideas, female audience was required. In Lerner's analysis, women mystics and cloistered nuns were the first to achieve such audiences. She traces the first documentation of an individual woman's life to the seventh-century writing of *The Life of St. Radegund,* by the nun Baudovinia.[16] Lerner points to this writing as the beginning of a long tradition of "sister books" in which younger nuns paid homage to their predecessors through written biographies. Although the primary impetus for these writings may have been the spreading of religious views or providing heroic images for sister nuns to emulate, they function significantly as the earliest written record of women's history. It is no accident that female clusters supporting women of note were often religious: during many different historical moments, the argument for women's equality often rested on theological and biblical grounds.[17]

In addition to being in the church, such female networks also emerged within courts and families of nobility, where women of wealth had access to education. Lerner writes of one such group of matriarchs, "we see in this clustering an inter-generational laying-on of hands by which the transmittal of knowledge to women becomes a family tradition."[18] Female clusters, female networks, and social spaces are the shoulders on which future generations of women *could have* stood, had they been aware of their inheritance.

However, as Lerner points out, most of their writings were lost without a trace to the women who followed.

> For over a thousand years, women reinterpreted the biblical texts in a massive feminist critique, yet their marginalization in the formation of religious and philosophical thought

prevented this critique from ever engaging the minds of men who had appointed themselves as the definers of divine truth and revelation.[19]

She concludes that individual efforts could not lead to collective advancement, because "women did not know that other women before them had already engaged in this enterprise of re-thinking and re-vision."[20]

Similarly, Rosemary Radford Ruether notes that alternative visions of community structured around egalitarian practices existed within early Christian traditions. These were never completely submerged within orthodoxy, but neither were they made fully visible. She summarizes the situation, which borders on being tragic:

> Nevertheless, fragments of the alternative vision were continually rediscovered in Christian history by women mystics, female religious communities, and popular Christian movements, some of which came to be defined as "heretical." A host of such popular movements in the late Middle Ages constantly *came close to rediscovering* a countercultural egalitarian Christianity opposed to the patriarchal and hierarchical church.[21]

Evidence of women thinking, writing, and publishing throughout history — work done against formidable odds in order to claim their worth and autonomy — is available to us now as a result of the modern women's movement. A primary goal of that movement has been to retrieve and interpret these hidden strains of women's thought and activity — to make of it a usable past. Armed with that usable past, women of today have what women of past generations lacked: the ability to move from private realms to transform public spheres.

Female clusters on the fringes of the church became centers for the flourishing of women's intellectual and theological capacities. From that fringe, they contributed significantly to the slow but inevitable building of voices that could finally be heard at the centers of power and authority. We also know that women in those female clusters were not all adults. Girls entered convents, cloisters, and monasteries at young ages. Although they may be difficult to hear, girls' voices entered that chorus as well. I imagine such female clusters revived in contemporary communities of faith, where, finally standing on the shoulders of giants, women and girls might hear their voices carry farther than they ever have before.

God-Talk at the Crossroads *of Souls*

In the four story sessions of girlfriend theology, girls and women talked about their lives, their feelings, their faith, and their ongoing action, meeting at the crossroads *of souls*. In doing so, they painted a picture of God using their worlds, bodies, and images. What emerged, however, is not so much a finished product as it is an ongoing process — not the blossom but the blooming.[22]

In the first story, we accompanied Emma on her journey of grief. We remembered the innocent bliss of playground friendships and experienced horror that such a friendship could end with a suicide. We found hope in the image of "church" as a group of friends gathering spontaneously to acknowledge their loss and offer mutual support, in spite of the failure of the designated church to do so. We gasped with Emma when she realized she was wearing the shoes of her deceased friend. When she named the sacred significance of the shoes on her feet, we all stood with Emma on holy ground for one still moment of recognition.

In the second story, Cathy took us with her to a remote swimming hole where she and her friend caught a glimpse of what heaven might be like. As we entered Cathy's world, we imagined ourselves floating on that red raft, staring into the clouds and locking eyes with the Holy One. At the same time, we felt the threat of Bigfoot lurking in the woods and the pervasive knowledge that, as women, we cannot float "freely, boldly, and adventurously" wherever we wish.[23] In a brief moment of forgetting that pernicious reality, we glimpsed "a foretaste of glory divine." Our bodies were the source of that glimpse, revealing to us that our lives are like fifth gospels, sites where God continues to reveal God's self to us.

In the third story, our eyes burned from the smoke of a lingering fire that killed Hannah's relatives. We stood with Hannah as three caskets were lowered into the ground and one young girl faced a lonely recovery. We saw God in the image of the girl's father, a young

Hispanic man who had tried to escape from a gang, but found there was no way out. In the midst of the fire he rescued his daughter by shielding her with his body. We honored the moment when Katie stepped forward, remembered the members of her family who had died from gang violence, and prophetically brought this image to speech.

In the final story, we revisited times when we hated our bodies and worried about our weight. We felt compulsion for perfection as a driving force, causing us to forget our capacity to question standards of achievement or beauty. Then, with Sarah, one day, we saw. We saw the scars on another human body, and we felt compassion — the kind of compassion that enables the transcending of social boundaries into a space where solidarity can happen. We celebrated Sarah's sacramental moment, the moment in which God's presence was made real through another person's wound. We smiled when Sarah shared her fascination that God was not the distant father but more like her, a compassionate one who feels pain. And when it was all over, none of us were quite ready to leave the comforting presence of a newfound female cluster.

The seven theological assertions I made at the beginning of this project changed as I proceeded. I struggled to let them reflect the specific notions about God to which the girls testified. As I carefully listened to what the girls and women said, I revised the assertions. Many of them are embedded in the brief summaries above, but the list bears repeating:

1. God is mysteriously omnipresent, but not magically omnipotent. Although we cannot explain it, God *is* at work within human tragedies to create healing potential. God may not fix things, but neither does God abandon us (story #3 and story #4).

2. God feels our pain and cries with us (story #3 and story #4).

3. We have direct access to God through our bodies (story #1 and story #2).

4. Our lives are like "fifth gospels." Our life stories are sacred texts where God continues to reveal God's self (story #1 and story #2).

5. We go to church to "*share* God, but not find God." Religious institutions can affirm our hunches about God but do not usually introduce us to God for the first time (story #1 and story #2).

6. God is most fully alive (incarnated) in us when our eyes are open to the pain of others (story #4).

7. Church, at its best, is a community of compassion, a resource in our healing, and a potential agent of change in the world (story #1 and story #4).

This list provides only the briefest sketch of a richly textured portrait of the God who emerged at the crossroads *of souls* where girls and women met. In many ways, this God is different from the God most of the girls inherited from their faith traditions. My collaborators had made many of those changes before they agreed to take part in girlfriend theology. The work of transforming traditions was not altogether new to them, but the girls seemed to breathe a collective sigh of relief at being able to speak out loud these potentially "unorthodox" images of God and have them be embraced, affirmed, and urged onward. The women, likewise, enjoyed moments when one of their hard-won theological transformations was greeted with a resounding "aha."

The God at the crossroads *of souls* is not the fortress, the rock, the king, or the writer of an unalterable plan for human history. This God moves and breathes within us and beyond us. This God reflects our passions and inspires new action in the world. When God takes on new shapes and forms, we change as well. Human bodies — *all* human bodies — take on new significance. They are not trivial or base but are avenues to the holy, means by which a living, moving, breathing God continues to express God's self in an ever-evolving creation. The image of the church alters as well. It, too, becomes alive and flexible, moving to adapt to evolving patterns of human behavior. It is not a place to go only for answers but a gathering of companions who bring their questions, their needs, and their passions for transforming the world.

This picture of God and God's relationship to humans is woefully incomplete. Numerous categories of theology do not surface here. Given time, I could have enlarged this initial picture with additional glimpses that emerged in the other nine story sessions — talk of vocation and calling, creation and ecology, and global networks of solidarity. The rest of the list — as long as infinity itself — is left to be written. What other characteristics of the God-human relationship might emerge if women and girls continue to meet — not only at the crossroads of female development, where the border separating "us" from "them" becomes very thin — but also at the crossroads *of souls?* At this crossroads, the border between "self" and "other" becomes less marked.[24] In this space, "her life crosses mine, and there is no name for it."[25] This space is best described with a story.

In My Grandmother's Garden[26]

On the afternoon of the day my grandmother died, the trees in my father's orange grove burst into fragrant bloom, the surest sign of a Florida spring. That night, I fell asleep in the bed of my adolescence. Strawberry season was in full swing, and my Hispanic neighbors celebrated in the light of an almost-full moon. I could hear their lively, thumping guitar music on the other side of the barbed wire fence.

A day later, I performed my grandmother's memorial service, just as she and I had planned. We were a small circle of family and friends gathered by the lake in her backyard, where for years she had rescued stray cats and fed hot dogs to a wild blue heron. As we told each other about her life, a hawk watched from a nearby tree, then took flight. A butterfly drifted lightly above. My eldest daughter handed out tissues when she noticed tears, and my youngest daughter tested unfamiliar laps. I fingered a piece of sea glass, and read aloud these words, which I had found scribbled in the margins of my grandmother's journal dated 1964, a year after I was born: "God is so large he requires all life to express himself." My soul whispered an amen: God *is* that large. He is and She is.

There, in my grandmother's garden, I gave thanks for my inheritance: for the women in my life who had helped me find voice; for those friends and teachers who taught me to cross borders in search of good soil; for the midwives who had helped me birth babies and ideas; for the ancient ones, Amazon women upon whose shoulders I stand when I don my priestly robe to witness to the Holy One in our midst; and for the chorus of women's voices that have "brought us this far on the way."[27]

I also gave thanks for the girls with whom I had recently journeyed. They gave me new eyes to see "church" as a quiet circle gathered in the midst of grief. They gave me a renewed image of God as father to stand beside my hard-won image of God as mother. They gave me a sacramental way of viewing another person's pain. And they gave me a resounding reminder that God *still* waits for human bodies through which to express God's self, writing fifth gospels again and again.

They have more to give. Girls' visions of God will transform the world. Their day will come. It has already.

Appendix

Guidelines for
Facilitating Girlfriend Theology,
and Frequently Asked Questions

In the pages that follow, I share step-by-step guidelines for facilitating girlfriend theology and answer some frequently asked questions. I will walk through two handouts that introduce the method.

For the purposes of these guidelines, two categories of context apply. The first context is an all-female group that closely adheres to the overarching purposes of feminist education of girls. The second context is one in which the feminist agenda takes a back seat to a human agenda, adapting the method to include men and boys in the act of communal meaning-making. The first context I call "girlfriend theology"; the second I call "story theology." The handouts are adaptable to the varying contexts and may be photocopied.

Before explaining the handouts, I answer a few frequently asked questions.

1. **Can I start a girlfriend theology group of my own? What kind of special training does it require?**

The facilitator must be someone who feels extremely at ease leading theological discussion and who has a nonjudgmental approach to conversations about God. Naturally, levels of comfort in leading small groups vary, as does ease in tackling theological issues. The best facilitator will be someone who is very comfortable in the pastoral role, is not afraid to interject her thoughts gently but authoritatively, and is careful to censor herself or other adults from monopolizing the conversation if youth are present. Usually, this means someone who has had some seminary training or has a breadth of experience in a related field, such as counseling or teaching. It is important to have a Bible and a concordance on hand. Sometimes a participant will think of a story from scripture, but they might not remember the details. If the details are important to making the theological connections, the facilitator may pause to consult the texts.

When facilitating a group, I take notes on the conversation. If people stray too far from the four-step method, I gently point it out and lead them back to the task at hand. I frequently find this happening in step two. People are quick to move beyond "experience near" and into the thoughts and images of "experience distant." If we have not dealt with feelings, I stand and say, "Tracy, you've introduced an important image here. Can I ask you to hold on to that for a minute while we remember to listen to our feelings? What were we *feeling* while we listened?"

A common lapse also occurs in step three. People sometimes avoid theological imagery, staying in a more literary conversation. This calls for the facilitator to step into the priestly role. I remind them to look for images of God by standing and repeating one of the questions from the handout, such as "Where is God in the story? What biblical stories or images does it call to mind?" Standing signals that I have stepped out of the role of participant and into the role of facilitator.

On occasion, I have encountered stories about evil. On those occasions, it is hard to find traces of God. It is important, in this instance, for the facilitator not to push persons to find God imagery where there is none. It is appropriate to acknowledge the reality of evil when it is indeed apparent.

It is also important that the facilitator and other adults refrain from the impulse to "fix" an interpretation offered by a youth. Emerging voices are sometimes tender. It is important to gently massage a new idea without applying too much pressure.

When starting a new group, I usually invite someone who has already experienced the method to be the first storyteller. This takes pressure off the new participants and allows the seasoned participant to practice any expertise she's gained from prior experiences. For more information on guidelines for providing a hospitable classroom, refer to "Embodied Pedagogy: The Girlfriend Theology Classroom" in chapter 7.

2. Does the storyteller take part in the conversation? Does the facilitator?

Yes. Both the storyteller and the facilitator are active participants. The storyteller should be encouraged to abstain from adding content to the story itself, once it has been read. I like to say that once the story has been shared, it no longer belongs to the storyteller. She has shared it, and it has become our communal property. The story, as given, has a beginning, middle, and end. It is not appropriate to ask the storyteller, "What happened next?" It is sometimes necessary, however, to ask a question for clarification around a confusing or unclear element of the story.

The storyteller's entry into the back-and-forth conversation is critical. The facilitator, too, should participate. Occasionally, a participant stretches to articulate a meaning that seems new or unfamiliar. This is when the facilitator draws on her usable past of history, tradition, and theological interpretation to add to the new image, acting as a midwife to its emergence. This is the teachable moment. It is best seized enthusiastically but briefly.

3. How might this method be adapted? Can it be used with mixed genders? Would it work as a way to help volunteer youth counselors examine the beliefs and practices that inform their ministry? What about as an ongoing small-group curriculum for junior or senior high youth groups?

Yes, it adapts easily to different contexts. It can be used with mixed genders. When doing so, I call it "story theology" and use the same four-step method. I have used this method effectively with volunteer youth counselors as a way of helping them learn to think theologically and as a way for them to build community with one another. In advance, I solicited stories from each of my ten volunteers. We met monthly for food and fellowship. I set aside forty minutes of our time together to do story theology. At first, I chose stories that did not call for a lot of self-disclosure. As the group bonded and grew more trusting, I used the stories that called forth deeper levels of engagement.

Even though I have not used the method this way for over ten years, I still remember images that surfaced through this time together. It was a meaningful way for these dedicated adults to support one another's spiritual growth and reflect on their ministry with youth. Over time they reported to me that story theology helped them begin to *think* theologically more often in the course of everyday life.

It *could* be used as a small-group curriculum for a youth group, but it would be important to recruit qualified facilitators to meet with each group. Also, it is important to remember that this method is *not* Bible study. It can, however, help foster a desire for Bible study in young people who have not been attracted to traditional methods of Bible study. I have found that the method creates an appetite for Bible reading. In other words, when through girlfriend theology someone comes to an "aha" moment in which a Bible story seems incredibly relevant to their life story, they sometimes uncover a desire to know more about the Bible, its origins, meanings, and history. I call this Bible study "from the bottom up," because it begins with life experience and moves toward the Bible, as opposed to traditional Bible studies that begin with the text and move toward life application.

4. What size should a group be? How often should it meet? For what duration?

The ideal size for a group is from eight to ten people. When a mixed-age group is new, it is best to have two adults for every six to eight youth so that youth voices are not overpowered by adults. Additional adults could be added as the youth gain confidence in their voice and ability. In this way, the method could become a way for youth to be in ministry *to* and *with* adults of a congregation.

I have used several formats for groups: an eight-week session; a retreat weekend; monthly meetings. The important step is to begin with an hour of introduction, explaining the method carefully, using the handouts below, and trying to reduce the expectation that the story needs to be a finely crafted work of art. (For more on getting stories, see below.)

On this initial meeting, I strongly suggest including a story session. This allows participants to get a feel for the method immediately, reinforcing the steps by actually engaging in them. This means the facilitator should have a few stories submitted from participants ahead of time, so that she has the luxury of choosing the most appropriate one with which to begin. It can be helpful to begin with the story of an adult co-facilitator, to take the pressure off youth who may be unsure of how to go about choosing or writing a story.

I allow one hour for each story session, but this varies greatly from group to group. Mixed-gender groups seem to take less time, usually finishing in about forty-five minutes. Groups who know each other well, or who have regularly immersed themselves in theological conversation, usually enjoy a more relaxed pace and can take up to seventy-five minutes. When I am facilitating, I progress toward the next step in the method when everyone who wants to speak has spoken. I move on to step four and toward closure when I feel that the energy around a story seems to have peaked. I'd rather end while the images still seem full of life and energy than to leave the impression that we have wrung a story dry.

5. **How do you go about getting stories? What makes for a good story?**

This is the advice I send to participants in advance of our first session:

> In preparation for our session on "Girlfriend Theology: Glimpsing the Holy in Our Everyday Lives," I am inviting you to write a story (one-page, single-spaced) about an event in your life that you would not mind sharing with others. It can be about almost anything: a special adventure with a friend, a first date, a spoiled birthday, a dream you had long ago, a recent moment when you experienced the holy. It **does** need to be in writing, and can be e-mailed to me five days before our meeting.
>
> We will be looking for signs of God in the story — so leave the interpretations to us.
>
> There are a few things the story **should not** be about. It should not be about a moment of religious conversion: extremely overt references don't leave us enough room to play. It also **should not** be a story you have told repeatedly in a small group or therapeutic setting. If you are in the midst of an extremely difficult

or painful life crisis, find a pastor or counselor with whom to talk. Elements of that story are still ongoing and **should not** be shared in this setting.

We are looking for a fresh slice-of-life story about some event in your life that feels like it might have meaning. Try to retell it in as much detail as possible, using your best descriptive writing to depict smells, feelings, colors, etc. Here are some brief descriptions of stories that have worked well in the past:

- A woman's story about a glistening spring day when, as a teenager, she gathered with her brothers on a tree branch for a family portrait.

- A boy's story about taking a walk to the cemetery with an elderly neighbor whose husband had died six months before.

- A teenage girl's story about the day her boyfriend woke her up early in the morning to take her to a hilltop where she could see the sunrise.

- A woman's story about a dream that came to her the summer after her twin sister died of leukemia.

- A teenage girl's story about a day she went swimming with a friend and all was right with the world.

When leading a group of adults engaged in youth ministry, I ask them to think of a story from their own adolescence. In general, I will get people thinking about the story they might tell by asking them to reflect upon a time in the last six months that they have felt God's presence, stood on holy ground, or experienced an event that still seems to be at work in them.

It is mandatory that the facilitator read the stories in advance. For the first few sessions with a new group, I choose ones that seem to have especially evocative imagery. Sometimes participants choose to submit a second story after they have experienced the method. I assume that the process itself reminded them of a story they wanted to tell.

Narrative to Accompany Handout #1

When I facilitate girlfriend theology for the first time, I begin with this handout. I call it "brushstrokes" because, like a Claude Monet painting, it gives a general impression of the scene. These one-sentence descriptions allow participants to get an overview of what they are about to experience. I invite participants in the circle to take turns reading a sentence from the handout, pausing after each one to allow for my comments. I am mindful that some people are not comfortable speaking out loud in front of a group. This nonthreatening first step of reading a sentence is a way to ease the quieter voices into participation and allows the facilitator to hear each spoken voice. After each sentence, I interject an explanatory remark as follows:

> Girlfriend theology is adults listening to youth; youth listening to each other; all listening for the presence of God.

It's important to remember that in mixed-age groups, priority must always be given to the youngest voices. We must listen to them before filling up the airspace with adult voices! Sometimes, right after the story has been read or in the midst of the conversation, there will be a bit of silence. Relax into the silence. Remember, it has been said that silence is God's first language.

> Girlfriend theology is a way to create community out of diversity.

I once thought "community" meant a bunch of people like me sitting around enjoying our similarities. Then I tasted true community, the kind that emerges when people from different walks of life experience each other's stories at a heartfelt level. This method helps foster that kind of deep community because it begins with our stories — which are more easily entered into than our politics, our dogmas, or our beliefs.

> Girlfriend theology invites the Christian practice of testimony — as we seek to tell the truths of our lives out loud to one another.

When we share our stories and memories, we enter into the ancient Christian practice of testimony. We hear one another's stories and help weave them together into a tapestry that gives life meaning. It's not just the big stories of life that deserve our testimony. Sometimes it is the little stories, the quiet, almost-forgotten moments where glimpses of God are hiding.

Girlfriend theology never happens the same way twice.

Sometimes the meanings we find are amazing. Sometimes they are more mundane. Trust the process, and don't be disappointed by having huge expectations.

Girlfriend theology is risky.

It asks us to be vulnerable, to share thoughts and feelings that we sometimes keep safely locked away. Share only what you feel comfortable sharing, especially until the group has developed a level of trust. Likewise, try to honor the feelings of others. If you share something that you would like the group to keep confidential, by all means, let us know.

Girlfriend theology is by girls, about girls, for girls, and with girls. But it is not limited to girls. God calls boys and men, girls and women to move away from gendered stereotypes and into fullness of life. Yes?

If there's a man here today, we welcome you! Girlfriend theology is not exclusively for women, it just started there. We honor your willingness to join in this experience.

As you become comfortable facilitating this method, you will probably have comments you wish to interject. These are the ones I have found helpful when using the method with groups of girls and women. If using it with a group including men and boys, I would change "girlfriend" to "story" and eliminate references to gender. Likewise, if using the method with a group of adults only, I would eliminate references to youth.

GIRLFRIEND THEOLOGY
is adults listening to youth;
youth listening to each other;
all listening for the presence of God.

GIRLFRIEND THEOLOGY
is a way to create community
out of diversity.

GIRLFRIEND THEOLOGY
invites the Christian practice of testimony —
as we seek to tell the truths of our lives
out loud to one another.

GIRLFRIEND THEOLOGY
never happens the same way twice.

GIRLFRIEND THEOLOGY
is risky.

GIRLFRIEND THEOLOGY
is by girls, about girls, for girls, and with girls.
But it is not limited to girls.
God calls boys and men, girls and women
to move away from gendered stereotypes
and into fullness of life.
Yes?

Narrative to Accompany Handout #2

After walking through Brushstrokes, I turn to this chart describing the four steps of the method. The following comments are ones I usually add when I am using this handout to introduce these steps to a new group of participants.

Step One: I will set a simple altar with a cloth, a candle, and a piece of local nature such as a flower, leaf, rock, or seashell. I will light the candle just before the storyteller begins, to signal that we are entering sacred time.

I will hand out a copy of the story before it is told, but please keep it turned over while the story is being read. Don't be tempted to read ahead. Focus on the storyteller while she is reading. When she finishes, if you need to refresh your memory of some detail, you can turn the story over and consult the written version.

Step Two: I always place my hand over my heart as I introduce this step, to remind us that it begins with our bodies. I encourage you to pay attention to what you are feeling in your body, such as increased heart rate, changes in breathing, tearfulness, heavy sighs, etc. These are sometimes our best clues to articulating feelings. Points of identification refer to times when you might say something like, "I identified with the part of your story where you got in the car and started driving."

This step is like playing with a beach ball — we bounce words and ideas back and forth, reminding each other of feelings we experienced during the story. This is not a time to censor yourself. The goal is to get the entire range of feelings out on the table.

I also compare this step to making seafood gumbo. We are putting a lot of different ingredients into the pot and letting them simmer together. Out of this simmering pot will arise the images, symbols, and motifs that lead us to the next step.

Step Three: This is the heart of the method. I'll ask you to imagine the Bible you carry around in your head — your canon within the canon. Where does the story, its images, or symbols touch part of scripture? Does it remind you of Moses and the burning bush? the woman caught in adultery? Ruth and Naomi as they charted the next stage of their journey? Again, share what comes to mind without too much censoring. Someone else will probably pick up on your idea and expand it. It's okay to gently interrupt each other: that happens in the process of communal meaning-making. It's also okay to acknowledge when someone seems to be entering into a prophetic moment of speaking the truth of her life out loud for the first time, or with heightened passion. The group usually becomes silent and makes room for these moments when they happen.

In addition to biblical images, I also invite images from epic cultural stories (e.g., *The Lord of the Rings* or *Star Wars*) and stories from other religious traditions. This is a way of welcoming "seekers" or others who have not been steeped in Christian tradition. Obviously, if using the method with a multifaith group, I would add specific references to the holy texts of the groups represented. In this step, I ask questions such as: Does this story remind you of a theological term that it seems to redefine or to which it gives new meaning? What title would you give this story? And finally, at some point during this step, I ask: Where is God in this story? What does God look like here? I may keep bringing this up if it seems as though we want to avoid it.

Step Four: This is the "so what" part of the method. Is there anything we've talked about here that you want to underline? Did you have an "aha" moment? Is there something you want to continue thinking about, or something that will change the way you act in the future? I usually refer to the story about Emma's friend Rachel I recounted in chapter 3. In step four, these girls made a commitment to one another never to commit suicide. They acknowledged that the story of Rachel's suicide heightened their awareness of the risks of mental illness and the importance of seeking treatment. The story session helped them determine future action. This is a stark example: usually it is more subtle. I remember statements such as, "I will always think of that little girl climbing up into your lap whenever I hear the word 'grace.'" I will remind you that we don't all come to the same conclusions. Don't try to force anyone into seeing the story your way. Once the storyteller has told her story, it becomes all of our stories. We are each free to draw our own conclusions from the conversation that follows.

GIRLFRIEND THEOLOGY: THE METHOD

Step One: Hearing the Story

- Set a simple altar. Light a candle.
- Pass out copies of the story.
- Listen as the storyteller reads the story.

Step Two: Experience Near

- Share feelings, memories, associations.
- Share points of identification.
- Note key images, themes, symbols.

Step Three: Experience Distant

- What is the meaning of this story?
- Tease out theological themes, biblical stories, Christian practices, or echoes of other religious traditions.
- Where is God in this story? What title would you give it?

Step Four: Going Forth

- How does what we've learned here change the way you practice your faith?
- Reinforce any "aha" moments.
- Remain open to different meanings.

Notes

Introduction

1. See the "Merchants of Cool" Web site at www.pbs.org.

2. For an excellent summary of this, see "The New Gender Gap" in Craig Kennet Miller and MaryJane Pierce Norton, *Making God Real for a New Generation: Ministry with the Millennials Born from 1982 to 1999* (Nashville: Discipleship Resources, 2003), 18–20.

3. Dan Kindlon and Michael Thompson, *Raising Cain: Protecting the Emotional Life of Boys* (New York: Ballantine Books, 1999), xix.

4. Dorothy Bass, ed., *Practicing Our Faith: A Way of Life for a Searching People* (San Francisco: Jossey Bass, 1997), xi.

5. Dorothy Bass and Don C. Richter, *Way to Live: Christian Practices for Teens* (Nashville: Upper Room Books, 2002), and accompanying Web site, www.waytolive.org.

6. This gap was first brought to my awareness through conversations with Margaret Ann Crain and Jack Seymour and is reported in their book *Yearning for God: Reflections of Faithful Lives* (Nashville: Upper Room Books, 2003).

7. Beverly Jean Smith, "Raising a Resister," in *Women, Girls, and Psychotherapy: Reframing Resistance*, ed. Carol Gilligan, Annie G. Rogers, and Deborah L. Tolman (Binghamton, N.Y.: Haworth Press, 1991), 137.

Chapter 1 / Vespers Whispered under a Full Moon

1. Michael Warren, in *Youth, Gospel, Liberation* (San Francisco: Harper & Row, 1987), provides a discussion of liberation theology and youth ministry.

2. Carol Gilligan and Lyn Mikel Brown, *Meeting at the Crossroads: Women's Psychology and Girls' Development* (New York: Ballantine Books, 1992).

3. Ibid. See also American Association of University Women, *Girls in the Middle: Working to Succeed in School* (Washington, D.C.: AAUW, 1996); American Association of University Women, *How Schools Shortchange Girls* (Washington, D.C.: AAUW, 1992); and Mary Pipher, *Reviving Ophelia: Saving the Selves of Adolescent Girls* (New York: Ballantine Books, 1994).

4. Gilligan and Brown, *Meeting at the Crossroads*, 41.

5. Mary Field Belenky, Blythe McVicker Clinchy, Nancy Rule Goldberger, and Jill Mattuck Tarule, *Women's Ways of Knowing: The Development of Self, Voice,*

and Mind (New York: Basic Books, 1986), 145. The understanding of silencing as a psychological and political phenomenon affecting young women and adolescents is named by Belenky and her colleagues as one of five perspectives from which women know and view the world. Based on research that includes late-adolescent women, they characterize silence as a denial of self and a dependence on external authority. Political implications of this silence include the lack of their voice in public realms that shape social policy. Drawing on similar sources, Warren, in *Youth, Gospel, Liberation,*, names silence among youth as a pervasive sense of viewing themselves as having no power or agency to shape public actions. Warren argues that the lack of a group public voice among youth operates to keep their religious experience confined within private concerns, rather than moving it into forms of participation that engage society.

6. Carol Lee Flinders, *At the Root of This Longing: Reconciling a Spiritual Hunger and a Feminist Thirst* (San Francisco: Harper & Row, 1998), 277.

7. This belief reflects the position of feminist theology, creation spirituality, and other postmodern movements that reject the body/soul split of classical Western theology. In the same vein, these movements also reject rigid dualisms between the secular and the sacred, affirming them rather as different dimensions of the same reality. See Rosemary Radford Ruether, *New Woman, New Earth: Sexist Ideologies and Human Liberation* (Minneapolis: Seabury, 1975), and Matthew Fox, *Original Blessing* (Santa Fe: Bear & Co., 1983). This belief also reflects the thinking of process theologian John Cobb, who critiques the professionalization of theology and calls for its redefinition as "practical Christian thinking" in *Reclaiming the Church: Where the Mainline Church Went Wrong and What to Do about It* (Louisville: Westminster John Knox Press, 1997), 2–7.

8. Resistance literature "emphasizes that individuals are not simply acted upon by abstract structures, but negotiate, struggle, and create their own meaning." Katherine Weiler, *Women Teaching for Change* (Boston: Bergin and Garvey, 1988), 8. See also Sharon D. Welch, *Communities of Resistance and Solidarity: A Feminist Theology of Liberation* (Maryknoll, N.Y.: Orbis Books, 1985); Sharon D. Welch, *A Feminist Ethic of Risk* (Minneapolis: Fortress Press, 1990), 141–45; and Peter McClaren, "Multiculturalism and the Post-Modern Critique: Toward a Pedagogy of Resistance and Transformation," in *Between Borders: Pedagogy and the Politics of Cultural Studies*, ed. Henry Giroux and Peter McLaren (New York: Routledge, 1994), 200.

9. Beverly Jean Smith, "Raising a Resister," in *Women, Girls, and Psychotherapy: Reframing Resistance*, ed. Carol Gilligan, Annie G. Rogers, and Deborah L. Tolman (Binghamton, N.Y.: Haworth Press, 1991), 137. For a sustained look at the lives of African American teenage girls, see select chapters in Evelyn L. Parker, *Trouble Don't Last Always: Emancipatory Hope among African American Adolescents* (Cleveland: Pilgrim Press, 2003).

10. Hyo-Jung Kim, "Do You Have Eyelashes?" in *Women, Girls, and Psychotherapy,* 201.

11. In using the term "womanism," I refer to a body of literature by contemporary African American scholars — especially works by Katie Geneva Cannon, Jacqueline Grant, Delores Williams, and Emilie Townes — who challenge interlocking systems of oppression including racism, classism, homophobia, and ecological abuse. The womanist movement traces its roots to the black feminist movement of the nineteenth century, when women such as Maria Stewart, Sojourner Truth, and Anna Julia Cooper voiced the multiple oppressions of black female life. See Karen Baker-Fletcher, "Womanist Voice," in *Dictionary of Feminist Theologies,* ed. Letty M. Russell and J. Shannon Clarkson (Louisville: Westminster John Knox Press, 1996), 316–17.

12. Nelle Morton, *The Journey Is Home* (Boston: Beacon Press, 1985), ix. A few notable exceptions include the works of Maria Harris, *Women and Teaching: Themes for a Spirituality of Pedagogy* (New York: Paulist Press, 1988); Bonnie Miller-McLemore, *Also a Mother: Work and Family as Theological Dilemma* (Nashville: Abingdon Press, 1994); Carol Lakey Hess, *Caretakers of Our Common House: Women's Development in Communities of Faith* (Nashville: Abingdon Press, 1997); and Rosemary Radford Ruether, *Women-Church: Theology and Practice of Feminist Liturgical Communities* (San Francisco: Harper & Row, 1985). Ruether's work includes rituals for girls at puberty, persons leaving home for the first time, and women coming out as lesbians, all of which may happen during adolescence.

13. I am indebted to a personal conversation with Dr. Linda Vogel, November 15, 1996, for some of the possible reasons cited here.

14. Elliot W. Eisner, *The Educational Imagination* (New York: Macmillan, 1979), provides a discussion of explicit, implicit, and null curriculum.

15. Alice Walker, *In Search of Our Mothers' Gardens* (San Diego: Harcourt Brace Jovanovich, 1983), xi–xii.

16. bell hooks, *Yearning: Race, Gender and Cultural Politics* (Boston: South End Press, 1990), 41.

17. Smith, "Raising a Resister," 143. For more on the role of resistance within black women's domestic spheres, see Toinette Eugene, "Moral Values and Black Womanist Thought," *Journal of Religious Thought* 41, no. 2 (1984–85): 2–34.

18. Tracy Robinson and Jane Victoria Ward, "A Belief in the Self Far Greater Than Anyone's Disbelief: Cultivating Resistance among African American Female Adolescents," in *Women, Girls, and Psychotherapy: Reframing Resistance*, ed. Carol Gilligan, Annie G. Rogers, and Deborah L. Tolman (Binghamton, N.Y.: Haworth Press,, 1991), 87–103.

19. Jane Victoria Ward, "High Self-Esteem/Low Achievement: The AAUW Findings on Black Girls Growing Up" (paper presented at a symposium on the psychology of girls and the culture of schools, Temple University, Philadelphia, 1993). In Robinson and Ward, "A Belief in the Self," the authors name high teen pregnancy rates, over-representation in the juvenile justice system, a rise in obesity, and high rates of school failure among African American girls as unhealthy survival strategies they adopt in an attempt to resist "a school system they experience as both disrespectful of, and irrelevant to, their lives."

20. Emily Hancock, *The Girl Within* (New York: Fawcett Books, 1989).

21. I use the term "feminism" aware that women of color are often excluded from the body of literature considered formative of that movement. I consider the work of women of color — those who call themselves womanists and *mujeristas,* as well as Asian feminists — as foundational to my understanding of feminism and feminist theology.

22. Jack L. Seymour, Margaret Ann Crain, and Joseph V. Crockett, *Educating Christians: The Intersection of Meaning, Learning, and Vocation* (Nashville: Abingdon Press, 1993), 29.

23. Robert O'Gorman, "Latin American Theology and Education," in *Theological Approaches to Christian Education,* ed. Jack L. Seymour and Donald E. Miller (Nashville: Abingdon Press, 1990), 95.

24. Rebecca Chopp, *Saving Work: Feminist Practices of Theological Education* (Louisville: Westminster John Knox Press, 1995), 73.

25. Gilligan and Brown, *Meeting,* 24.

26. Flinders, *At the Root of This Longing,* 95.

27. Mary Elizabeth Moore, *Education for Continuity and Change* (Nashville: Abingdon Press, 1983), 121.

28. Hess, *Caretakers of Our Common House,* 74.

29. Margaret Ann Crain and Jack L. Seymour, "The Ethnographer as Minister: Ethnographic Research in Ministry," *Religious Education* 91 (Summer 1996): 299–315.

30. Diane L. Wolf, "Situating Feminist Dilemmas in Fieldwork," in *Feminist Dilemmas in Fieldwork,* ed. Diane L. Wolf (Boulder, Colo.: Westview Press, 1996), 4.

31. G. Stanley Hall, *Adolescence: Its Psychology, and Its Relations to Physiology, Anthropology, Sociology, Sex, Crime, Religion, and Education* (New York: Appleton, 1904).

32. Judith Torney-Purta, "Youth in Relation to Social Institutions," in *At the Threshold: The Developing Adolescent,* ed. S. Shirley Feldman and Glen R. Elliott (Cambridge, Mass.: Harvard University Press, 1990), 457–77.

33. Mihaly Csikszentmihalyi and Mark Freeman, "Adolescence and Its Recollection: Toward an Interpretive Model of Development," *Merrill-Palmer Quarterly* 32, no. 2 (April 1986): 167–85; Paul C. Vitz, "The Use of Stories in Moral Development: New Psychological Reasons for an Old Educational Model," *American Psychologist* 45, no. 6 (June 1990): 709–20; and Mark B. Tappan and Martin J. Packer, eds., *Narrative and Storytelling: Implications for Understanding Moral Development* (San Francisco: Jossey-Bass, 1991).

34. Norman K. Denzin and Yvonna S. Lincoln, eds., *Handbook of Qualitative Research* (London: SAGE Publications, 1994).

35. For a discussion of this turn in the field of anthropology, see Ruth Behar, *Translated Woman: Crossing the Border with Esperanza's Story* (Boston: Beacon Press, 1993), 320–42; Ruth Behar, *The Vulnerable Observer: Anthropology That Breaks Your Heart* (Boston: Beacon Press, 1996); Anna Lowenhaupt-Tsing, *In the Realm of the Diamond Queen* (Princeton, N.J.: Princeton University Press, 1993);

and Roger N. Lancaster, *Life Is Hard: Machismo, Danger, and the Intimacy of Power in Nicaragua* (Berkeley: University of California Press, 1994).

36. Donna Haraway, "Situated Knowledges: The Science Question in Feminism and the Privilege of the Partial Perspective," *Feminist Studies* 14, no. 3 (Fall 1988): 58.

37. Kamala Visweswaran, *Fictions of Feminist Ethnography* (Minneapolis: University of Minnesota, 1994), and Deborah E. Reed-Danahay, *Auto/Ethnography: Rewriting the Self and the Social* (Oxford, England: Berg, 1997).

38. Visweswaran, *Fictions of Feminist Ethnography,* 105.

39. Wolf, "Situating Feminist Dilemmas," 14.

40. Ibid., 27. See also Sue Middleton, *Educating Feminists: Life Histories and Pedagogy* (New York: Teachers College Press, 1993), 67.

41. The metaphors writers use to describe research subjects say much about the mutuality, or lack thereof, through which they approach the "other." Whereas "informant" connotes an inside operative smuggling information out, metaphors such as dance, harmonizing, or music-making describe an ethnographic relationship that strives to acknowledge and minimize an imbalance of power. Clifford Geertz, *Works and Lives: The Anthropologist as Author* (Stanford, Calif.: Stanford University Press, 1989), and José Limón, *Dancing with the Devil: Society and Cultural Poetics in Mexican-American South Texas* (Madison: University of Wisconsin Press, 1991).

42. Autobiography is also a primary context for scholars in the field of theology. See Jung Young Lee, *Marginality: The Key to Multicultural Theology* (Minneapolis: Fortress Press, 1995), 7.

43. For these steps in the research process, I followed the model of "meta-ethnography" outlined by Ada María Isasi-Díaz in "*Mujerista* Theology's Method: A Liberative Praxis, a Way of Life," in *Mestizo Christianity: Theology from the Latino Perspective,* ed. Arturo J. Bañuelas (Maryknoll, N.Y.: Orbis Books, 1995). As I reviewed the transcripts, I coded for key metaphors and generative theological themes. I then translated these themes through the writing process, checking back with my collaborators for accuracy of my interpretations. This method receives fuller description in chapter 6.

Chapter 2 / Future Homemakers and Feminist Awakenings

1. Nelle Morton, *The Journey Is Home* (Boston: Beacon Press, 1985), 201–6.

2. These words by Spanish poet Federico García Lorca tell of a man journeying on horseback to the Andalusian town of Córdoba. They translate "Córdoba. Distant and alone. Black mare, huge moon.... "

3. Throughout this project, I use the word "voice" in keeping with the multi-layered usage of the term in the works of Carol Gilligan and Lyn Mikel Brown. Voice refers first to literal utterances, grounded in the body. Voice also refers to the psychological capacity to "say what we know" in a relationship, rather than to silence true feelings in an effort to conform to social norms. When women's and girls' voices are silenced, they go underground, a problem emblematic of women's depression. Carol

Gilligan and Lyn Mikel Brown, *Meeting at the Crossroads: Women's Psychology and Girls' Development* (New York: Ballantine Books, 1992), 19–23.

4. Maya Angelou, *I Know Why the Caged Bird Sings* (New York: Bantam Books, 1969), 80–85. In these pages, Angelou tells of one of her early mentors, describing her as a "lifeline." The importance of mentors in the lives of young girls cannot be underemphasized. As Mary Pipher writes, "Many women tell stories of what saved them from the precipice. . . . Girls can be saved by a good school, a good teacher, or a meaningful activity. Many women report that when they were in adolescence, they had someone they could really talk to, who encouraged them to stay true to who they really were." Mary Pipher, *Reviving Ophelia: Saving the Selves of Adolescent Girls* (New York: Ballantine Books, 1994).

5. This reflects an institutionalization of feminist consciousness, a process Gerda Lerner traces as fundamental to women's emancipation throughout history. Without the creation of such institutions, individual women deprived of a female tradition do not share the male advantage of standing "on the shoulders of giants." See Gerda Lerner, *The Creation of Feminist Consciousness: From the Middle Ages to Eighteen-seventy* (New York: Oxford University Press, 1993). The intersection between this dynamic and girlfriend theology will receive fuller treatment in chapter 8. Although I initially envisioned my audience as churches only, I came to adopt the term "communities of faith" to include a wider spectrum of the Judeo-Christian heritage. Women within church and synagogue hold the power to better institutionalize feminist consciousness, especially as it relates to theology.

6. Rebecca Chopp, *Saving Work: Feminist Practices of Theological Education* (Louisville: Westminster John Knox Press, 1995), 85.

7. Morton, *The Journey Is Home*, 205.

8. Morton acknowledges her indebtedness to Paulo Freire, who makes a similar point from the perspective of Latin American peasants in *Pedagogy of the Oppressed* (New York: Herder & Herder, 1970).

9. Sharon D. Welch, *A Feminist Ethic of Risk* (Minneapolis: Fortress, 1990), 18.

10. Chopp, *Saving Work*, 85.

11. Martin Heidegger, *Being and Time*, trans. J. Macquarrie and C. Robinson (New York: Harper and Row, 1962), 177. For a discussion of shifting views of the self in modernity and postmodernity, see Dan McAdams, *The Stories We Live By: Personal Myths and the Making of the Self* (New York: William Morrow, 1993), and Anthony Giddens, *Modernity and Self-Identity: Self and Society in the Late Modern Age* (Stanford, Calif.: Stanford University Press, 1991).

12. Jack Seymour, Margaret Ann Crain, and Joseph V. Crockett, *Educating Christians: The Intersection of Meaning, Learning, and Vocation* (Nashville: Abingdon Press, 1993), 23.

13. Ibid.

14. Tom Beaudoin, *Virtual Faith: The Irreverent Spiritual Quest of Generation X* (San Francisco: Jossey-Bass, 1998), 52.

15. Henry A. Giroux, *Fugitive Cultures: Race, Violence, and Youth* (New York: Routledge, 1996), 50.

16. Beth Burbank, "Reflecting upon Stories as a Way of Doing Theology in CPE," *Journal of Supervision and Training in Ministry* 9 (1987): 151, 147–57.

17. Thomas Groome, *Sharing Faith* (San Francisco: HarperSanFrancisco, 1991), 147.

18. Anne Streaty Wimberly, *Soul Stories: African American Christian Education* (Nashville: Abingdon Press, 1994).

19. Zora Neale Hurston, *Dust Tracks on a Road* (San Francisco: HarperCollins, 1996), 15.

20. The term "girlfriend theology" first surfaced in this group as we talked about the process. I'm grateful to these collaborators for the gift of this generative descriptor.

21. Jerome Bruner, *On Knowing: Essays for the Left Hand* (Cambridge, Mass.: Harvard University Press, 1969), 121.

22. Ann L. Brown, "Design Experiments: Theoretical and Methodological Challenges in Creating Complex Interventions in Classroom Settings," *Journal of the Learning Sciences* 2, no. 2 (1992): 141–78.

23. I have changed the names of all the participants, except my own, to protect their anonymity. I paid a twenty-dollar stipend to the girls in the second group for travel expenses. The girls in the first and third groups did not incur travel expenses by taking part. I paid Peg and Sarah, two of the adult women with graduate degrees in theology, for their time. I did not pay Lisa, as she integrated the research project into her paid position as a youth minister.

24. Alice Walker, *The Color Purple* (New York: Washington Square Press, 1982), 176.

Chapter 3 / God-Talk across Religious Borders

1. Sara Shandler, *Ophelia Speaks: Adolescent Girls Write About Their Search for Self* (New York: Harper Perennial, 1999), 258.

2. R. J. Zwi Werblowsky and Geoffrey Wigoder, eds., *The Oxford Dictionary of the Jewish Religion* (New York: Oxford University Press, 1997), 468.

3. Rosemary Radford Ruether, *Women-Church: Theology and Practice of Feminist Liturgical Communities* (San Francisco: Harper & Row, 1985), 58–61.

4. Ibid., 91.

5. Rebecca Chopp, *Saving Work: Feminist Practices of Theological Education* (Louisville: Westminster John Knox Press, 1995), 14. See also Jerome Berryman, *Godly Play: A Way of Religious Education* (San Francisco: HarperSanFrancisco, 1991), 11. Story theology bears characteristics of Godly play, in that it provides "a place of spontaneity where one does not need to be compliant or acquiescent."

6. Chopp, *Saving Work,* 14.

7. Ibid., 46

8. Alice Walker, *The Color Purple* (New York: Washington Square Press, 1982), 176.

9. Judith Siqueira, untitled editorial in *In God's Image* 13, no. 4 (Winter 1994): 2–4.

10. Pui Lan Kwok, "Mothers and Daughters, Writers and Fighters," in *Frontiers in Asian Christian Theology: Emerging Trends,* ed. R. S. Sugirtharaja (Maryknoll, N.Y.: Orbis Books, 1994), 153.

11. Siqueira, *In God's Image,* 3.

12. Mary Field Belenky, Blythe McVicker Clinchy, Nancy Rule Goldberger, and Jill Mattuck Tarule, *Women's Ways of Knowing: The Development of Self, Voice, and Mind* (New York: Basic Books, 1986), 145.

13. Carter Heyward, *Touching Our Strength: The Erotic as Power and the Love of God* (San Francisco: HarperCollins, 1980), 93–94.

14. Ibid.

15. See Erik Erikson, *The Life Cycle Completed: A Review* (New York: W. W. Norton, 1982), and James Fowler, *Stages of Faith: The Psychology of Human Development and the Quest for Meaning* (New York: Harper & Row, 1981).

16. Tom Beaudoin, *Virtual Faith: The Irreverent Spiritual Quest of Generation X* (San Francisco: Jossey-Bass, 1998), 34.

Chapter 4 / Collecting Sea Glass

1. Mary Pipher, *Reviving Ophelia: Saving the Selves of Adolescent Girls* (New York: Ballantine Books, 1994), 22.

2. Katie Haegele, "Pack a Punch," *Feminista!* 3, no. 8 (February 2000): 1–6.

3. Ibid.

4. Susan Faludi, *Backlash: The Undeclared War on American Women* (New York: Crown, 1991), xix.

5. Carol Lee Flinders, *At the Root of This Longing: Reconciling a Spiritual Hunger and a Feminist Thirst* (San Francisco: Harper & Row, 1998), 97.

6. These influences are affected by culture and combine to make up the microsystems, mesosystems, exosystems, and macrosystems affecting a person's development. See Urie Bronfenbrenner, *The Ecology of Human Development* (Cambridge, Mass.: Harvard University Press, 1979).

7. Robert Kegan, *The Evolving Self: Problem and Process in Human Development* (Cambridge, Mass.: Harvard University Press, 1982), 255–60. While Kegan's theories of development have undergone significant revision in the twelve years since the publication of this book, his image of natural therapies remains useful in describing the emulative process of formal curricula of therapy and education. See Robert Kegan, *In Over Our Heads: The Mental Demands of Moral Life* (Cambridge, Mass.: Harvard University Press, 1994), 219–21.

8. Ibid.

9. See Carol Gilligan, *In a Different Voice: Psychological Theory and Women's Development* (Cambridge, Mass.: Harvard University Press, 1982).

10. Mary Catherine Bateson, *Composing a Life* (New York: Plume, 1990), 4.

11. Flinders, *At the Root of This Longing,* 45.

12. Kathleen Norris, *The Cloister Walk* (New York: Riverhead Books, 1996), xvii.

13. Flinders, *At the Root of This Longing*, 45.

14. Sharon Welch, *Communities of Resistance and Solidarity: A Feminist Theology of Liberation* (Maryknoll, N.Y.: Orbis Books, 1985), 35–42.

15. Nam-Soon Kang, "Creating 'Dangerous Memory': Challenges for Asian and Korean Feminist Theology," *Ecumenical Review* 49, no. 1 (January 1998): 21–31.

16. In drawing attention to the nonneutrality of these stories, I contend that all education carries with it a particular perspective. See Paulo Freire, *Pedagogy of the Oppressed* (New York: Herder & Herder, 1970).

17. Katie Geneva Cannon, *Katie's Canon: Womanism and the Soul of the Black Community* (New York: Continuum, 1995), 78–91; and Alice Walker, *In Search of Our Mothers' Gardens* (San Diego: Harcourt Brace Jovanovich, 1983), xi–xii.

18. Kegan, *The Evolving Self*, 258.

19. Audre Lorde, "An Open Letter to Mary Daly," in *Sister Outsider* (Freedom, Calif.: Crossing Press, 1984), provides a provocative discussion of the responsibility of white women to educate themselves about race and racism.

20. See Peggy McIntosh, "White Privilege: Unpacking the Invisible Knapsack," in *Peace and Freedom* (July–August 1989): 10–12.

21. Maya Angelou, *I Know Why the Caged Bird Sings* (New York, Bantam, 1969), 80–85.

22. Jerome Berryman, *Godly Play: A Way of Religious Education* (San Francisco: HarperSanFrancisco, 1991), 103.

23. bell hooks, *Yearning: Race, Gender and Cultural Politics* (Boston: South End Press, 1990), 41. "Homeplace" is only one among many womanist/feminist themes that could enter fruitfully into dialogue with this story. I will explore others in chapter 6. (bell hooks intentionally uses lowercase letters in the spelling of her name.)

24. Ibid.

25. Ibid.

26. Ibid., 44.

27. Kathleen Thompson, "Maya Angelou," in *Black Women in America: An Historical Encyclopedia,* ed. Darlene Clark Hine, Elsa Barkley Brown, and Rosalyn Terborg-Penn (Bloomington: Indiana University Press, 1994), 36–38.

28. Nelle Morton, *The Journey Is Home* (Boston: Beacon Press, 1985), 202.

29. Tracy Robinson and Janie Victoria Ward, "A Belief in the Self Far Greater Than Anyone's Disbelief: Cultivating Resistance among African American Female Adolescents," in *Women, Girls and Psychotherapy: Reframing Resistance,* ed. Carol Gilligan, Annie G. Rogers, and Deborah L. Tolman (Binghamton, N.Y.: Haworth Press, 1991), 95.

30. Patricia Hill Collins, "The Meaning of Motherhood in Black Culture and Black Mother-Daughter Relationships," in *Double Stitch: Black Women Write about Mothers & Daughters,* ed. Patricia Bell-Scott, Beverly Guy-Sheftall, Jacqueline Jones Royster, Janet Sims-Wood, Miriam DeCosta-Willis, and Lucie Fulz (Boston: Beacon

Press, 1991), 47. See also Stanlie James, *Theorizing Black Feminisms: The Visionary Pragmatism of Black Women*, ed. Stanlie M. James and Abena P. A. Busia (London: Routledge, 1993), 44–54.

31. For a discussion of engaged pedagogy as holistic practice, see bell hooks, *Teaching to Transgress* (New York: Routledge, 1994), 13–22.

32. Audre Lorde, *Zami: A New Spelling of My Name* (Watertown, Mass.: Persephone Press, 1982), 3.

33. Ibid., 4.

34. Kathy Peiss, "Beauty Culture," in *Black Women in America: An Historical Encyclopedia*, ed. Darlene Clark Hine, Elsa Barkley Brown, and Rosalyn Terborg-Penn (Bloomington: Indiana University Press, 1994), 103

35. Walker, *In Search of Our Mothers' Gardens*, xii.

36. As quoted by Cannon, *Katie's Canon*, 178.

37. Ibid., 90.

38. Ibid., 79.

39. Ibid.

40. Regina Austin, "Sapphire Bound" (paper presented at the American Association of Law Schools Workshop for Women in Legal Education, Washington D.C., October 1987), 15.

41. Alice Walker, *The Color Purple* (New York: Washington Square Press, 1982), 176.

42. Annie Dillard, *An American Childhood* (New York: Harper and Row, 1987), 88–90.

43. Ntozake Shange, *For Colored Girls Who've Considered Suicide When the Rainbow Is Enuf* (New York: Macmillan, 1977), 63.

44. Walker, *In Search of Our Mothers' Gardens*, xii.

45. Nellie Y. McKay, "Autobiography," in *Black Women in America: An Historical Encyclopedia*, ed. Darlene Clark Hine, Elsa Barkley Brown, and Rosalyn Terborg-Penn (Bloomington: Indiana University Press, 1994) 55–59.

46. Ibid.

47. Carolyn Heilbrun, *Writing a Woman's Life* (New York: Ballantine Books, 1989), 117.

48. Darlene Clark Hine, class lecture, Northwestern University Avalon Lecture, March 8, 1997.

49. McKay, "Autobiography," 59.

50. Lorde, *Sister Outsider,* 36–39.

51. Robinson and Ward, "A Belief in the Self," 102.

Chapter 5 / God-Talk in the Midst of Violence and Death

1. I include eating disorders as part of a long list of violent behaviors, including self-mutilation (known as "cutting"), that girls inflict upon themselves as a way of coping with sex-role expectations. Eating disorders claim the lives of up to a thousand girls a year in the United States. See Jennifer Egan, "The Thin Red Line," *New*

York Times Magazine (July 27, 1997): 21–46, and Carol Lakey Hess, *Caretakers of Our Common House: Women's Development in Communities of Faith* (Nashville: Abingdon Press, 1997), 132–35.

2. Centers for Disease Control and Prevention, National Center for Injury Prevention, "Violence in the United States," www.cdc.gov. Although still high, homicide rates among youth have been declining steadily since a peak in 1993, according to Thomas B. Cole, "Ebbing Epidemic: Youth Homicide Rate at a 14-year Low," *Journal of the American Medical Association* 281, no. 1 (January 1999).

3. Six of the fifteen stories collected in my research focused on death and/or violence, including suicide, eating disorders, murder, and domestic abuse.

4. Jürgen Habermas, "A Review of Gadamer's *Truth and Method*," in *The Hermeneutic Tradition: From Ast to Ricoeur*, ed. Gayle L. Ormiston and Alan D. Schrift (Albany: State University of New York Press, 1990), 213–44.

5. See Virginia Ramey Mollenkott, *The Divine Feminine: The Biblical Imagery of God as Female* (New York: Crossroad, 1991), for a plethora of biblically grounded images of God growing out of feminist critique of "God the father" imagery.

6. Mary Daly, *Beyond God the Father: Toward a Philosophy of Women's Liberation* (Boston: Beacon Press, 1973), 13.

7. Ruth Duck, *Gender and the Name of God: The Trinitarian Baptismal Formula* (New York: Pilgrim Press, 1990), 43–51.

8. Elisabeth Schüssler-Fiorenza, *In Memory of Her: A Feminist Theological Reconstruction of Christian Origins* (New York: Crossroad, 1987), 151.

9. Rosemary Radford Ruether, *New Woman, New Earth: Sexist Ideologies and Human Liberation* (Minneapolis: Seabury, 1975), 67–69.

10. For a summary of essentialism as a topic germane to feminist theology, see Ellen T. Armour, "Essentialism," in *Dictionary of Feminist Theologies*, ed., Letty M. Russell and J. Shannon Clarkson (Louisville: Westminster John Knox Press, 1996), 88. For a more in-depth discussion of essentialism as a topic within feminist scholarship in general, see Diana Fuss, *Essentially Speaking: Feminism, Nature, and Difference* (New York: Routledge, 1990).

11. Sallie McFague, *Metaphorical Theology: Models of God in Religious Language* (Philadelphia: Fortress Press, 1982), 159.

12. Ibid., 9.

13. Ibid., 21.

14. Ibid., 177.

15. A study by Joyce Mercer found feminist theology's stress on God's imminence limiting to adolescent females. (Joyce Mercer, "Gender, Violence and Faith: Adolescent Girls and the Theological Anthropology of Difference" [PhD diss., Emory University, 1997]). The girls in my research, by contrast, often embraced images of God's imminence as a welcome counterpoint to the images of a predominately transcendent God they had inherited from popular culture and their religious traditions. This is not to imply that transcendent images of God did not seem important to my

collaborators: the girls in my study seemed to affirm *both* characteristics in God and exhibited little difficulty in holding the two in tension.

16. John B. Cobb Jr., *Lay Theology* (St. Louis, Mo.: Chalice Press, 1994), 109.

17. Gustavo Gutiérrez, *A Theology of Liberation* (Maryknoll, N.Y.: Orbis Books, 1988), 106.

18. The Youth Theology Institute is an annual four-week gathering of high-school youth at Emory University's Candler School of Theology. It was the first of many programs sponsored by the Fund for Theological Education and the Eli Lilly Foundation with the intent of recruiting adolescents to the study of theology.

19. Gutiérrez, *A Theology of Liberation*, 106, and Ada María Isasi-Díaz, *Mujerista Theology: A Theology for the Twenty-first Century* (Maryknoll, N.Y.: Orbis Books, 1996), 92–94.

20. Dwight W. and Linda J. Vogel, *Sacramental Living: Falling Stars & Coloring Outside the Lines* (Nashville: Upper Room Books, 1999), 24.

21. Roberta Bondi, *Memories of God: Theological Reflections on a Life* (Nashville: Abingdon Press, 1995), 28.

22. McFague, *Metaphorical Theology*, 165.

23. Ibid., 186.

24. Howard Thurman, *The Search for Common Ground: An Inquiry into the Basis of Man's Experience of Community* (Richmond, Ind.: Friends United Press, 1986), 76–77.

25. Starhawk, *Dreaming the Dark* (Boston: Beacon Press, 1982), 26. Emphasis added.

26. McFague, in *Metaphorical Theology*, 152, provides a helpful distinction between the feminist theologian as reformer versus revolutionary.

Chapter 6 / *Slipping Through the Barbed Wire Fence*

1. Louis Freedberg, "Borderline Hypocrisy: Do We Want Them Here, or Not?" *Washington Post*, February 6, 2000, sec. B, 1. Freedberg writes provocatively of his crossing of the U.S./Mexican border with a dozen Mexicans as part of a yearlong exploration into U.S. immigration laws.

2. Sharon D. Welch, *A Feminist Ethic of Risk* (Minneapolis: Fortress Press, 1990), 68. Welch defines an ethic of risk as follows: "Within an ethic of risk, actions begin with the recognition that far too much has been lost and there are no clear means of restitution. The fundamental risk constitutive of this ethic is the decision to care and to act, although there are no guarantees of success. Such action requires immense daring and enables deep joy." In quoting this definition, I follow the lead of Linda Moody, *Women Encounter God: Theology across the Boundaries of Difference* (Maryknoll, N.Y.: Orbis Books, 1996), 151–52.

3. Many other women's voices of theology — those coming from Africa, Latin America, and other third-world contexts — could be useful in girlfriend theology. Out of necessity, I have limited my discussion to the work of specific authors or groups of authors within these three contexts.

4. Ada María Isasi-Díaz, *Mujerista Theology: A Theology for the Twenty-first Century* (Maryknoll, N.Y.: Orbis Books, 1996), 172.

5. American Association of University Women, *Girls in the Middle: Working to Succeed in School* (Washington, D.C.: AAUW, 1996), 31.

6. Rosemary Radford Ruether, *Women and Redemption: A Theological History* (Minneapolis: Fortress Press, 1998), 235.

7. Ada María Isasi-Díaz, "*Mujerista* Theology's Method: A Liberative Praxis, a Way of Life," in *Mestizo Christianity: Theology from the Latino Perspective,* ed. Arturo J. Bañuelas (Maryknoll, N.Y.: Orbis Books, 1995), 179.

8. Ibid., 161.

9. Isasi-Díaz, *Mujerista Theology,* 65–73.

10. Hyun Kyung Chung , *Struggle to Be the Sun Again: Introducing Asian Women's Theology* (Maryknoll, N.Y.: Orbis Books, 1990), 23.

11. Ruether, *Women and Redemption,* 263.

12. Chung, *Struggle,* 7.

13. Nam-Soon Kang, "Creating 'Dangerous Memory': Challenges for Asian and Korean Feminist Theology," *Ecumenical Review* 49, no. 1 (January 1998): 21–31.

14. Pui Lan Kwok, "Mothers and Daughters, Writers and Fighters," in *Frontiers in Asian Christian Theology: Emerging Trends,* ed. R. S. Sugirtharaja (Maryknoll, N.Y.: Orbis Books, 1994), 147–55.

15. Judith Siqueira, untitled editorial in *In God's Image* 13, no. 4 (winter 1994): 3.

16. Chung, *Struggle,* 5.

17. Ibid., 104–9.

18. Ibid., 42–43.

19. Ibid., 49.

20. Alice Walker, *In Search of Our Mothers' Gardens* (San Diego: Harcourt Brace Jovanovich, 1983), xi–xii.

21. Toinette Eugene, class lecture at Garrett-Evangelical Theological Seminary, Evanston, Ill., October 1, 1997.

22. Walker, *In Search of Our Mothers' Gardens,* xi–xii.

23. bell hooks, *Yearning: Race, Gender, and Cultural Politics* (Boston: South End Press, 1990), 41–49.

24. Katie Geneva Cannon, *Katie's Canon: Womanism and the Soul of the Black Community* (New York: Continuum, 1995), 91–100.

25. Isasi-Díaz, *Mujerista Theology,* 16–21.

26. Toinette M. Eugene, "Appropriation/Reciprocity," in *Dictionary of Feminist Theologies,* ed. Letty M. Russell and J. Shannon Clarkson (Louisville: Westminster John Knox Press, 1996), 15–16.

27. Ibid.

28. Chung, *Struggle,* 89.

29. Gloria Anzaldúa, *Borderlands/La Frontera: The New Mestiza* (San Francisco: Aunt Lute Books, 1987), 59–60.

30. Carolyn G. Heilbrun, *Writing a Woman's Life* (New York: Ballantine Books, 1989), 96.

31. Olive Schreiner, *The Story of an African Farm* (Oxford: Oxford University Press, 1992), 38.

Chapter 7 / Breast-Feeding Women and Vegan Girls

1. Carol Gilligan and Lyn Mikel Brown, *Meeting at the Crossroads: Women's Psychology and Girls' Development* (New York: Ballantine Books, 1992), 14.

2. My experience here resonates with that of Bonnie Miller-McLemore, who writes, "Daily, I become entangled in the ambiguous oppositions between so-called public and private life. On the one hand, my 'private' vocation as devoted mother collides head-on with my religious and feminist hopes for justice and equality in a 'public' world not structured for, and even hostile to children. On the other hand, my 'public' vocation as professor clashes with my religious and maternal desires for creation, nurturing, and sustenance in the 'private' world of child's play and domestic routine. My life refuses to fall into the traditional dichotomy between private and public arenas that Western society has fostered." Bonnie Miller-McLemore, *Also a Mother: Work and Family as Theological Dilemma* (Nashville: Abingdon Press, 1994), 30–31.

3. Wendy M. Wright, "Wreathed in Flesh and Warm," *Weavings* 12, no. 1 (January–February 1987): 18–27.

4. Adriana Hernández, *Pedagogy, Democracy, and Feminism: Rethinking the Public Sphere* (Albany: State University of New York Press, 1997), 10.

5. According to the Vegan Society, veganism is defined as "a way of living which seeks to exclude, as far as possible and practical, all forms of exploitation of and cruelty to, animals for food, clothing, or any other purpose. In dietary terms, it refers to the practice of dispensing with all animal produce — including meat, fish, poultry, eggs, animal milks, honey, and their derivatives." www.JewishVegan.com.

6. Potential health risks of veganism include vitamin B-12 and iron deficiencies. These have the short-term effect of fatigue. Vegans who use proper supplemental vitamins avoid these risks. See Ursula Donovan and Rosalind Gibson, "Dietary Intakes of Adolescent Females Consuming Vegetarian, Semi-Vegetarian, and Omnivorous Diets," *Journal of Adolescent Health* 18 (1996): 292–300.

7. Paul Ricoeur, *The Conflict of Interpretations: Essays in Hermeneutics* (Evanston, Ill.: Northwestern University Press, 1974), 289.

8. Sara Shandler, *Ophelia Speaks: Adolescent Girls Write About Their Search for Self* (New York: Harper Perennial, 1999).

9. Joan Jacobs Brumberg, *The Body Project: An Intimate History of American Girls* (New York: Random House, 1997), xvii–xx. Brumberg's study compares diaries and journals of contemporary female adolescents with those from nineteenth-century white America. She finds adolescent female angst about bodies to be persistent across time, but that "it is the historical moment that defines *how* [a girl] reacts to her changing flesh." Earlier women's mention of their bodies refers to efforts to avoid vanity and self-indulgence. The "cult of true womanhood" deemed

self-control, service to others, and belief in God to be more important than beauty. Contemporary journals of adolescent girls, Brumberg writes, show persistent preoccupation with bodies — including weight, complexion, clothes, and piercings — as second only to peer relationships.

10. Henry A. Giroux, *Fugitive Cultures: Race, Violence, and Youth* (New York: Routledge Press, 1996), 5.

11. Hyo-Jung Kim, "Do You Have Eyelashes?" in *Women, Girls, and Psychotherapy: Reframing Resistance,* ed. Carol Gilligan, Annie G. Rogers, and Deborah L. Tolman (Binghamton, N.Y.: Haworth Press, 1991).

12. Rebecca Carroll, *Sugar in the Raw: Voices of Young Black Girls in America* (New York: Crown, 1997), 33.

13. See Henry A. Giroux and Peter McLaren, eds., *Between Borders: Pedagogy and the Politics of Cultural Studies* (New York: Routledge Press, 1994); Henry A. Giroux, Colin Lankshear, Peter McClaren, and Michael Peters, eds., *Counternarratives: Cultural Studies and Critical Pedagogies in Postmodern Spaces* (New York: Routledge Press, 1996); bell hooks, *Teaching to Transgress: Education as the Practice of Freedom* (New York: Routledge Press, 1994); and Mary Field Belenky, Blythe McVicker Clinchy, Nancy Rule Goldberger, and Jill Mattuck Tarule, *Women's Ways of Knowing: The Development of Self, Voice, and Mind* (New York: Basic Books, 1986).

14. hooks, *Teaching to Transgress,* 6.

15. Giroux and McLaren, *Between Borders,* 196.

16. Tom Beaudoin, *Virtual Faith: The Irreverent Spiritual Quest of Generation X* (San Francisco: Jossey Bass, 1998), 11.

17. Ibid., 198.

18. Giroux and McClaren, *Between Borders,* 39.

19. hooks, *Teaching to Transgress,* 196.

20. Ibid., 13–22.

21. This concept receives fuller elaboration in Maria Harris, *Women and Teaching: Themes for a Spirituality of Pedagogy* (New York: Paulist Press, 1988), 83.

22. Belenky, et al., *Women's Ways,* 214–29.

23. Harris, *Women and Teaching;* Michael Warren, *Youth, Gospel, Liberation* (San Francisco: Harper & Row, 1987); Mary Elizabeth Mullino Moore, *Teaching From the Heart: Theology and Educational Method* (Minneapolis: Fortress Press, 1991); and Daniel Schipani, *Religious Education Encounters Liberation Theology* (Birmingham, Ala.: Religious Education Press, 1988). These religious educators mostly fall under the category of "Educating for Social Transformation" in the typography of the field offered in Jack L. Seymour, *Mapping Christian Education: Approaches to Congregational Learning* (Nashville: Abingdon Press, 1997). For the most part, they draw directly on Paulo Freire's work, or adaptations of it within the realm of religious education. It is rare to find religious educators who trace their postmodern critique through the field of critical education and cultural studies.

24. John B. Cobb Jr., *Reclaiming the Church: Where the Mainline Church Went Wrong and What to Do about It* (Louisville: Westminster John Knox Press, 1997).

25. Paulo Freire, *Pedagogy of the Oppressed* (New York: Herder & Herder, 1970), 63. Examples of religious education as the banking model abound, especially within mainstream denominations' confirmation classes. Introduction to the Christian faith in this initiation into church membership often focuses on the memorization of scripture and creeds, without equal attention to forming spirituality, creating meaningful community, or acknowledging doubt about faith traditions.

26. Jack L. Seymour, Margaret Ann Crain, and Joseph V. Crockett, *Educating Christians: The Intersection of Meaning, Learning, and Vocation* (Nashville: Abingdon, 1993), 113–31.

27. I borrow the term "public theologians" from the grant proposal of the Youth Theology Institute at Candler School of Theology, Emory University, Atlanta, Georgia.

28. Megan Bolen, *Feeling Power: Emotions and Education* (New York: Routledge Press, 1999), 176. See also the concept of web pedagogy in Susan Willhauck and Jacqulyn Thorpe, *The Web of Women's Leadership: Recasting Congregational Ministry* (Nashville: Abingdon, 2001), 108.

29. Seymour, Crain, and Crockett, *Educating Christians*, 96–112.

30. This open-ended process resembles the type of inquiry described by Anne Game as a "disturbing pleasure" in which "the risks of infinity, with hints of madness ... are far preferable to the safety (and possibly bad faith) of closure." *Undoing the Social: Towards a Deconstructive Sociology* (Toronto and Buffalo: University of Toronto Press, 1991), 191.

31. This attention to bodily comfort is in stark contrast to what I remember of my own religious and secular education as an adolescent and young adult. It brings to mind bell hooks's comment: "When I first became a teacher and needed to use the restroom in the middle of class, I had no clue as to what my elders did in such situations." *Teaching to Transgress*, 191.

32. Emilie Townes provides a helpful metaphor for this kind of exchange. The "ring shout" of traditional black religious practice allows for diverse voices within a space of equality. Unlike a monologue or a chorus, the ring shout is not performance-based and does not require harmony. "Voices of the Spirit: Womanist Methodologies in Theological Disciplines," *Womanist* 1 (Summer 1994): 1–2.

33. On the experience of literally being hushed, journalist Ann Taylor Fleming writes, "Down the corridors of my preteen years, the word I remember hearing the most was 'hush' or some variation on it, a quashing chorus of 'shhs' that inevitably greeted one of my characteristically high-decibel riffs on the world and served to intensify my feeling of choking." *Motherhood Deferred: A Woman's Journey* (New York: G. P. Putnam's Sons, 1994), 170.

34. Kathleen Norris defines prophets as "the carriers of hope through disastrous times." This is a fitting image for adolescent prophets, who can describe a landscape adults are often unable to see. *The Cloister Walk* (New York: Riverhead Books, 1996), 45.

35. See Stephanie Paulsell, *Honoring the Body: Meditations on a Christian Practice* (San Francisco: Jossey-Bass, 2002).

36. Thomas Groome defines praxis, in part, as "the consciousness and agency that arise from and are expressed in any and every aspect of people's 'being' as agent-subjects-in-relationship, whether realized actions that are personal, interpersonal, sociopolitical, or cosmic." *Sharing Faith* (San Francisco: HarperSanFrancisco, 1991), 135. See also Rebecca S. Chopp, "Praxis as the Shape of Theology," in *Dictionary of Feminist Theologies*, ed. Letty M. Russell and J. Shannon Clarkson (Louisville: Westminster John Knox Press, 1996), 222.

37. For a thorough discussion of some of the specific developmental issues facing adolescent girls coming out as lesbians, see Beth Zemsky, "Coming Out against All Odds: Resistance in the Life of a Young Lesbian," in *Women, Girls and Psychotherapy: Reframing Resistance*, ed. Carol Gilligan, Annie G. Rogers, and Deborah L. Tolman (Binghamton, N.Y.: Haworth Press, 1991), 185–99. See also Gerald Unks, *The Gay Teen: Educational Practice and Theory for Lesbian, Gay, and Bisexual Adolescents* (New York: Routledge Press, 1995) and Leanne McCall Tigert and Timothy Brown, *Coming Out Young and Faithful* (Cleveland: Pilgrim Press, 2001).

38. Ruth Behar, in telling about a year of her girlhood spent in a body cast, writes eloquently of this, stating that "the body is a homeland — a place where knowledge, memory, and pain is stored by the child." *The Vulnerable Observer: Anthropology That Breaks Your Heart* (Boston: Beacon Press, 1996), 30.

39. Carol Lakey Hess, *Caretakers of Our Common House: Women's Development in Communities of Faith* (Nashville: Abingdon Press, 1997), 131.

40. Becky Wangsgaard Thompson, "'A Way Outa No Way': Eating Problems among African-American, Latina, and White Women," *Gender and Society* 4 (December 1992): 50.

41. Greg Critser, "Let Them Eat Fat: The Heavy Truths about American Obesity," *Harper's Magazine* (March 2000): 41–47.

42. Tracy Robinson and Janie Victoria Ward, "A Belief in the Self Far Greater Than Anyone's Disbelief: Cultivating Resistance among African American Female Adolescents," in *Women, Girls, and Psychotherapy: Reframing Resistance,* ed. Carol Gilligan, Annie G. Rogers, and Deborah L. Tolman (Binghamton, N.Y.: Haworth Press, 1991), 95.

43. Barrant W. Walsh and Paul M. Rosin, *Self-Mutilation: Theory, Research and Treatment* (London: The Guilford Press, 1988).

44. Jennifer Egan, "The Thin Red Line," *New York Times Magazine,* July 27, 1997, 21–40.

45. Ibid., 22.

46. Dusty Miller, *Women Who Hurt Themselves: A Book of Hope and Understanding* (New York: Basic Books, 1994), 3.

47. Egan, "The Thin Red Line," 22.

48. I borrow the term "body/selves" from Carter Heyward, *Touching Our Strength: The Erotic as Power and the Love of God* (San Francisco: HarperCollins, 1980), 93. It allows me to speak of our embodied natures without furthering the dichotomy implied by the distinct words "body" and "self."

49. Behar, *The Vulnerable Observer,* 131.

Chapter 8 / God-Talk at the Crossroads of Souls

1. Gerda Lerner, *The Creation of Feminist Consciousness: From the Middle Ages to Eighteen-seventy* (New York: Oxford University Press, 1993), 220–46.

2. Joy G. Dryfoos, *Safe Passage: Making It through Adolescence in a Risky Society* (New York: Oxford University Press, 1998), 39, 262.

3. Patricia Hersch, *A Tribe Apart: A Journey into the Heart of American Adolescence* (New York: Ballantine Publishing Group, 1998), 30.

4. Ibid., 364.

5. Joan Jacobs Brumberg, *The Body Project: An Intimate History of American Girls* (New York: Random House, 1997), 209.

6. Joyce Mercer, "Gender, Violence, and Faith: Adolescent Girls and the Theological Anthropology of Difference" (PhD diss., Emory University, 1997), 473.

7. Carol Lee Flinders, *At the Root of This Longing: Reconciling a Spiritual Hunger and a Feminist Thirst* (San Francisco: Harper & Row, 1998), 65. Emphasis added.

8. Carol Gilligan and Lyn Mikel Brown, *Meeting at the Crossroads: Women's Psychology and Girls' Development* (New York: Ballantine Books, 1992), 232.

9. Patricia Hill Collins, "The Meaning of Motherhood in Black Culture and Black Mother-Daughter Relationships," in *Double Stitch: Black Women Write about Mothers & Daughters*, ed. Patricia Bell-Scott, Beverly Guy-Sheftall, Jacqueline Jones Royster, Janet Sims-Wood, Miriam DeCosta-Willis, and Lucie Fultz (Boston: Beacon Press, 1991), 47.

10. Beverly Jean Smith, "Raising a Resister," in *Women, Girls, and Psychotherapy: Reframing Resistance*, ed. Carol Gilligan, Annie G. Rogers, and Deborah L. Tolman (Binghamton, N.Y.: Haworth Press, 1991).

11. Brumberg, *The Body Project,* 198.

12. Sondra Higgins Matthaei, *Faith Matters: Faith Mentoring in the Faith Community* (Valley Forge, Pa.: Trinity Press International, 1996), 20.

13. Lerner, *The Creation of Feminist Consciousness,* 274.

14. Ibid., 220.

15. Sidonie Smith, "Who's Talking/Who's Talking Back? The Subject of Personal Narrative," in *Signs: Journal of Women in Culture and Society* 18, no. 2 (Winter 1993): 392–407.

16. Lerner, *The Creation of Feminist Consciousness,* 249.

17. Rosemary Radford Ruether, *Women and Redemption: A Theological History* (Minneapolis: Fortress Press, 1998), 5–7.

18. Lerner, *The Creation of Feminist Consciousness,* 220–29.

19. Ibid., 275.

20. Ibid.

21. Rosemary Radford Ruether, *Sexism and God-Talk: Toward a Feminist Theology* (Boston: Beacon Press, 1986), 35. Emphasis added.

22. Jerome Berryman, *Godly Play: A Way of Religious Education* (San Francisco: HarperSanFrancisco, 1991), 103.

23. Ruth Behar, *The Vulnerable Observer: Anthropology That Breaks Your Heart* (Boston: Beacon Press, 1996), 130.

24. See Carolyn Kay Steedman, *Landscape for a Good Woman: A Story of Two Lives* (New Brunswick, N.J.: Rutgers University Press, 1986), 11–22; and Behar, *The Vulnerable Observer,* 131, for discussion of the dissolution of borders between girlhood and womanhood and between self and other in the ethnographic enterprise.

25. Kathleen Norris, *The Cloister Walk* (New York: Riverhead Books, 1996), 173.

26. The imagery here recalls several sources, including Alice Walker, *In Search of Our Mothers' Gardens* (San Diego: Harcourt Brace Jovanovich, 1983), and Ada María Isasi-Díaz, *Mujerista Theology: A Theology for the Twenty-first Century* (Maryknoll, N.Y.: Orbis Books, 1996).

27. James Weldon Johnson, "Lift Every Voice and Sing," in *The United Methodist Hymnal* (Nashville: United Methodist Publishing House, 1989), 519. This hymn is also known as the Black National Anthem.

Bibliography

American Association of University Women. *Girls in the Middle: Working to Succeed in School*. Washington, D.C.: AAUW, 1996.

———. *How Schools Shortchange Girls*. Washington, D.C.: AAUW, 1992.

Angelou, Maya. *I Know Why the Caged Bird Sings*. New York: Bantam Books, 1969.

Anzaldúa, Gloria. *Borderlands/La Frontera: The New Mestiza*. San Francisco: Aunt Lute Books, 1987.

Armour, Ellen T. "Essentialism." In *The Dictionary of Feminist Theologies*, ed. Letty M. Russell and J. Shannon Clarkson. Louisville: Westminster John Knox Press, 1996.

Austin, Regina. "Sapphire Bound." Paper presented at the American Association of Law Schools Workshop for Women in Legal Education, Washington D.C., October 1987.

Baker-Fletcher, Karen. "Womanist Voice." In *Dictionary of Feminist Theologies*, ed. Letty M. Russell and J. Shannon Clarkson. Louisville: Westminster John Knox Press, 1996.

Bass, Dorothy, ed. *Practicing Our Faith: A Way of Life for a Searching People*. San Francisco: Jossey-Bass, 1997.

Bass, Dorothy, and Don C. Richter. *Way to Live: Christian Practices for Teens*. Nashville: Upper Room Books, 2002.

Bateson, Mary Catherine. *Composing a Life*. New York: Plume, 1990.

Beaudoin, Tom. *Virtual Faith: The Irreverent Spiritual Quest of Generation X*. San Francisco: Jossey-Bass, 1998.

Behar, Ruth. *Translated Woman: Crossing the Border with Esperanza's Story*. Boston: Beacon Press, 1993.

———. *The Vulnerable Observer: Anthropology That Breaks Your Heart*. Boston: Beacon Press, 1996.

Belenky, Mary Field, Blythe McVicker Clinchy, Nancy Rule Goldberger, and Jill Mattuck Tarule. *Women's Ways of Knowing: The Development of Self, Voice, and Mind*. New York: Basic Books, 1986.

Berryman, Jerome. *Godly Play: A Way of Religious Education.* San Francisco: HarperSanFrancisco, 1991.

Bolen, Megan. *Feeling Power: Emotions and Education.* New York: Routledge, 1999.

Bondi, Ruth. *Memories of God: Theological Reflections on a Life.* Nashville: Abingdon, 1995.

Bronfenbrenner, Urie. *The Ecology of Human Development.* Cambridge, Mass.: Harvard University Press, 1979.

Brown, Ann L. "Design Experiments: Theoretical and Methodological Challenges in Creating Complex Interventions in Classroom Settings." *Journal of the Learning Sciences* 2, no. 2 (1992): 141–78.

Brown, Lyn Mikel. "Telling a Girl's Life." In *Women, Girls, and Psychotherapy: Reframing Resistance,* ed. Carol Gilligan, Annie G. Rogers, and Deborah L. Tolman. Binghamton, N.Y.: Haworth Press, 1991.

Brumberg, Joan Jacobs. *The Body Project: An Intimate History of American Girls.* New York: Random House, 1997.

Bruner, Jerome. *On Knowing: Essays for the Left Hand.* Cambridge, Mass.: Harvard University Press, 1969.

Burbank, Beth. "Reflecting upon Stories as a Way of Doing Theology in CPE." *Journal of Supervision and Training in Ministry* 9 (1987): 151, 147–57.

Cannon, Katie Geneva. *Katie's Canon: Womanism and the Soul of the Black Community.* New York: Continuum, 1995.

Carroll, Rebecca. *Sugar in the Raw: Voices of Young Black Girls in America.* New York: Crown, 1997.

Centers for Disease Control and Prevention, National Center for Injury Prevention, "Violence in the United States," www.cdc.gov.

Chopp, Rebecca. "Praxis as the Shape of Theology." In *Dictionary of Feminist Theologies,* ed. Letty M. Russell and J. Shannon Clarkson. Louisville: Westminster John Knox Press, 1996.

———. *Saving Work: Feminist Practices of Theological Education.* Louisville: Westminster John Knox Press, 1995.

Chung, Hyun Kyung. *Struggle to Be the Sun Again: Introducing Asian Women's Theology.* Maryknoll, N.Y.: Orbis Books, 1990.

Cobb, John B., Jr. *Lay Theology.* St Louis, Mo.: Chalice Press, 1994.

———. *Reclaiming the Church: Where the Mainline Church Went Wrong and What to Do about It.* Louisville: Westminster John Knox Press, 1997.

Cole, Thomas B. "Ebbing Epidemic: Youth Homicide Rate at a 14-year Low." *Journal of the American Medical Association* 281, no. 1 (January 1999).

Collins, Patricia Hill. "The Meaning of Motherhood in Black Culture and Black Mother-Daughter Relationships." In *Double Stitch: Black Women Write about Mothers & Daughters,* ed. Patricia Bell Scott, Beverly Guy-Sheftall, Jacqueline Jones Royster, Janet Sims-Wood, Miriam DeCosta-Willis, and Lucie Fulz. Boston: Beacon Press, 1991.

Crain, Margaret Ann, and Jack L. Seymour. "The Ethnographer as Minister: Ethnographic Research in Ministry." *Religious Education* 91 (Summer 1996): 299–315.

———. *Yearning for God: Reflections of Faithful Lives.* Nashville: Upper Room Books, 2003.

Critser, Greg. "Let Them Eat Fat: The Heavy Truths about American Obesity." *Harper's Magazine* (March 2000): 41–47.

Csikszentmihalyi, Mihaly, and Mark Freeman. "Adolescence and Its Recollection: Toward an Interpretive Model of Development." *Merrill-Palmer Quarterly* 32, no. 2 (April 1986): 167–85.

Daly, Mary. *Beyond God the Father: Toward a Philosophy of Women's Liberation.* Boston: Beacon Press, 1973.

———. *Pure Lust: Elemental Feminist Philosophy.* San Francisco: HarperSanFrancisco, 1992.

Denzin, Norman K., and Yvonna S. Lincoln, eds. *Handbook of Qualitative Research.* London: SAGE Publications, 1994.

Dillard, Annie. *An American Childhood.* New York: Harper and Row, 1987.

Donovan, Ursula, and Rosalind Gibson. "Dietary Intakes of Adolescent Females Consuming Vegetarian, Semi-Vegetarian and Omnivorous Diets." *Journal of Adolescent Health* 18 (1996): 292–300.

Duck, Ruth. *Gender and the Name of God: The Trinitarian Baptismal Formula.* New York: Pilgrim Press, 1990.

Dryfoos, Joy G. *Safe Passage: Making It through Adolescence in a Risky Society.* New York: Oxford University Press, 1998.

Egan, Jennifer. "The Thin Red Line." *New York Times Magazine,* July 27, 1997, 21–46.

Eisner, Elliot W. *The Educational Imagination.* New York: Macmillan, 1979.

Erikson, Erik. *The Life Cycle Completed: A Review.* New York: W. W. Norton, 1982.

Eugene, Toinette M. "Appropriation/Reciprocity." In *Dictionary of Feminist Theologies,* ed. Letty M. Russell and J. Shannon Clarkson. Louisville: Westminster John Knox Press, 1996.

———. "Moral Values and Black Womanist Thought." *Journal of Religious Thought* 41, no. 2 (1984–85): 2–34.

Faludi, Susan. *Backlash: The Undeclared War on American Women.* New York: Crown, 1991.

Fleming, Ann Taylor. *Motherhood Deferred: A Woman's Journey.* New York: G. P. Putnam's Sons, 1994.

Flinders, Carol Lee. *At the Root of This Longing: Reconciling a Spiritual Hunger and a Feminist Thirst.* San Francisco: Harper & Row, 1998.

Fowler, James. *Stages of Faith: The Psychology of Human Development and the Quest for Meaning.* New York: Harper & Row, 1981.

Fox, Matthew. *Original Blessing.* Santa Fe: Bear & Co., 1983.

Freedberg, Louis. "Borderline Hypocrisy: Do We Want Them Here, or Not?" *Washington Post,* February 6, 2000, sec. B, 1.

Freire, Paulo. *Pedagogy of the Oppressed.* New York: Herder & Herder, 1970.

Fuss, Diana. *Essentially Speaking: Feminism, Nature, and Difference.* New York: Routledge, 1990.

Game, Anne. *Undoing the Social: Towards a Deconstructive Sociology.* Toronto and Buffalo: University of Toronto Press, 1991.

Geertz, Clifford. *Works and Lives: The Anthropologist as Author.* Stanford, Calif.: Stanford University Press, 1989.

Giddens, Anthony. *Modernity and Self-Identity: Self and Society in the Late Modern Age.* Stanford, Calif.: Stanford University Press, 1991.

Gilligan, Carol. *In a Different Voice: Psychological Theory and Women's Development.* Cambridge, Mass.: Harvard University Press, 1982.

Gilligan, Carol, and Lyn Mikel Brown. *Meeting at the Crossroads: Women's Psychology and Girls' Development.* New York: Ballantine Books, 1992.

Giroux, Henry A. *Fugitive Cultures: Race, Violence, and Youth.* New York: Routledge, 1996.

Giroux, Henry A., Colin Lankshear, Peter McClaren, and Michael Peters, eds. *Counternarratives: Cultural Studies and Critical Pedagogies in Postmodern Spaces.* New York: Routledge, 1996.

Giroux, Henry, and Peter McClaren, eds. *Between Borders: Pedagogy and the Politics of Cultural Studies.* New York: Routledge, 1994.

Groome, Thomas. *Sharing Faith.* San Francisco: HarperSanFrancisco, 1991.

Gutiérrez, Gustavo. *A Theology of Liberation.* Maryknoll, N.Y.: Orbis Books, 1988.

Habermas, Jürgen. "A Review of Gadamer's *Truth and Method.*" In *The Hermeneutic Tradition: From Ast to Ricoeur,* ed. Gayle L. Ormiston and Alan D. Schrift. Albany: State University of New York Press, 1990.

Haegele, Katie. "Pack a Punch." *Feminista!* 3, no. 8 (February 2000): 1–6.

Hall, G. Stanley. *Adolescence: Its Psychology, and Its Relations to Physiology, Anthropology, Sociology, Sex, Crime, Religion, and Education.* New York: Appleton, 1904.

Hancock, Emily. *The Girl Within.* New York: Fawcett Books, 1989.

Haraway, Donna. "Situated Knowledges: The Science Question in Feminism and the Privilege of the Partial Perspective." *Feminist Studies* 14, no. 3 (Fall 1988): 58–72.

Harris, Maria. *Women and Teaching: Themes for a Spirituality of Pedagogy.* New York: Paulist Press, 1988.

Heidegger, Martin. *Being and Time.* Trans. J. Macquarrie and C. Robinson. New York: Harper and Row, 1962.

Heilbrun, Carolyn. *Writing a Woman's Life.* New York: Ballantine Books, 1989.

Hernández, Adriana. *Pedagogy, Democracy, and Feminism: Rethinking the Public Sphere.* Albany: State University of New York Press, 1997.

Hersch, Patricia. *A Tribe Apart: A Journey into the Heart of American Adolescence.* New York: Ballantine Publishing Group, 1998.

Hess, Carol Lakey. *Caretakers of Our Common House: Women's Development in Communities of Faith.* Nashville: Abingdon Press, 1997.

Heyward, Carter. *Touching Our Strength: The Erotic as Power and the Love of God.* San Francisco: HarperCollins, 1980.

Hine, Carlene Clark. Class lecture, Northwestern University Avalon Lecture, March 8, 1997.

hooks, bell. *Teaching to Transgress: Education as the Practice of Freedom.* New York: Routledge, 1994.

———. *Yearning: Race, Gender and Cultural Politics.* Boston: South End Press, 1990.

Hurston, Zora Neale. *Dust Tracks on a Road.* San Francisco: HarperCollins, 1996.

Isasi-Díaz, Ada María. *En La Lucha/In the Struggle: Elaborating a Mujerista Theology.* Minneapolis: Fortress Press, 1993.

———. *Mujerista Theology: A Theology for the Twenty-first Century.* Maryknoll, N.Y.: Orbis Books, 1996.

———. "*Mujerista* Theology's Method: A Liberative Praxis, a Way of Life." In *Mestizo Christianity: Theology from the Latino Perspective,* ed. Arturo J. Bañuelas. Maryknoll, N.Y.: Orbis Books, 1995.

James, Stanlie. *Theorizing Black Feminisms: The Visionary Pragmatism of Black Women,* ed. Stanlie M. James and Abena P. A. Busia. London: Routledge, 1993.

Johnson, James Weldon. "Lift Every Voice and Sing." In *The United Methodist Hymnal.* Nashville: United Methodist Publishing House, 1989.

Kang, Nam-Soon. "Creating 'Dangerous Memory': Challenges for Asian and Korean Feminist Theology." *Ecumenical Review* 49, no. 1 (January 1998): 21–31.

Kegan, Robert. *The Evolving Self: Problem and Process in Human Development.* Cambridge, Mass.: Harvard University Press, 1982.

———. *In Over Our Heads: The Mental Demands of Moral Life.* Cambridge, Mass.: Harvard University Press, 1994.

Kim, Hyo-Jung. "Do You Have Eyelashes?" In *Women, Girls, and Psychotherapy: Reframing Resistance,* ed. Carol Gilligan, Annie G. Rogers, and Deborah L. Tolman. Binghamton, N.Y.: Haworth Press, 1991.

Kindlon, Dan, and Michael Thompson. *Raising Cain: Protecting the Emotional Life of Boys.* New York: Ballantine Books, 1999.

Kingsolver, Barbara. *Small Wonders.* New York: HarperCollins, 2002.

Kwok, Pui Lan. "Mothers and Daughters, Writers and Fighters." In *Frontiers in Asian Christian Theology: Emerging Trends,* ed. R. S. Sugirtharaja. Maryknoll, N.Y.: Orbis Books, 1994.

Lancaster, Roger N. *Life Is Hard: Machismo, Danger, and the Intimacy of Power in Nicaragua.* Berkeley: University of California Press, 1994.

Lee, Jung Young. *Marginality: The Key to Multicultural Theology.* Minneapolis: Fortress Press, 1995.

Lerner, Gerda. *The Creation of Feminist Consciousness: From the Middle Ages to Eighteen-seventy.* New York: Oxford University Press, 1993.

Limón, José. *Dancing with the Devil: Society and Cultural Poetics in Mexican-American South Texas.* Madison: University of Wisconsin Press, 1991.

Lorde, Audre. *Sister Outsider.* Freedom, Calif.: Crossing Press, 1984.

———. *Zami: A New Spelling of My Name.* Watertown, Mass.: Persephone Press, 1982.

Lowenhaupt-Tsing, Anna. *In the Realm of the Diamond Queen.* Princeton, N.J.: Princeton University Press, 1993.

Matthaei, Sondra Higgins. *Faith Matters: Faith Mentoring in the Faith Community.* Valley Forge, Pa.: Trinity Press International, 1996.

McAdams, Dan. *The Stories We Live By: Personal Myths and the Making of the Self.* New York: William Morrow, 1993.

McClaren, Peter. "Multiculturalism and the Post-Modern Critique: Toward a Pedagogy of Resistance and Transformation." In *Between Borders: Pedagogy and the Politics of Cultural Studies,* ed. Henry Giroux and Peter McLaren. New York: Routledge, 1994.

McFague, Sallie. *Metaphorical Theology: Models of God in Religious Language.* Philadelphia: Fortress Press, 1982.

McIntosh, Peggy. "White Privilege: Unpacking the Invisible Knapsack." *Peace and Freedom* (July–August 1989): 10–12.

McKay, Nellie Y. "Autobiography." In *Black Women in America,* ed. Darlene Clark Hine, Elsa Barkley Brown, Rosalyn Terborg-Penn. Bloomington: Indiana University Press, 1994.

Mercer, Joyce. "Gender, Violence and Faith: Adolescent Girls and the Theological Anthropology of Difference." PhD diss., Emory University, 1997.

Middleton, Sue. *Educating Feminists: Life Histories and Pedagogy.* New York: Teachers College Press, 1993.

Miller, Craig Kennet, and MaryJane Pierce Norton. *Making God Real for a New Generation: Ministry with Millennials Born from 1982 to 1999.* Nashville: Discipleship Resources, 2003.

Miller, Dusty. *Women Who Hurt Themselves: A Book of Hope and Understanding.* New York: Basic Books, 1994.

Miller-McLemore, Bonnie. *Also a Mother: Work and Family as Theological Dilemma.* Nashville: Abingdon Press, 1994.

Mollenkott, Virginia Ramey. *The Divine Feminine: The Biblical Imagery of God as Female.* New York: Crossroad, 1991.

Moody, Linda. *Women Encounter God: Theology across the Boundaries of Difference.* Maryknoll, N.Y.: Orbis Books, 1996.

Moore, Mary Elizabeth. *Education for Continuity and Change.* Nashville: Abingdon Press, 1983.

———. *Teaching From the Heart: Theology and Educational Method.* Minneapolis: Fortress Press, 1991.

Morton, Nelle. *The Journey Is Home.* Boston: Beacon Press, 1985.

Norris, Kathleen. *The Cloister Walk.* New York: Riverhead Books, 1996.

O'Gorman, Robert. "Latin American Theology and Education." In *Theological Approaches to Christian Education,* ed. Jack L. Seymour and Donald E. Miller. Nashville: Abingdon Press, 1990.

Parker, Evelyn L. *Trouble Don't Last Always: Emancipatory Hope among African American Adolescents.* Cleveland: Pilgrim Press, 2003.

Paulsell, Stephanie. *Honoring the Body: Meditations on a Christian Practice.* San Francisco: Jossey-Bass, 2002.

Peiss, Kathy. "Beauty Culture." In *Black Women in America: An Historical Encyclopedia,* ed. Darlene Clark Hine, Elsa Barkley Brown, and Rosalyn Terborg-Penn. Bloomington: University of Indiana Press, 1994.

Pipher, Mary. *Reviving Ophelia: Saving the Selves of Adolescent Girls.* New York: Ballantine Books, 1994.

Reed-Danahay, Deborah E. *Auto/Ethnography: Rewriting the Self and the Social.* Oxford, England: Berg, 1997.

Ricoeur, Paul. *The Conflict of Interpretations: Essays in Hermeneutics.* Evanston, Ill.: Northwestern University Press, 1974.

Robinson, Tracy, and Jane Victoria Ward. "A Belief in the Self Far Greater Than Anyone's Disbelief: Cultivating Resistance among African American Female Adolescents." In *Women, Girls, and Psychotherapy: Reframing Resistance,* ed. Carol Gilligan, Annie G. Rogers, and Deborah L. Tolman. Binghamton, N.Y.: Haworth Press, 1991.

Ruether, Rosemary Radford. *New Woman, New Earth: Sexist Ideologies and Human Liberation.* Minneapolis: Seabury, 1975.

———. *Sexism and God-Talk: Toward a Feminist Theology.* Boston: Beacon Press, 1986.

———. *Women and Redemption: A Theological History.* Minneapolis: Fortress Press, 1998.

———. *Women-Church: Theology and Practice of Feminist Liturgical Communities.* San Francisco: Harper & Row, 1985.

Schipani, Daniel. *Religious Education Encounters Liberation Theology.* Birmingham, Ala.: Religious Education Press, 1988.

Schreiner, Olive. *The Story of an African Farm.* Oxford: Oxford University Press, 1992.

Schüssler-Fiorenza, Elisabeth. *In Memory of Her: A Feminist Theological Reconstruction of Christian Origins.* New York: Crossroad, 1987.

Seymour, Jack L. *Mapping Christian Education: Approaches to Congregational Learning.* Nashville: Abingdon Press, 1997.

Seymour, Jack L., Margaret Ann Crain, and Joseph V. Crockett. *Educating Christians: The Intersection of Meaning, Learning, and Vocation.* Nashville: Abingdon Press, 1993.

Shandler, Sara. *Ophelia Speaks: Adolescent Girls Write About Their Search for Self.* New York: Harper Perennial, 1999.

Shange, Ntozake. *For Colored Girls Who've Considered Suicide When the Rainbow Is Enuf.* New York: Macmillan, 1977.

Siqueira, Judith. Untitled editorial. In *In God's Image* 13, no. 4 (Winter 1994): 2–4.

Smith, Beverly Jean. "Raising a Resister." In *Women, Girls, and Psychotherapy: Reframing Resistance,* ed. Carol Gilligan, Annie G. Rogers, and Deborah L. Tolman. Binghamton, N.Y.: Haworth Press, 1991.

Smith, Sidonie. "Who's Talking/Who's Talking Back? The Subject of Personal Narrative." In *Signs: Journal of Women in Culture and Society* 18, no. 2 (Winter 1993): 392–407.

Starhawk. *Dreaming the Dark*. Boston: Beacon Press, 1982.

Steedman, Carolyn Kay. *Landscape for a Good Woman: A Story of Two Lives*. New Brunswick, N.J.: Rutgers University Press, 1986.

Tappan, Mark B., and Martin J. Packer, eds. *Narrative and Storytelling: Implications for Understanding Moral Development*. San Francisco: Jossey-Bass, 1991.

Thompson, Becky Wangsgaard. " 'A Way Outa No Way': Eating Problems among African-American, Latina, and White Women." *Gender and Society* 4 (December 1992): 50.

Thompson, Kathleen. "Maya Angelou." In *Black Women in America: An Historical Encyclopedia*, ed. Darlene Clark Hine, Elsa Barkley Brown, and Rosalyn Terborg-Penn. Bloomington: Indiana University Press, 1994.

Thurman, Howard. *The Search for Common Ground: An Inquiry into the Basis of Man's Experience of Community*. Richmond, Ind.: Friends United Press, 1986.

Tigert, Leanne McCall and Timothy Brown. *Coming Out Young and Faithful*. Cleveland: Pilgrim Press, 2001.

Torney-Purta, Judith. "Youth in Relation to Social Institutions." In *At the Threshold: The Developing Adolescent*, ed. S. Shirley Feldman and Glen R. Elliott. Cambridge, Mass.: Harvard University Press, 1990.

Townes, Emilie. "Voices of the Spirit: Womanist Methodologies in Theological Disciplines." *Womanist* 1 (Summer 1994): 1–2.

Unks, Gerald. *The Gay Teen: Educational Practice and Theory for Lesbian, Gay, and Bisexual Adolescents*. New York: Routledge, 1995.

Visweswaran, Kamala. *Fictions of Feminist Ethnography*. Minneapolis: University of Minnesota, 1994.

Vitz, Paul C. "The Use of Stories in Moral Development: New Psychological Reasons for an Old Educational Model." *American Psychologist* 45, no. 6 (June 1990): 709–20.

Vogel, Dwight D., and Linda J. Vogel. *Sacramental Living: Falling Stars & Coloring Outside the Lines*. Nashville: Upper Room Books, 1999.

Walker, Alice. *The Color Purple*. New York: Washington Square Press, 1982.

———. *In Search of Our Mothers' Gardens*. San Diego: Harcourt Brace Jovanovich, 1983.

Walsh, Barrant W., and Paul M. Rosin. *Self-Mutilation: Theory, Research and Treatment*. London: Guilford Press, 1988.

Ward, Jane Victoria. "High Self-Esteem/Low Achievement: The AAUW Findings on Black Girls Growing Up." Paper presented at a symposium on the psychology of girls and the culture of schools, Temple University, Philadelphia, 1993.

Warren, Michael. *Youth, Gospel, Liberation*. San Francisco: Harper & Row, 1987.

Weiler, Katherine. *Women Teaching for Change*. Boston: Bergin and Garvey, 1988.

Welch, Sharon D. *Communities of Resistance and Solidarity: A Feminist Theology of Liberation.* Maryknoll, N.Y.: Orbis Books, 1985.

———. *A Feminist Ethic of Risk.* Minneapolis: Fortress Press, 1990.

Werblowsky, R. J. Zwi, and Geoffrey Wigoder, eds. *The Oxford Dictionary of the Jewish Religion.* New York: Oxford University Press, 1997.

Westfield, Lynne N. *Dear Sisters: A Womanist Practice of Hospitality.* Cleveland: Pilgrim Press, 2001.

Willhauck, Susan, and Jacqulyn Thorpe. *The Web of Women's Leadership: Recasting Congregational Ministry.* Nashville: Abingdon, 2001.

Wimberly, Anne Streaty. *Soul Stories: African American Christian Education.* Nashville: Abingdon Press, 1994.

Wolf, Diane L., ed. *Feminist Dilemmas in Fieldwork,* Boulder, Colo.: Westview Press, 1996.

Wright, Wendy M. "Wreathed in Flesh and Warm." *Weavings* 12, no. 1 (January–February 1987): 18–27.

Zemsky, Beth. "Coming Out against All Odds: Resistance in the Life of a Young Lesbian." In *Women, Girls and Psychotherapy: Reframing Resistance,* ed. Carol Gilligan, Annie G. Rogers, and Deborah L. Tolman. Binghamton, N.Y.: Haworth Press, 1991.

Index

adolescence, 21, 65, 135, 163
adolescent girls
  psychology of, 1, 145, 79
  stories of, 21, 29, 30, 42, 53
African American women, 14, 17, 73, 77–78, 82, 148
American Academy of Religion (AAR), 139
American Association of University Women (AAUW), 29, 122
American Childhood, An, 84
Angelou, Maya, 74, 77–80, 83, 194n4
anorexia nervosa. *See* eating disorders
Anzaldúa, Gloria, 140
Asian American women, 14, 74, 136, 146, 166
Asian-feminist theology, 129–35
  han, 133
  hyun jang, 132
  importance of community in, 134
Austin, Regina, 83
autobiography
  of girls, 18, 20, 21, 102
  as literary construction of self, 88
  as resource for theology, 89, 121, 133, 193n42
  of women, 24, 66, 72–75, 88–89, 121
autoethnography, 21–23, 24, 26, 66

barbed wire fence, 118
barriers to adult-adolescent relationship, 167

Bass, Dorothy, 6
Bateson, Mary Catherine, 70
Beaudoin, Tom, 65, 149
beer commercial, 67
Behar, Ruth, 160, 205n38
Belenky, Mary Field, 149, 152, 190n5
Berriozabal, Maria Antonietta, 121
Berryman, Jerome, 195n5
Bible. *See* scripture
blacks. *See* African Americans
body
  as form of voice, 157–60
  image of female, 53, 82, 104, 106, 171
  language, 39, 60, 155
  as primary, 12, 25, 160, 205n48, 205n38
  as resource in theology, 40, 57, 61, 63, 84–84, 87, 145–47, 158
  safety of the female, 58–59, 144, 159
Bondi, Roberta, 113
border crossing, 42, 64–64, 118–22, 129, 139–41, 145, 174–75
border pedagogy, 150–51, 153
boys, 5–6, 12
Breakfast Club, The, 109, 111
breast-feeding, 142–45
breath, as theological image, 60
Bronfenbrenner, Urie, 196n6
Brown, Lyn Mikel, 9, 12, 166, 193n3
Brumberg, Joan Jacobs, 165

Buddhism, 59, 151
Burbank, Beth, 34

Cannon, Katie Geneva, 82, 84, 138
Catherine of Siena, St., 29
Centers for Disease Control and
    Prevention, 199n2
Chopp, Rebecca, 19, 30–33, 51, 52
Christology, 128
Chung, Hyun Kyung, 129, 131–33
church
    curriculum of, 16, 29, 80, 127
    feminist consciousness within, 163,
        169, 170
    images of, 4, 49, 53, 63, 171, 175
    as a source of meaning-making, viii,
        5, 12
    transformation of, 1, 30
    women-church, 51, 191n2, 195n3
Clinical Pastoral Education (CPE), 34,
    35
Cobb, John, 101
Color Purple, The, 52, 61
Columbine High School, 23
confidentiality, 155
confirmation, 11, 204n25
connected teaching, 151
covenant, theological theme of, 48, 52,
    64
communities of resistance, 31, 72
curriculum, 15, 19, 150, 179
cutting, 157–58
Csikszentmihalyi, Mihaly, 192n33
Crain, Margaret Ann, 20, 189n6
critical ethnography, 21, 22
critical pedagogy, 25, 146

Daly, Mary, 98, 135, 161
dangerous memory, 72, 90, 145, 197n15

death, 24, 48–50, 91–97, 101,
    162
DeLois, story about, 81
Denzin, Norman, 192n34
depression, vii, 1, 45, 47, 105, 193n3
diet. *See* eating disorders; veganism
Dillard, Annie, 84–87
dominant culture, 30, 87, 90
Duck, Ruth, 99
Dryfoos, Joy, 164

eating disorders, 91, 105, 115, 158
Ecumenical Association of Third
    World Theologians (EATWOT),
    129–33
Egan, Jennifer, 158
emanicipatory theology, 25, 73
    defined, 121
embodied pedagogy, 25, 147
    guidelines for, 154–56
engaged pedagogy, 151
epiphany, 57, 58
Erikson, Erik, 20
essentialism, 99, 199n10
ethic of risk, 121
ethnography, 123–24
Eugene, Toinette, 137
Evanston Review, The, 142
experience distant, 33, 47, 58
experience near, 22

Faludi, Susan, 69
fathers, 29, 81–82, 91
    imagery for God, 94–114
feelings, identifying, 13, 20, 33, 46–48,
    57, 63, 155, 171
female clusters, 2, 168, 170
feminist consciousness, 28, 72, 144

feminist theology
  correctives to, 12, 14, 121
  critique of white, 12, 138
  practical application of, 15
  themes of, 40, 51–53, 61–64, 101
  as transforming tradition, 19
fifth gospel, 40, 42, 53, 57–63, 130,
  171–75
Flinders, Carol Lee, 71, 165
formal operational thinking, 65, 135
Fowler, James, 196n15
Fox, Matthew, 190n7
Freire, Paulo, 146, 151, 194n8, 204n25
Future Homemakers of America, 27

gang violence, 94
Gertz, Clifford, 193n41
Giddens, Anthony, 194n11
Gilligan, Carol, 12, 19, 21, 70, 79, 160,
  166, 193n3
girlfriend theology
  as constructive theology, 23, 40
  defined, 17–18
  as a method of education, 23
  origin of term, 112, 195n21
  theological assertions of, 40, 172
girlfriends, 18
Giroux, Henry, 149–53
God-talk, 40, 48, 58, 116
  defined, 19
going forth, 34, 50, 61, 97, 111, 112,
  188
grief, 48–50, 162, 171
Grant, Jacquelyn, 137
Groome, Thomas, 35
Gutiérrez, Gustavo, 101

Habermas, Jürgen, 199n4
Hall, G. Stanley, 21

Haraway, Donna, 193n36
Harris, Maria
  "heard to speech," 23–31, 36, 40, 74,
  79, 156
Heidegger, Martin, 32
hermeneutic tradition, 98
Hersch, Patricia, 164, 166
Hess, Carol Lakey, 19
Heyward, Carter, 63
Hindu practices, 59, 65
Hispanics.
  men, 97, 119
  teenagers, 95
  women, 74 *See also mujerista* theology
historiography, embodied, 131
holding environment, 19
homeplace, 17, 77
hooks, bell, 78, 84, 149
Hurston, Zora Neale, 36, 82, 138

icons, 49
identity formation, 78, 141
I Know Why the Caged Bird Sings,
  74
images of God, viii, 87, 95–100, 134,
  172–73
inclusive language, 16
In God's Image, 129
Isasi-Díaz, Ada María, 122–23
isolation, feelings of, 106–7

Judaism, 48, 49
Judeo-Christian, 48, 116

Kang, Nam-Soon, 197n15
Kegan, Robert, 70
Kim, Hyo-Jung, 148
Kindlon, Dan, 189n3

Kohlberg, Lawrence, 20
Kwok, Pui Lan, 62, 130

Lee, Jarena, 88
Lerner, Gerda, 169
lesbian, 157
liberation theology, 72, 101
liberatory praxis, 25
literature, as substitute for religion, 71
Lion King, The, 3
Lorde, Audre, 80–82, 90, 135
Lowenhaupt-Tsing, Anna, 192n34

Matthaei, Sondra Higgins, 167
McAdams, Dan, 194n11
McClaren Peter, 149
McFague, Sallie, 99, 113–14
mentoring circles, 167–68
mentors, 2, 5, 24, 29, 66, 79
   faith mentors, 164–66
Mercer, Joyce, 165
"Merchants of Cool," 5
metaphorical theology. *See* McFague,
   Sallie
methodology of *Girlfriend Theology*
   characteristics of, 20–26, 27
   emphasis on storytelling, vii
   as religious education, 2, 5, 35, 39,
      80
   use of feelings in, 107
millennial generation, 33
Miller, Dusty, 159
Miller-McLemore, Bonnie, 191n12
minyan, theological theme of, 49, 64
Moody, Linda, 135
moon, significance of, for women, 9–10
Moore, Mary Elizabeth, 19
Morton, Nelle, 15, 29–31, 79

Moses, birth narrative of, 96
mothering ones, 79
mujerista theology, 112–13, 121–29
   la lucha in, 123
   lo cotidiano in, 125
   permítanme hablar in, 127

natural education, 69–70, 166
Norris, Kathleen, 197n12
No Way Out, 92

Obesity. *See* eating disorders
other-mothers, 79, 166

Parker, Evelyn L., 190n9
patriarchy, 13, 98, 99, 100, 102, 132,
   168
Paulsell, Stephanie, 205n35
pedagogy. *See* border pedagogy; critical
   pedagogy; embodied pedagogy;
   engaged pedagogy; feminist
   pedagogy
perfection, expectations of, 106, 110
physical abuse, 104, 115
Piaget, Jean, 20
Pipher, Mary, 189n3
postmodernity
   characteristics of, 65
   definitions of, 149–50
   in religious education, 152, 153
process theology, 101

Quaker, 33
qualitative research, 21

racism, 74, 82, 95, 120, 121, 139,
   141
reciprocity, 74, 139–40
relics, 157

religious education
  banking model of, 204n5
  feminist models of, 70, 79–80, 134,
    138–39
  girlfriend theology as method of, 2, 5,
    6, 17, 70, 79–80
  restructuring of, 149
  task of, 19
  as theological reflection, 35–36, 83,
    87
resistance, 13, 14, 17, 30, 72, 84, 160
Ricoeur, Paul, 202n7
Ruether, Rosemary Radford, 51, 99,
  170

Sabbath, 58
salvation, 31
Sapphire, 83
saving work, 30–33, 36
Schipani, Daniel, 203n23
Schüssler-Fiorenza, Elisabeth, 99
Scripture
  authority of, 62, 132
  function of, 3, 58, 117
  interpretation of, 125–28, 138, 145,
    152, 169
  stories from, 96, 110
  in theological reflection, 33, 35, 36,
    47, 59, 178, 186
sea glass, 89
self-esteem, 17, 47, 79
self-mutilation, 158
semantic derogation, 68–69
sexism, 14, 78, 84, 123, 136, 58,
  206n21
sexual maturation, 165
sexual orientation, 122, 128, 136, 157
sexual violence, 2, 78, 91, 99, 126,
  131–32, 158–59, 167

sexuality, positive notions of, 87–88,
  119
Seymour, Jack, 20
Shandler, Sara, 195n1
Shange, Ntozake, 84, 198n43
silence
  as imposed by others, vii, 11–14, 30,
    36, 74, 155, 165, 190n5, 193n3
  as sacred interlude, 30, 94, 154–55,
    183
sister books, 169
situated knowledge, 22
Siqueira, Judith, 42, 57
Smith, Beverly Jean, 14, 166
social boundaries, transcending of,
  106–7, 114
solidarity, 126–27
Starhawk, 116
suicide, vii, 1, 2, 42, 50, 91, 147, 156,
  171, 187

teachable moment, 62
television sportscast, 68
temples of meaning, 32
Teresa of Avila, St., 30, 85
testimony, as a Christian practice, 6–7
Then, One Day, I Saw, 103
theodicy, 46
theology, 18
  contemporary voices in, 20
  as meaning-making, 32
theological reflection, 22, 33–36, 63,
  83, 131–34, 140
Tigert, Leanne McCall
Tomorrow, Then, 53
Townes, Emilie, 191n11, 204n32
transformation of tradition, 11, 13, 19,
  30, 62, 90, 116, 172

usable past, 69, 71–72, 145

veganism, 142, 146
violence, 24, 91
Visweswaran, Kamala, 22
Vogel, Linda J., 191n13
voice
  finding one's, 28
  loss of, 12, 79
  resisting loss of, 14
  use of body as, 158

Walker, Alice, 52, 61, 84, 86, 136
Ward, Janie Victoria, 79
Warren, Michael, 189n1
water, as theological image, 59, 97

Welch, Sharon, 31, 72, 121
Wesley, John, 117
white feminism, 14–16, 19, 74, 136, 138–39
white privilege, 74, 120
Will You Be My Friend? 42
Willhauck, Susan, 204n28
Williams, Delores, 136, 137
Wimberly, Anne Streaty, 36
Wolf, Diane L., 22
womanist ethics, 136
womanist theology, 14, 16–17, 25, 74, 77–86, 135–41, 191n11
Women's Ways of Knowing, 149, 152, 189n4

Youth Theology Initiative (YTI) 38, 102